Computers
in
Mathematics Education

Computers
in
Mathematics Education

1984 Yearbook

Viggo P. Hansen
1984 Yearbook Editor
California State University—Northridge

Marilyn J. Zweng
General Yearbook Editor
University of Iowa

National Council of
Teachers of Mathematics

Library of Congress Cataloging in Publication Data:

Main entry under title:

Computers in mathematics education.

(Yearbook ; 1984)
Bibliography: p.
1. Mathematics—Computer-assisted instruction—
Addresses, essays, lectures. I. Hansen, Viggo P.
II. Zweng, Marilyn J. III. Series: Yearbook (National
Council of Teachers of Mathematics) ; 1984.
QA3.N3 1984 [QA20.C65] 510.7s [510'.7'8] 84-2037
ISBN 0-87353-210-4

Printed in the United States of America

Contents

Part 3: Teaching Mathematics through Programming

Part 4: Diagnostic Uses of the Computer

Part 5: Bibliography

Preface

The title of this NCTM 1984 Yearbook, *Computers in Mathematics Education,* reflects a most paradoxical situation. Certainly no branch of human knowledge has withstood the test of time better than mathematics. The Pythagorean theorem is as immutable today as it was the very day it first became apparent. However, the role of the computer in mathematics education is so mutable as to make this book about it obsolete even as it is being written. Mathematics teachers have witnessed in the span of a few years an incomprehensible number of suggestions on how to teach mathematics with computers. We might add that not only was the number of suggestions incomprehensible but so were many of the suggestions themselves. If we may borrow from marketing terminology, we might say that the bottom line is extremely exciting but not clearly in focus at this time. Perhaps this is exactly the same situation we see in general for this much heralded year of 1984.

It was into this maelstrom of paradoxes that many noble NCTM authors took up their battle stations. The range and depth of ideas submitted was indicative of the impact the computer is having on many of our teaching practices. New philosophical positions began to emerge; new language, more interactive teaching strategies, and different mathematics topics arose; and most gratifying of all was the inherent enthusiasm each author projected in his or her manuscript.

As we read and studied the many submitted articles, certain generalized assumptions began to appear. A few of these can be summarized as follows: (1) The computer is definitely here to stay in education, both in the classroom and in the home; (2) to date there is still a shortage of good software; (3) we are desperately in need of more research (this is critical and will be costly); (4) the integration of the computer into the curriculum is at best in its infancy; (5) cost factors, though coming down, are still a major factor; and (6) we are painfully reminded of the need for better teacher training in this area.

Lurking in these and other, similar assumptions are additional social concerns. Who will best be able to capitalize on this technology? What is going to be the role of industry in delivering hardware and software and cooperating with educators? Finally, who will be able to afford these sophisticated devices, especially if they can be used effectively in the home? For the most part these kinds of questions are not discussed in depth in this yearbook but are crucial issues for all of us to consider when viewing the total impact the computer will have on mathematics education.

Your 1984 Yearbook Committee, which was held to a very restricted number of pages, had to select and then heavily edit submitted material to make it fit. It was with great humility and regret that we could not include all the material given us. But we were refreshed by the abundance of ideas and enthusiasm all authors exhibited. NCTM can be proud of its membership. It was recently projected that Orwell's *Nineteen Eighty-Four* will be this year's best-seller. However, our survey forecasts that this yearbook, *Computers in Mathematics Education,* will capture that honor.

1984 Yearbook Committee

Shirley Frye, Scottsdale School District, Phoenix, Arizona

Gail Lowe, Conejo Valley Unified School District, Thousand Oaks, California

Henry Pollak, Central Services Organization for Regional Bell Operating Companies (formerly Bell Laboratories), Murray Hill, New Jersey

Robert Wisner, New Mexico State University, Las Cruces, New Mexico

Marilyn Zweng, University of Iowa, Iowa City, Iowa

There were simply too many people involved in the preparation of this book to list all of them. But you can be certain this committee knows who they are, and we are forever indebted to them for their assistance.

VIGGO P. HANSEN
1984 Yearbook Editor

Toward Comprehensive Instructional Computing in Mathematics

Larry L. Hatfield

THROUGHOUT the world educators are exploring the potential of the computer in instruction. Indeed, during more than twenty years of innovative efforts, we have seen considerably varied computer applications in instruction. Mathematics education has been among the most extensively explored areas of instruction, and there exists a broad base of experience and materials for mathematics instructional computing.

Let us examine a vision toward which the emerging emphasis on computers in instruction might progress. The vision may stimulate your conceptions of what might be feasible or desirable. It may suggest ideas for how to think about instructional computing in mathematics and how to consider the selection or creation of computing activities in your own classroom. Of course, it is not intended to be prescriptive, but rather provocative and suggestive of a mature approach to instructional computing in the mathematics classroom.

What Is Mathematics Instructional Computing?

Most of us realize that the computer has already assumed a ubiquitous role in our society. At first glance, it may seem obvious that the term *instructional computing* means any application of the computer that serves the goals and functions of instruction. But here we shall consider instructional computing in mathematics to include any application that gives either the student or the teacher direct contact with the computer and serves the goals and functions of mathematics instruction.

The past two decades have witnessed considerable exploratory innovations of computing in classrooms. You may be surprised at the wide range of applications that have been tried. But amid the growing flood of computer programs for instruction, one may identify some distinguishing characteristics. For the purposes of this article, we shall divide the domain of mathematics instructional computing into three broad categories: *student programming, computer-based instruction,* and *teacher utilities.*

Student programming

When mathematics learners construct their own computer programs, powerful learning experiences can occur. Indeed, many mathematics teachers have realized the apparent connections between the thinking involved in building, testing, correcting, and refining one's own computer algorithm and many aspects of mathematical thought. In addition, many mathematics educators have recognized the potential effects that solving a curriculum-oriented computer programming task can have on stimulating or enhancing understandings of a mathematical concept, problem, or procedure. It has seemed almost a natural relationship for computer programming to be taught within the mathematics curriculum; this may have led to serious distortions of our goals and objectives for a sound mathematical education. We know that students can learn to write computer programs; we must now consider the more critical questions about why our mathematics students should become engaged in such tasks.

Computer-based instruction

The distinguishing feature of *computer-based instruction* is the execution of a prepared computer program by the student or the teacher for the purposes of instructing. For the student the focus is on the *output* of the program, not on the program's code or logic. The student does not become involved with the program as an object, only as a generator of tasks, text, graphics, sounds, or stored records. Within this category we include eight types of uses: practicing, tutoring, simulating, gaming, demonstrating, testing, informing, and communicating. It should be noted that precise classification is difficult; these terms only suggest a working framework. Each use is described briefly.

Practicing. Computer-based practicing involves the student in rehearsing different elements of thinking and behaving to bring about more effective performance. Most educators believe that a student should engage in practice after certain meanings and understandings about a situation have been constructed. Thus, practice sessions at a computer should be predicated on a readiness to rehearse based on a background of meaning and motivation. This usually includes no attempt to present underlying explanations, although some computer-based practice programs attempt to incorporate brief reviews or diagnostic comments to be used when the student errs.

Tutoring. What is usually sought in computer-based tutoring is a high-fidelity simulation of a knowledgeable, sensitive, stimulating teacher's live instruction. Obviously, most examples of such computer programs fall considerably short of this intent. Yet a tutoring program may attempt to approximate a flow of activity similar to ordinary classroom discourse: an *introduc-*

tion, or overview of the session; *explanations* with examples and characteristics of the ideas being taught; *questions* aimed at checking the student's comprehension of the idea at different points in the development; differing *teaching branches* to be followed, depending on the student's responses; correct *feedback* and appropriate *reinforcement* following responses; and *records* of what and how the student performed during the session.

Simulating. Computer-based simulating involves the student in experiences with certain aspects of some true-to-life environment or phenomenon in ways that approximate the real events. The program incorporates certain features of the phenomenon through a model embodied in the program and its execution. It is usually possible to manipulate, interactively, various parameters or variables in order to examine the effects of choices or random factors. Mathematics instruction that incorporates simulating may include demonstrations of the phenomenon, explorations of the functional aspects of the underlying model, or applications of ideas being studied.

Gaming. Computer-based gaming for mathematics instruction is among the most stimulating uses for students. These computer programs, which are essentially a special kind of simulation, offer competitive situations in which one or more persons can play, score, and win. Our society abounds with electronic games; our focus on gaming should feature worthwhile learning activities related to the objectives, contents, and processes deemed integral to our mathematics curriculum. One unique focus could be on learning about a game as a system or structure.

Demonstrating. The mathematics teacher can execute a computer program to *demonstrate* an idea or a process. The computer can augment a presentation by generating examples, instances, summaries, counterexamples, illustrations, or questions. The machine can be made to produce such displays rapidly, accurately, and flexibly. The teacher needs to integrate such demonstrations into the overall development of instruction by stimulating, guiding, questioning, pacing, and directing.

Testing. In computer-based testing, the student interacts with a computer program that presents test items, accepts responses, and records and reports scores, all for the purpose of student evaluation. Such programs may simply display a single, stored test; more complex testing programs can generate multiple forms of a test from item pools or item forms, using prescribed or random criteria given by the teacher.

Informing. Students can access and query a stored computer-based reference system to gain information. In combination with video (for example, video cassettes and videodiscs), it is possible to provide high-speed access to textual as well as animated displays of information. Of course, the significant elements of instruction will still focus on how to use such information in the situations and challenges of mathematics.

Communicating. In computer-based instruction, communicating involves the use of a computer as a word-processing system by the student. Appropriate examples of such word-processing programs will be student-oriented, embodying not only the "forgiving" ways that compositions can be easily corrected and changed but also instructional helps with spelling, vocabulary, and grammar. Mathematics students involved in significant problematic projects could be expected to write and refine substantial reports of their efforts and results. Additionally, classroom "bulletin boards" that foster shared notices, both private and public, would be possible.

Teacher utilities

The third category of mathematics instructional computing employs computer programs executed by the teacher that serves as an electronic teacher's aide. The teacher's *utility* focus is on the output of the program. Within this category we include six types of uses: *generating tests, generating curriculum materials, scoring and analyzing tests, grading, managing,* and *communicating.* In general, these applications can enhance aspects of a teacher's responsibilities in planning, managing, evaluating, and reporting on instruction and learning. The computer programs usually feature interactive sessions in which stored files are retrieved, created, or updated.

What Are We Doing?

The computer has proved to be a provocative, motivating device in instruction. Students and teachers alike become excited and enthusiastic about the computer as a new tool in the classroom. However, we should briefly identify certain limitations or flaws in what has been attempted, as a basis for considering more mature manifestations for the future.

Rationales. Often, it appears, eager educators have acquired and used classroom computers simply to become part of the exciting computer age. Too little attention is given to the potential impacts of computing technology in relation to what we conceptualize education to be. We must now rethink the question, What can mathematics education become? Our rationales must acknowledge our goals and beliefs and consider heretofore unattainable purposes and procedures for educating. We must focus attention on learning as a person-centered, constructive process whose purpose is to build up and refine knowledge. Mathematics instruction must be in a context and include a process for involving the learner in problematic approaches that stimulate the development of a concept, a generalization, a procedure, or a solution. Accepting a challenge, constructing an understanding, and reflecting on the processes of thinking that might be used are all aspects of the problematic approach. A classroom computer can foster mathematical learning based on such constructivist, process-oriented, problem-solving approaches.

Roles. The changing roles of the teacher and the learner have not been carefully considered in our past efforts with instructional computing. Too often, mathematics teachers have been informers and students have been receivers. Indeed, the computer may be used as an interactive source of information. But it may also be used as a constructive context in which a learner solves, generalizes, abstracts, conjectures, searches, observes, simplifies, experiments, deduces, or remembers. Whether we mathematics teachers stimulate such processes through instructional computing will depend on the activities and tasks in which we involve our students. The teaching act may be changed, and it is to be hoped it will be changed in ways that capitalize on the computer as an instructional tool and that put the mathematics teachers into deep, personal interactions with the student. For example, in the domain of student programming, the teacher can become much more involved in setting *algorithmic tasks as problems to be solved* rather than modeling or dictating a single, inflexible procedure to be imitated by all students. The learning act may also be changed, and we hope it will be changed in ways that allow firsthand *experiences* with ideas significant to mathematical knowledge, personal *activity and responsibility* in building and refining one's own mathematics, and *individuality* in the ways and results of coming to know mathematics.

Development and research. Though our past efforts have been largely innovative, our approaches in developing classroom computing have been *single-use approaches.* That is, innovators have singled out one type of use, such as practicing or testing or student programming, to the exclusion of other kinds of instructional computing. Once a particular strategy for using the machine was identified, many of the pioneering developments sought to draw choice situations from school curricula that would permit the exhibition of that kind of computing use. In other words, school mathematics has been used to enhance the visibility of the computing application instead of the computer being used systematically to enhance mathematics curriculum. This has resulted in a sporadic, helter-skelter employment of the computer in perspectives too narrow to reflect the broad potentials of instructional computing.

Criticisms related to particular uses can be more specific. For example, mathematics educators have widely adopted student programming in the mathematics curriculum. Too often we have witnessed the isolated computer programming course as a mistaken approach:

1. As a "computer science" course, its primary objectives involve the learning of programming rather than mathematics.
2. As an upper-level elective, often with a prerequisite of algebra or an

even higher course, it delays computing and restricts it to an intellectu-ally elite subset.

3. As a course taught only by a specially prepared teacher, it fosters the attitude that computing has no place in any other part of the cur-riculum, thus obscuring its potential impact on all levels of mathemat-ics instruction.

4. Such a narrow implementation of programming portrays computing as an end rather than a means, and results in minimal impact on students.

Educators have also failed to analyze carefully the pedagogical and psy-chological bases for including programming tasks: the focus must be on stimulating and guiding students as they construct the ideas and processes we call mathematical knowledge. Curriculum developers have included com-puter-programming activities as optional enrichment rather than as signifi-cant situations embodying mathematical thinking essential to the goals of the curriculum.

Developing effective computer-based instruction can be a complex, time-consuming endeavor. We have all experienced productions that pre-sent poorly conceptualized and weakly operationalized forms of teaching and learning. When the capabilities and enhancements of the computer are not capitalized on, the machine becomes a shallow, electronic exposition. Artistic, sensitive, knowledgeable mathematics teachers must be involved in direct ways with the construction of effective computer-based mathematics instruction.

Little research has been undertaken to investigate the design of instruc-tional computing in mathematics or the effects of using diversified comput-ing in the classroom. A few studies have examined the relative effects of student programming on the learning of mathematics. Also, some evalua-tion studies have sought to identify the effectiveness of some forms of computer-based instruction, such as practicing or gaming. Overall, our knowledge base for developing or implementing instructional computing in mathematics is extremely thin, relying primarily on intuitive notions of "good" teaching.

Implementation. Teachers, students, principals, school boards, and par-ents eagerly desire the "computer age" for their schools. In seeking to begin, we can easily err. One serious mistake that can result is the absence of thoughtful *planning*. In an eagerness to get something started, little or no thought is given to how or why we should be using a classroom computer. Sometimes a top-down decision comes from an administrator; or the "iso-lated enthusiast" may be a teacher who tries to get something started. In any event, without comprehensive planning that attempts to build rationales and perspectives for integrating instructional computing throughout the mathe-matics curriculum, efforts for implementation have narrow, limited impact. Few teachers, few students, few curricular goals are affected.

Too often, educators have tunnel vision in viewing the implementation of instructional computing. Mathematics teachers have primarily accepted computer-programming, or perhaps practicing, usages. Students are typically allowed to use the computer in one way. These experiences can bear little or no relationship in the mind of the child to what might be going on in the learning activities of the regular classroom instruction of the day (e.g., when students go to a practicing session "down the hall" apart from the current mathematical studies, or when students solve computer-programming tasks that have no current relationship to the mathematics being studied). Thus, the *multiple uses* of the computer, *embedded* in the mainstream mathematical curriculum, have rarely been achieved.

Lastly, we must be sensitive to potential misuses and abuses of the computer. It is wrong to expect the computer to take over. Computers do not make good replacements for effective mathematics teachers. When using student programming, we must employ a constructive, problematic pedagogy; it violates the interactive, solving context to give completed computer programs to our students. When conducting any computer-based instruction session, we must realize that students will need preparation and follow-up if the session is to be an effective, integrated experience. In our classroom implementations we must avoid sporadic, hit-or-miss approaches and, instead, base our use of the computer on thoughtful, careful planning that embeds and integrates computing applications into the curricular goals and teaching strategies.

Multiusage Approaches

Goals

Instructional computing in mathematics must be determined through a careful construction of our planning for instruction. Classroom computing is a context of activity for learning and teaching; computers are tools to aid in the construction of knowledge of mathematics. You are well aware that any teaching context or aid must be fitted into plans for teaching *after* many thoughtful decisions have been made regarding the educational goals, objectives, and subject matter. To avoid the possible distortions to a sound mathematics curriculum that such an exciting, eye-catching technology as the microcomputer may produce, we must first determine what sorts of knowledges (ideas and processes) we seek to have students construct. Of course, we must be alert to the impacts of the computer on the discipline of mathematics and the myriad domains of mathematical applications in our culture. We must keep abreast of how the computing and informational technologies are altering the problems or tasks, as well as the solution strategies, that producers and consumers of mathematics employ. But any implementation of instructional computing must be preceded by careful decisions about the purposes and contents of our mathematics curricula.

Presuming that a thorough analysis of the aims and contents of the mathematics curriculum has been completed, then it is appropriate to consider the full range of the computer's potential for our instruction. The perspective of a *multi-use approach* is embodied in the following question to be posed for each instructional objective or topic:

> Of *all* the known ways that a computer can be used for instruction, which may be effective for the learning experiences we wish to provide in teaching a particular topic?

That is, for each objective or topic, we would consider each of the approaches within instructional computing (student programming, eight types of computer-based instruction, six types of teacher utilities) as potential applications of the computer.

Obviously, not all uses of instructional computing by either student or teacher can occur within all units of instruction. Indeed, it would be a serious distortion to force usages where they are not appropriate. But there are sensible and varied applications that can contribute substantively to the different aspects of learning and teaching mathematics. What is sought through the concept of *multiuse approaches* is a recognition of the rich, varied potential that instructional computing can offer as a context and a tool for furthering the goals and objectives of mathematics instruction.

Strategies

What are the appropriate tactics or strategies for developing a multiuse approach? The following advice may suggest ways to proceed:

1. Construct a comprehensive view of instructional computing, especially acknowledging a perspective of multiuse approaches. You will need to learn some computer programming and how to build student programming tasks appropriate to school mathematics learning. You will also need to learn to "play student" and "play teacher" to computer-based instruction programs.

2. In terms of your own commitments and classroom computing resources, set some sensible long-term goals. Ask, "What might mathematics learning and teaching in my classroom look like in three years?" To set goals, you will need to build visions.

3. In terms of your visions and goals, you will need to set some priorities. Ask, "What can I reasonably attempt first? Where would I like to be with my instructional computing in one year?" You might focus on certain topics and certain types of computing. You might decide to develop fairly extensive multiuse approaches for one or two topics or units of instruction during the first year. Or you might want to focus on developing one mode of computer usage for several topics.

4. Engage in mature curriculum planning in order to specify the approach. Decide on the goals and content of the curriculum. Only after these

decisions have been made should the computer decisions be formulated. Avoid the computer as a "tail wagging" distorter of the curriculum.

5. Construct a detailed list describing the computer programs that will be needed during the instruction of the unit. Can you select and acquire needed programs, or will you write them yourself?

6. Plan for the episodes involving computing sessions to occur within your overall lesson plans.

7. Reflect on, and evaluate, your instructional computing accomplishments in terms of your goals. Ask, "In what ways might my conduct of this instructional unit be improved next time through an enhanced application of computing?" Such self-evaluation is important; the complex innovations that comprehensive computing may make possible will probably evolve through a repeated "successive approximation" in our classroom.

Mathematics teachers stand at the threshold of a new era in education. Imagine how you might have felt if, as a teacher, you had learned of a technological breakthrough called a printing press, which would become an easy, inexpensive, reliable, comprehensive, graphical, dynamic instrument for transmitting information and stimulating learning! Computing technology constitutes such a revolution.

Meanwhile, it is *we* who face the challenge and excitement of exploring the potentials of the microcomputer in the classroom. What strategies are possible for implementing instructional computing? What steps are advisable? What cautions might we observe? How might instructional computing change mathematics education, allowing us to approach teaching in new ways? What traditional ideas and processes will the microcomputer make irrelevant? What new content emphases, such as algorithmics, might be amplified in our curricula? These are complex questions requiring our thoughtful, deliberate attention. Perhaps the most important step is simply to begin.

Yet during the pressure to "get something started," we must pause to realize the necessity to proceed rationally. Comprehensive planning at all levels, including the classroom, school system, state, and nation, is needed. Our vision of what mathematics educating *might be,* given the computational, literal, graphical, and analytical power of a classroom microcomputer, must be open and constructive. Mathematics teachers need to study state-of-the-art instructional computing—from the point of view of both the student and the teacher; staff development must be included in our comprehensive planning. And throughout our explorations we must avoid computing activities whose only basis may be "doing computing activities." Computing activities must fit into our mathematical instruction in terms of the goals and objectives, the mathematical knowledge to be built, the overall classroom framework as a social activity involving students and teacher, and the beliefs we hold regarding mathematics learning and teaching.

2

Computers: Challenge and Opportunity

Elizabeth M. Glass

IN THE next decade computers will be standard equipment in schools and as commonplace as the TV set in many homes. They will leave few facets of our personal lives untouched. Today's schoolchildren were born in the "computer age" and must leave school as computer-literate adults if they are to function in a computer-oriented society. The preservice education of elementary and secondary teachers in all disciplines must include the computer as an integral part of the teacher-training program. Adult education for computer literacy is growing in demand and becoming essential. The computer is no longer a mystique of the few or the private domain of scientists but a technological device demanding public awareness.

Rationale

Although the responsibility for computer education does not, and should not, rest solely with mathematics education, the innate mathematical basis of the technology—and experience with its use as a mathematical problem-solving tool—place a heavy burden on mathematics educators to provide leadership and chart direction for computer education.

Computer availability

Hardware. The development of the integrated circuit and the pursuit of miniaturization leading to today's chip has resulted in a revolution in computer hardware. Computer capabilities that were once restricted to very large, expensive hardware are now available in desktop computers priced within reach of classroom and household budgets. Hand-held machines with a single purpose or limited computer capabilities, such as the pocket calculator and hand-held electronic games, are available for under ten dollars.

Although schools have used large computers and minicomputers for instruction, they are now purchasing microcomputers for classroom use at a rapidly increasing rate. With the continued perfection of miniaturization inevitably resulting in lower cost, computer hardware is becoming even more generally available despite cutbacks of federal and state funds.

Software. Computer equipment has outdistanced instructional programs for computers, just as television sets were available long before the development of good commercial and educational programs for Instructional Television (ITV). All kinds of software have been produced and packaged by individuals, newly formed companies, and large computer projects. Some are educationally sound and well programmed. Others are poor. Presently, large book-publishing companies are making massive contributions to the development of software. In addition, there are many state and federally funded efforts to evaluate software. The production of software will increase rapidly, and, at the same time, more selection criteria and more formal evaluation tools will become available.

Types of programs

Drill and practice. Programs that give students practice in such areas as operations with whole numbers, number sequences, and factoring fall into the drill-and-practice category. Such programs are usually designed to pre-test the student and, on the basis of results, provide the appropriate level of practice. Records of the results are usually summarized, stored, and made available through the computer's output devices.

Tutorial programs. Programs that develop a new skill or concept are tutorial, or teaching, programs. These are usually small learning segments designed in carefully sequenced steps that require student participation. Such topics as solving equations, ratio and proportion, or area and perimeter lend themselves to this type of program.

Simulations. Programs can be written to simulate either a verifiable real-life situation or a situation that might exist. A computer program in science might simulate a laboratory experiment involving genetics or chemical reactions, which might be too time-consuming, too dangerous, or too expensive for actual experimentation in the classroom. In mathematics a computer can simulate the probable outcomes of a hundred tosses of a coin. Programs can also be written to simulate an imaginary situation that gives insight into the effect of manipulating various factors.

Games. Games can be purely recreational, but they can also meet clearly defined educational objectives. Both purposes have value, but the latter is more important for schools. Games that require logic or strategy play an important role in developing thinking skills crucial to learning, whatever the discipline. The skilled teacher can direct learning through games without stifling joy and creativity.

Computer benefits

The computer can do a number of things to help teachers. Consider the following:

Computers can individualize instruction. The ideal goal of education that has often eluded educators is one of addressing each student's individual needs. Even those programs providing one-to-one tutoring for low-achieving children are designed to help them cope with the class or grade curriculum rather than meet their individual needs. Differentiated assignments are often abandoned because of the great expenditure of time required of the teacher. Textbook materials are keyed for "slow, average, and fast" or "remedial, developmental, and enrichment" groups of learners, not for individual students. Instructional grouping and tracking subdivide the group but still do not address the individual.

Although ultimate individualization is the one-on-one model (e.g., Mark Hopkins, sitting on a log with a student), education had not approached this ideal prior to the interactive computer. Education has now replaced the log with the machine and, according to some, the teacher with a program. But lest some fear the technology, we should note that a person develops the program. Students can benefit from material appropriate to their personal needs, immediate feedback, instruction adjusted on the basis of analyzed response, and stimuli based on their differing modes of learning, whether verbal, visual, or audio. In addition to individualized developmental and practice exercises, the program can be personalized to identify and recall the student by name, a monumental task for some teachers with large classes.

Computers can manage instruction. Instruction and the management of instruction are intertwined in the classroom. A highly organized program of setting objectives, analyzing results, and reporting often leaves no time to teach. Teaching without organization and assessment is chaotic and inefficient. In fact, it may be regressive rather than progressive. The computer can be used effectively to prescribe instructional tasks, assess results, analyze responses, compare student progress over time, store information for immediate recall, and prepare reports. Reports can be personalized—there is no need to write the names of thirty students more than once. With the computer as an extra hand, the teacher has time to *think* and to *teach.*

Computers can teach concepts. Higher-level concepts and skills, especially those involving the interrelationships of various elements, are difficult to teach or to learn from a book. Simulated experiences on a computer make them more easily achievable. The computer is far more effective and efficient than a teacher in helping individuals develop higher-level concepts through analyzing a problem, gaming, and perceiving spatial relationships.

Computers can perform calculations. The computer is the most powerful, most efficient, and fastest calculating tool ever devised. It can perform long, tedious calculations in seconds, particularly in mathematics; chalkboards of calculations necessary for a single result can be stored in a program, displayed systematically, and repeated or recalled at will. In algebra the computer can evaluate a system of equations, plot them on a screen, and give the solution, all in a matter of seconds. How often have students missed the forest while focusing on the trees? Because complicated calculations can be performed with speed and accuracy, new fields of mathematics are being developed and discovered.

Computers can stimulate student learning. The phenomenal growth in the production and sale of both simple and sophisticated electronic hardware demonstrates the general popularity of computer technology. The beep of the electronic device is a familiar sound at home and at school. The active learner participation required by the computer makes it far exceed television in its potential for motivating the learner. The challenge of human against machine—the individual beating the system—is an ever-present and personal one. The motivation, even in an arithmetic practice set, is positive. A failure is not repeated, does not go unheeded, and is not displayed for all to see. Moreover, the computer opens doors and motivates all students, particularly the gifted, to achieve greater learning independence and greater creativity.

The computer's limitations

A computer has limitations. There are certain things it is *not.* It is not, for instance, a panacea, an add-on, or a replacement for the teacher.

A panacea. The computer is not a panacea; it will not solve all problems facing education. Such claims have been made in the past for both television and programmed learning, only to result in unmet expectations. The danger exists that some will promote the view that computer technology is capable of delivering a total mathematics program, particularly in the mode of computer-assisted instruction (CAI). If this happens, even full use of the technology for providing motivation, enrichment, and creativity can result in a curriculum that is limited, regimented, and regressive.

An add-on. The computer is not another piece of audiovisual hardware to be used as just an add-on and, thereby, assist the teacher only with remedial students or provide enrichment only for the gifted and talented. Used to its full potential, the computer can become an integral part of the curriculum at all grade levels and for all children. It needs to be thought of as both a tool and a medium for instruction, not as something that is added on to the existing curriculum in appropriate places.

A replacement for the teacher. Despite the cries of those who fear that education will be dehumanized and machines will replace teachers, the computer will, in fact, only enhance the role of the teacher. The computer itself is an inanimate piece of hardware until it is programmed and controlled by humans. Even computers that "talk" to other computers depend on people. The role of the teacher will change notably, but the importance of the teacher will be magnified. Teachers will be freed from myriad nonteaching duties, as never before, to pursue the art of teaching.

Conclusion

The National Council of Teachers of Mathematics (1980), in *An Agenda for Action,* has recommended that mathematics programs of the 1980s must take full advantage of the power of computers at all grade levels. *Priorities in School Mathematics: Executive Summary of the PRISM Project* (NCTM 1981) noted that lay people give stronger support for increased emphasis on the use of computers than professionals do. Since mathematics educators have more knowledge of computer technology and more experience with it in the classroom than their colleagues in other subject areas, the responsibility rests heavily on their shoulders to take full advantage of the available technology. Limiting the use of computers to a single mode, designing programs that give priority or restrict their use to mathematics, or failing to let the technology become an agent for curriculum change in the 1980s and beyond will not meet the challenge. Because mathematics educators have the knowledge of and experience with this technology in its educational infancy, they have a most crucial opportunity for leadership. The opportunity to provide the leadership and chart the direction not only of mathematics education but for all education of future generations is waiting. But not for long. The challenge is now; the responsibility is heavy. Mathematics educators can, and should, seize the opportunity.

REFERENCES

National Council of Teachers of Mathematics. *An Agenda for Action: Recommendations for School Mathematics of the 1980s.* Reston, Va.: The Council, 1980.
———. *Priorities in School Mathematics: Executive Summary of the PRISM Project.* Reston, Va.: The Council, 1980.

3

A Compass-and-Computer Perspective on Technology

David Clough Lukens

W HEN we face the question, "How will technology affect our teaching of mathematics?" We would do well to remember that technology has been a part of mathematics for a long time. We can look at history to get some perspectives on the uses and effects of technology.

There is a story that several philosophers visited René Descartes, the father of analytic geometry. They were very interested in his geometrical discoveries and asked to see his drawing instruments. He rummaged in his desk and brought out an old, rusty pair of compasses and a dented ruler. The philosophers asked how such discoveries as his could have been made with such obviously imperfect tools. Descartes replied that the tools suggested things to one's reason but never replaced reason.

There is also a story about Victor Poncelet, a later French mathematician, who was expert at geometrical constructions. He invented a graphical solution to an engineering problem that had baffled contemporary French mathematicians, including Laplace, who had tried algebraic solutions. Poncelet's solution could be done in the field by the captain of engineers and required only careful drawing for an adequate solution.

These stories show the two uses of technology in mathematics: suggesting things to our reasoning powers and finding solutions to problems. As we consider the technology of computers in our mathematics classrooms, it would be well to reflect on the uses of technology.

We use computers to solve problems, and we spend time teaching our students how to connect their problems with instructions the computer will understand. We can distinguish, then, between using the computer to solve a problem and analyzing the problem to fit it to the computer. The latter process helps us see things about the problem. This process of seeing does not depend on the proper functioning of the computer, merely on our knowledge of its software.

Likewise, the ruler and compass need not be perfect for us to use them to illustrate our proof of a theorem. The lines are straight and continuous and the circle equidistant from its center, not because we have good tools, but

15

because we define them that way. But the ruler and compass do more for us. We use the ruler and compass to illustrate our definition of line and circle, but we get our definitions from all the lines and circles we have drawn with those instruments. For example, when we think of continuity to reach a definition of it, we think of all the lines we have drawn or could draw, and from those actual lines we abstract the idea of a mathematical line—one of no width, of perfect straightness, of perfect continuity. It is true that looking at pictures of lines can feed the imagination and provide the material from which the mind can make its abstractions. But experience shows that the handling of technology, the physical gestures of drawing, are more effective than merely gazing at pictures for providing the raw material for abstractions.

Another piece of history illustrates this. Galileo proved the law of falling bodies (distance fallen from rest is proportional to the square of the time of fall) mathematically and experimentally. His mathematical proof assumed that speed was a continuously changing variable, an assumption not widely accepted at the time. He was familiar with continuous magnitudes from Euclidian geometry and from his work with the geometric and military compass (fig. 3.1), which he designed (Drake 1978).

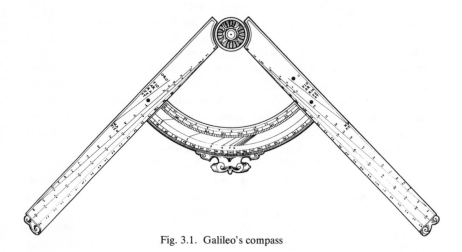

Fig. 3.1. Galileo's compass

The compass contained

> pairs of lines graduated according to the relative densities of various metals and stones, and according to the cube-root relation of diameter to volume. With these two scales, knowing the proper charge for a cannon of any bore and a ball of any material, gunners could quickly obtain the equivalent charge for any other bore and material of ball. Galileo called this the "problem of caliber," solved up to this time only approximately by referring to empirical tables with considerable risk of burst guns and wasted trial shots. (P. 39)

The important thing about this piece of mathematical technology was that it enabled its user to deal with a continuous variable. The engineer in the field might not have appreciated this mathematical fact, but a skilled and perceptive mathematician such as Galileo did appreciate it. The cannon balls could be of any size whatever, and the number of sizes was infinite. Likewise, the compasses could be set for any angle between 0 degrees and 90 degrees. The number of angles an engineer would use in his lifetime was indeed finite, but the continuity of the angle and its infinite divisibility were potentially there.

When Galileo analyzed the motion of a falling body and the relation of its speed to time, he discussed the infinite divisibility of time and the continuous change of speed in terms that could have been learned with the compass. For each *time*, there is a *speed;* for each *speed,* there is a *time;* for any two times there is a time in between, and its corresponding speed is between the speeds corresponding to the original two times.

To establish a relationship between time and distance in uniformly accelerated motion, Galileo first showed that the same distance is traveled in the same time by (1) an object accelerating uniformly from rest and (2) an object moving uniformly with half the final speed of the uniformly accelerating body. The diagram he used (fig. 3.2) is of interest to mathematicians. *AB* represents the time in which an object moves with uniform acceleration from rest through the space *CD. BE* represents the maximum final speed and *BF,* half of that speed. The lines from *AB* to *AE,* parallel to *BE,* represent the "increasing degrees of speed after the instant *A*." The lines from *AB* to *GF* represent the

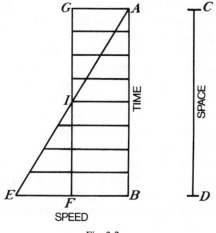

Fig. 3.2

unchanging speeds with which the uniform motion is performed. The two aggregates of parallel lines are equal, since *FEI* is equal to *GAI* and the trapezoid *BFIA* is common. Hence, Galileo's physical conclusion about speeds, times, and distance.

The figure illustrates Galileo's use of one-to-one correspondence between continuous things.

> Each instant and all instants of time *AB* correspond to each point and all points of line *AB,* from which points the parallels drawn and included within triangle *AEB* represent increasing degrees of the increased speed, while the parallels contained within the parallelogram represent in the same way just as many degrees of speed not increased but equable. . ." (Galilei, pp. 165–66).

The technology Galileo invested and the mathematical reasoning go together. Both involve an appeal to a one-to-one correspondence between continuous acts. I suggest that Galileo's familiarity with the geometric and military compass—a piece of technology—gave him a feeling for continuous variation that was essential to the invention of his proof.

Galileo's contemporaries rejected his idea of continuous change and said that the speed changed by discrete (although imperceptible) steps. The argument hinges on two questions that must be clearly distinguished. One is physical: "Does nature change continuously?" The mathematician, as mathematician, is silent on that point. The other question is, "Can continuous change be analyzed mathematically?" Galileo did it; and after him, Newton and Leibniz invented the calculus (independently) to deal with continuous change. Most of Galileo's contemporaries insisted that continuous change must be dealt with by approximating such a change by a series of very small but discrete steps.

This series of small, discrete steps is exactly how a computer shows a line on its screen (fig. 3.3). Both images are composed of finite steps; neither is a continuous line.

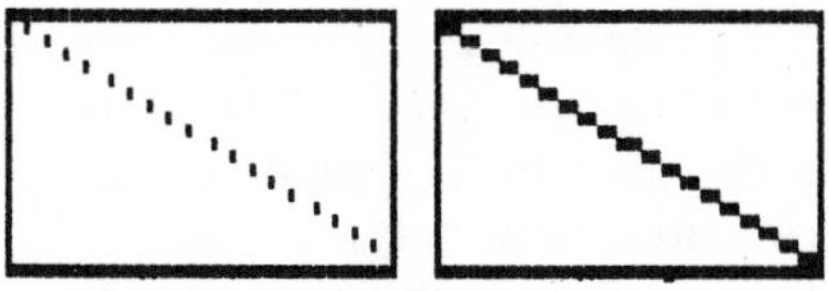

Fig. 3.3

If we ask one engineer to solve a problem on a computer and another to solve the same problem graphically, they will get the same answer within whatever tolerance is appropriate. To be useful, engineering solutions must be within tolerances, but they need not be exact. So computers, calculators, slide rules, and military compasses are used by engineers and judged on their ease, speed, and convenience.

But when we use then in our teaching, we are introducing to the student not only a tool but also a source of images of mathematical things. Just as Galileo's military compass gaven him an image from which he could firmly grasp the concept of continuous change, so the computer gives us images enabling us to grasp the concept of discrete entities.

What I see here is a danger to the teaching of the whole of mathematics unless the images from computers are balanced by images from the ruler and compass. Discrete mathematics is a very important part of mathematics, rich and useful. The student needs to be introduced to it and helped to become master of the computer. But it is not the whole of mathematics; continuous magnitudes and their study form the other half of mathematics. The fact that a computer can approximate a continuous function with a high degree of accuracy must not distract us from the fact that it is not continuous and gives discrete images of things.

When students must deal with continuity and appeal to their own grasp of the concept of continuity, computer pictures are deceptive. The images from a ruler and compass are needed here. The computer is a complicated adding machine, and it works only with an integral domain. It cannot handle even the continuity of rational numbers, much less the completeness of the reals, because it handles only a finite number of digits.

The computer pictures in figure 3.3 *suggest* that lines are composed of dots and that the slope of a line is always the ratio between two integers. Although this can be denied by the teacher, the image remains with the student. We need to be aware of this persisting image and provide other suitable images so the student can deal with the continuum on its own terms, just as we deal with discrete quantities by using the digital computer.

REFERENCES

Drake, Stillman. *Galileo at Work: His Scientific Biography.* Chicago: University of Chicago Press, 1978.
Galilei, Galileo. *Two New Sciences.* Translated with introduction and notes by Stillman Drake. Madison, Wis.: University of Wisconsin Press, 1974.

4

Imperatives and Possibilities for New Curricula in Secondary School Mathematics

James Fey
M. Kathleen Heid

THE microelectronics of computers offer hope of major breakthroughs in all school programs. There is, however, a special relationship between computers and mathematics. It was the search for a tool to perform rapid arithmetic and logical operations that led to modern computers.

The instructional roles of computers have been classified by Robert Taylor (1980) in three categories—tutor, tool, and tutee. Most of the original computer activity in mathematics education concentrated on the computer as tutee. Mathematics teachers, hypothesizing that students who wrote programs to guide computation (tutor the computer) would gain a deeper understanding of conventional mathematics, first viewed computer mathematics as a course in programming and numerical analysis. Thomas Dwyer's SOLO-Mode computing and Seymour Papert's Turtle Geometry have suggested new possibilities for the computer-as-tutee role, but student programming (usually for able students who have completed three years of college-preparatory mathematics in high school) is probably still the most common form of computer activity in secondary school mathematics. On a second side of Taylor's triad, work with computer-assisted instruction has long held promise of effective, efficient tutoring by machine. Much of the current developmental work involving microcomputers—such as using clever graphics, simulation, games, and dynamic demonstrations for teaching difficult mathematical concepts and skills—seems to fit in the computer-as-tutor category.

Recent research at the University of Maryland has focused on the implications of computers as mathematical tools. Despite the rich variety of propo-

Work on this paper was supported in part by NSF Award No. SED-8024425 in the joint National Science Foundation–National Institute of Education Program on Mathematics Education Using Information Technology. Any opinions, findings, conclusions, or recommendations expressed herein are those of the authors and do not necessarily reflect the views of the National Science Foundation or the National Institute of Education.

sals and developmental efforts seeking to use computers for mathematics teaching, the actual content of most secondary mathematics programs today is remarkably similar to that of thirty years ago. Students still spend years honing their skills in arithmetic, algebraic manipulations and equation solving, calculations and manipulation of trigonometric functions, and procedures for differentiation and integration of elementary functions in calculus. Unfortunately, many attain only limited and temporary mastery of these skills, and one has to be highly optimistic to believe that computers will be the instructional key unlocking the door to overcoming the deficiencies in learning that have persisted for many years despite the best efforts of gifted teachers.

Looking at the current capabilities of widely available computing equipment and software and making only modest projections of likely future developments, one is forced to question the content and emphases in school mathematics programs today. Must students still acquire the traditional collection of mathematical skills and ideas to operate intelligently in the computer-enhanced environment for scientific work? Are there new skills or understandings that should take prominent roles in courses preparing students for mathematical demands that lie in the twenty-first century?

This article reports the answers and further questions that have evolved in several years of curriculum analysis, software development, and classroom testing of several innovative computer-based curricula.

What Computers Can Do

It has long been possible to write and store small programs on the personal calculator. Technical journals are filled with descriptions of calculator programs that yield solutions to a wide variety of applied mathematics problems. Calculator programs have also been written to solve the type of problems commonly encountered in students' early exposures to mathematics. However, the exciting capabilities of programmable calculators are no match for the seemingly endless list of applications now possible on low-cost microcomputers. At last within the financial reach of every school system are computers and programs capable of performing a range of mathematical procedures that could consume the entire mathematics careers of even the most mathematically inclined. The graphics capabilities of even a small microcomputer system make possible a powerful array of two-dimensional representations. The somewhat more limited applications of three-dimensional graphics now available for the microcomputer add still more potential for the classroom, and present progress in lowering the cost of other graphics hardware may bring previously inaccessible graphics systems into the classroom in the near future (Whitted 1982).

Possibilities for classroom use of preprogrammed computer software are boundless. There is something for everybody (Gilder 1980; Poole and

Borchers 1979; Spectrum Software 1981). The middle school student can find programs that compute prime factors or greatest common denominators, convert measurements from English to metric, or compute the day of the week for any given date. For the business mathematics student, there are programs to answer virtually any question about investments, mortgages, depreciation, loans, taxes, or check writing, as well as programs that solve linear programming and other optimization problems. Systems such as VISICALC can demonstrate across an entire range of financial summaries the effect of a change in a single entry (Branscomb 1982). With the right program, the geometry student can—

- find the area and volume of almost any two- or three-dimensional geometric figure;
- compute the measures of the missing parts of given figures;
- perform geometric transformations;
- even prove theorems.

An inexpensive Versa-Writer or graphics tablet would add to all this the ability to calculate the area of a closed geometric figure simply by tracing its shape with a drawing arm. Adding a three-dimensional graphics tablet would permit rotating and rescaling representations of three-dimensional objects, imagined or real.

The algebra student will find fascinating tools in programs in curve plotting (with considerable variety of scaling and transformation options), linear and curvilinear interpolation, and root finding, as well as programs to solve large systems of linear equations and perform matrix operations and operations on complex numbers. For calculus students, programs to estimate limits, derivatives, and integrals are readily available. Programs to compute permutations and combinations as well as do sophisticated simulations are available for the probability student. Statistics students will have no trouble locating programs to compute probabilities for given values in any of the common distributions, perform a superb variety of statistical tests, or complete a regression analysis on a given set of data. Countless other applications are undoubtedly being created daily. The possibilities seem endless. A justifiably optimistic projection of the future might forecast microcomputer adaptation of a variety of programs available for larger systems, including those that handle mathematical programming, differential equations, linear algebra, optimization methods, and even portions of abstract algebra (Fox, Hall, and Schryer 1978; Lawson et al. 1979; Machura and Sweet 1980; Wardlaw 1978).

For the purist who would cavalierly relegate such programs to the engineer's domain, recent developments in artificial intelligence provide an undeniably potent counterexample. Programs now available for use on the microcomputer can perform almost all the symbolic manipulation necessary in academic mathematics classes through first-year calculus. The most powerful and widely available of these programs, muMath, leaves even the most stubborn sceptic in wonder (Pavelle, Rothstein, and Fitch 1981; Steen 1981; Wilf 1982).

MuMath is designed to do rational arithmetic and symbolic algebra and calculus. An arithmetician might test the powers of muMath with such commands as—

? 5/9 + 7/12;

The program would respond immediately with

@: 41/36

Further tests would produce these results:

? $(-72) \wedge (1/3)$;
@: $-2 * 9 \wedge (1/3)$
? 20!;
@: 2432902008176640000 [muMath produces up to 611-digit answers]
? 20!/18!;
@: 380
? $2 \wedge 2 \wedge 5 + 1$;
@:4294967297
? $(2 \wedge 2 \wedge 5 + 1)/641$;
@: 6700417

Imagine the progress a budding number theorist could make.

The algebra student would delight in such muMath performances as this:

? SOLVE $((4*T + 5)/(10*T - 7) == (2*T + 3)/(5*T - 7),T)$;
@: $[T = -14/19]$
? $((A \wedge (-1/6))*(B \wedge (3/2))) \wedge 12 / ((A \wedge (2/3))*(B \wedge (3/5))) \wedge 9$;
@: $B \wedge (117/5)/A \wedge 8$
? TRGEXPD $(SIN(2*X + Y), -15)$;
@: $2*COS(X) \wedge 2 * SIN(Y) + 2*COS(X)*COS(Y)*SIN(X) - SIN(Y)$

MuMath calculus answers the frequent lament of calculus teachers that round-off errors produce misleading results (Gordon 1979; Miel 1980). MuMath does not give answers in decimal form. If answers are not integral fraction functions, radicals, or pi, whatever is appropriate is used, as shown in the preceding example. Calculus students could use muMath to give suitable answers to most of the examination questions they encounter in their first year. Here are muMath results on a few University of Maryland examination questions:

? LIM$(((SIN(3*X)) + 4*X \wedge 2)/X,X,0)$;
@: 3

(*Translation:* $\lim_{x \to 0^+} \dfrac{\sin(3x) + 4x^2}{x} = 3$)

? LIM((3 + X $\wedge$ (1/2))/(X − 9), X, 9, TRUE);
@: MINF

(*Translation:* $\displaystyle\lim_{x \to 9^-} \left(\frac{3 + \sqrt{x}}{x - 9} \right) = -\infty$)

The word "TRUE" in the statement of the problem indicates that the limit 9 is to be approached from below. The absence of TRUE in the preceding examples instructs muMath to approach from above.

DIF (DEFINT (T∗ (1 − T $\wedge$ 5) $\wedge$ (1/2), T, 1, −2∗X) ,X);
4∗X ∗ (1 + 32∗X $\wedge$ 5) $\wedge$ (1/2)

(*Translation:* $\displaystyle\frac{d}{dx} \int_{1}^{-2x} t\sqrt{1 - t^5}\ dt = 4x\sqrt{1 + 32x^5}$)

If an algorithm or symbol manipulation is taught to secondary school or calculus students, in all likelihood there is a microcomputer program that will perform the procedure. If the desired program is not now available for the microcomputer, the near future will most likely see its creation. Technology will soon be ready to supply the classroom with user-friendly versions of any of these programs. Easy-to-use, low-cost programs will perform most of the skills that today's students spend hours practicing. If schools allowed students to use the considerable computer power available, drastic curricular revisions would be in order. The challenge of the computer revolution rests squarely at the door of the mathematics classroom.

Pending Curricular Change

What are the ways that secondary school mathematics curricula might properly change to reflect the innovations in the technology available for doing mathematical tasks? In this section we shall outline what appear to be some of the most promising directions for new curricula and the questions raised by those proposals. We hope to stimulate research-and-development activity to assess the virtues and difficulties in each.

As a prototype, we shall focus on the usual topics of elementary algebra. In judging the merit of any particular mathematical fact, concept, skill, or principle, we have applied the basic criterion that students of emerging curricula should at least acquire the understanding and skill needed to solve the problems within reach of successful algebra students today—assuming that computers and appropriate programs are permitted as working tools.

In some sense, secondary mathematics begins with the abstraction of arithmetic operations and principles to algebra. In an algebra course we introduced (students) to the use of variables, equations, inequalities, the rules or symbolic syntax needed to express relations among variables, and the symbol manipulation for wresting information from given conditions. A typical sequence of topics follows:

1. Operations and properties of real numbers
2. Variables, expressions, and open sentences
3. Linear equations and inequalities
4. Operations on polynomials
5. Fractional expressions and equations
6. Irrational numbers and radical expressions
7. Systems of open sentences in two variables
8. Quadratic equations and inequalities
9. Functions, relations, and graphs

Are all these concepts and skills essential?

Topics of diminished importance

Without doubt, the focus of most class time in elementary algebra is the array of *procedures* for transforming algebraic expressions and solving equations and inequalities. The required transformations follow a few general principles that have been programmed for the computer. As a consequence, it is possible to use the computer to extend the course by including much more difficult applications of the usual procedures. It seems more sensible, however, to reduce sharply the time spent training students to perform as efficient, reliable algebra machines. It seems *unnecessary,* for example, for students to become facile in solving such expressions as these:

$$19n - 11 - 12n - 5 = 5$$
$$16 - 8n \leq n - 20$$
$$|5 - 3(2 - z)| \leq 8$$
$$x^2 + 5x + 6 = 0$$
$$\frac{3}{x^2 - 1} + \frac{1}{x + 1} = 0$$
$$\begin{cases} 3x + 2y = 7 \\ x - y = 1 \end{cases}$$

But learning the skills requisite for these strategies and manipulations might be necessary for other reasons. It might be that learning these skills is an essential phase in building important understandings of variables, function, and the problem-solving applications of algebra, although this is not supported by any research evidence. Whereas an algebra course that asks students to master only the very simplest of such manipulations and that uses computers for complex work offers promise of savings in curriculum space, we do not know if significant understandings would be lost. This problem ought to be studied.

Topics of continued importance

Algebraic ideas and skills that retain their importance in a computer-enhanced environment for mathematics are those that contribute to the *formulation of problems* for subsequent manipulative solution or to the *interpretation of results* from algebraic transformations. The mathematical modeling process—whether fitting a linear equation to some simple word problem or finding multiple constraints and an objective function in linear programming—involves a variety of skills and understandings that have traditionally received too little attention amid the techniques of algebra.

Nearly every quantitative situation to which an algebraic model applies includes one or more variables and some functions or relations placing conditions on those variables. To operate effectively in such situations, students must develop broad abilities and more specific skills in three important phases of activity:

1. When students venture outside the mathematics classroom and away from the comforting guidance of their text with its problems neatly partitioned into appropriate sections, they have great difficulty in *recognizing the ingredients of situations to which their mathematical skills might apply*. It seems essential that students acquire well-developed intuition about the structure of problem settings to which their various mathematical tools apply. This kind of intuition seems to come from extensive experience and reflection on that experience. Reducing the time devoted to manipulative skills would free time for applied problem solving, whereas the graphic and calculating capabilities of computers would help students explore the shapes of graphs of various algebraic functions and relations. The result should be better reasoning in the *problem identification* stage of applications, which is of critical importance.

2. The *translation of the conditions of the problem or situation into mathematical form* for algebraic calculations involves concepts, reasoning processes, and technical skills that have always been judged important but not often effectively taught. Although students in algebra seem to learn how to perform elaborate symbolic gymnastics, recent research suggests that even very successful students have a flawed understanding of the concept of variable. The translation of the problem's conditions into algebraic expressions requires a sound understanding of variable usage. It further requires ease with the rules of syntax for expressions (order of operations) and the common computer usage of those rules. In constructing appropriate algebraic models, students must use precise language and take care to determine relevant and extraneous information (and get some experience in seeking needed information not already displayed in the problem statement). All these objectives are expressed for algebra courses today, but in reality they are neither the focus nor the significant outcomes of the courses.

Not only can computer use create time needed for careful construction of mathematical models, but computers make it feasible to formulate more realistically the functions and relations that fit problem data. For most common algebra problems the given numbers and conditions lead in a clear-cut way to writing an equation or inequality or system of such conditions. In practice, however, applied questions much more commonly appear like the following:

> Given below are market research data on a new product. Find a relation between price and projected sales that fits these data and project the sales if the price is set at $5.50.

Price:	$3	4	5	6	7
Sales:	100	80	65	40	10

The first step in approaching this problem calls for fitting a function to data that are only approximately linear. Some sort of least-squares curve fitting is necessary. The idea is fairly simple, but the theory behind the least-squares technique seems too sophisticated for algebra students. With computers the difficult calculations can be done easily while demonstrating a realistic problem-solving strategy.

3. When students work on applied problems, their answers are seldom subjected to even the simplest tests of reasonableness. When computers are used to assist with calculations, it is still essential to *interpret and check the results*. Students must be adept at performing estimates, checking answers by substitution in conditions, and asking themselves whether an answer is plausible in the context of the problem setting; moreover they must be inclined to do these things. To perform this validation, they must be comfortable with using measurement units, substituting in formulas, and again, careful in their use of algebraic symbolism.

Moreover, sensible interpretation of results requires an understanding of how modeling assumptions have influenced the results. (Did a simplifying assumption really invalidate the conclusions or explain the counterintuitive solution?) Another phase of modeling that is not often done in mathematics classes but that occurs regularly in realistic situations is sensitivity analysis. If one or more of the problem-setting conditions change, how will the solution be affected? For instance:

> Suppose the relation between price (p) and sales (s) of a product is given by $s = -20p + 1000$, and costs (c) are related to sales by $c = 5s + 750$. Find the sales, cost, revenue, and profit for various price levels and find the optimum price.

This problem requires following the effect of changes in one variable through a sequence of related conditions. The questions are very natural in real applications, but students with a traditional background in algebra find them difficult. The difficulty might simply be the complexity of chasing many variables around, but our own research suggests that the "find x" orientation of algebra that focuses on the manipulative skills has not prepared students for the more common task of studying the interplay of conditions, for thinking about functional relationships.

The frequent use of algebra in a function or relation context also makes the interpretation of graphical information very important. For instance, in the preceding business situation, graphs of the cost, revenue, and profit functions will commonly be displayed simultaneously. Students must be adept at making correct interpretations of the shapes of those graphs to find max/min points, intercepts, and so forth, and to explain the meaning of those critical points in the applied situation at hand. This might sound like much more advanced course content than first-year algebra students could absorb. Our exploratory classes indicate the contrary; many students who are not good at the manipulative aspects of symbolic algebra can use good quantitative reasoning when interpreting the results of computer-generated computations or graphs. These experiences suggest to us the possibility of radically different organizations for the material in algebra syllabi.

New structures for algebra topics

One of the most common beliefs of mathematics teachers is the hypothesis that the mastery of calculational skills (in arithmetic, algebra, or calculus) must precede applications or problem solving. Teachers hold the view that if students were asked to spend much of their time simply formulating applied problems without having the tools to get some of the answers, they would have a poor experience indeed. But if one allowed computational aids in the manipulative aspects of answer finding, courses would not have to be organized to develop extensive technical skills before encountering realistic or appealing problem materials. It is conceivable that a first course in algebra could stress the basic *concepts* of variable, function, relation, and equation/inequation conditions. The manipulative skills could be the focus of a later course for students who find need for that ability to pursue more creative uses of algebra. Some other attractive alternative organizations for an algebra course might focus on problem finding and problem making with, again, realistic applications of mathematics.

Conclusions

As hand-held arithmetic calculators have spread to nearly every facet of contemporary society, their capabilities have brought into serious question the emphasis elementary mathematics instruction places on speed and accuracy with computational algorithms. The demonstrable and projected potential of computers raises identical questions about the focuses of secondary school mathematics courses like algebra, trigonometry, and calculus. Several alternative curricula for these courses can be constructed now, and the implications of changing the content and emphasis in each area should be studied carefully. Our preliminary work at the University of Maryland suggests that at least one model of the proposed new curricula has great potential. Students who have previously been stymied by the difficulty of acquiring various manipulative skills have learned and successfully used advanced mathematical ideas. The promise and risks of curricular changes such as those outlined above must be studied carefully and extensively to guide our choices in the years ahead.

REFERENCES

Birnbaum, Joel S. "Computers: A Survey of Trends and Limitations." *Science,* 12 February 1982, pp. 760–65.

Branscomb, Lewis M. "Electronics and Computers: An Overview." *Science,* 12 February 1982, pp. 755–60.

DeRosa, J. H. "Printing Calculator Normalizes Data, Makes Graphical X-Y Plot." *Electronic Design,* 6 December 1979, p. 126.

Fox, P. A., A. D. Hall, and N. L. Schryer. "PORT Mathematical Subroutine Library." *ACM Transactions in Mathematical Software* 4 (June 1978):104–26.

Gilder, Jules H. *Basic Computer Programs in Science and Engineering.* Rochelle Park, N.J.: Hayden Book Co., 1980.

Gordon, Sheldon P. "Discrete Approach to Computer-oriented Calculus." *American Mathematical Monthly* 86 (May 1979):386–91.

Kahan, W. "Personal Calculator Has Key to Solve $f(x) = 0$." *Didactic Programming* 2 (Winter-Spring 1980):36–42.

Lawson, C. L., R. J. Hanson, D. R. Kincaid, and F. T. Krogh. "Basic Linear Algebra Subprograms for FORTRAN Usage." *ACM Transactions in Mathematical Software* 5 (September 1979):308–23.

Machura, Marek, and Roland A. Sweet. "A Survey of Software for Partial Differential Equations." *ACM Transactions in Mathematical Software* 6 (December 1980):461–88.

Miel, George. "Calculator Calculus and Round-Off Errors." *American Mathematical Monthly* 87 (April 1980):243–52.

Morgan, Chris. "Keeping Our Technological Edge." *Byte* 7 (August 1982):6–18.

Pavelle, Richard, Michael Rothstein, and John Fitch. "Computer Algebra." *Scientific American,* December 1981, pp. 136–52.

Poole, Lou, and Mary Borchers. *Some Common Basic Programs.* 3d ed. Berkeley, Calif.: Osborne/McGraw-Hill, 1979.

Spectrum Software. *Mathematics Series: Statistical Analysis I, Numerical Analysis, Matrix, 3D Surface Plotter.* Sunnyvale, Calif.: Spectrum Software, 1981.

Steen, Lynn A. "Computer Calculus." *Science News* 119 (1981):250–51.

Taylor, Robert P., ed. *The Computer in the Classroom: Tutor, Tool, Tutee.* New York: Teachers College Press, 1980.

Wardlaw, William P. "Computer-aided Intuition in Abstract Algebra." *Computers and Education* 2 (1978):247–57.

Whitted, Turner. "Some Recent Advances in Computer Graphics." *Science,* 12 February 1982, pp. 755–74.

Wilf, Herbert S. "The Disc with the College Education." *American Mathematical Monthly* 89 (January 1982):4–8.

5

The Impact of Computers: A Syllabus

Edward T. Ordman

MEMPHIS State University, drawing on the resources of large undergraduate and graduate programs in computer science, has established a survey course on the impact of computers for upper-level nontechnical students. The syllabus and reading list for this course may suggest topics for reading or in-service courses for teachers that are different from the relatively common "introduction to programming."

It is increasingly accepted that all teachers, perhaps all college graduates, and possibly even all high school graduates, should have some acquaintance with computers. Although a brief introduction to computer programming is often proposed, many such introductions fail to address the issue of how computers actually affect society or specific institutions.

During the early 1980s, Memphis State University's Department of Mathematical Sciences developed a computer literacy course intended for nontechnical students at the senior or graduate level. This course was intended, not as a programming course, but as a broad overview of computer science, computer applications, and the impact of computers on organizations and society.

The project reported here was a joint activity with Charles Brandon, Stanley Franklin, Hugh McHenry, and Austin Smith. It was supported by Memphis State University and other donors. Staff for the first offerings of the course included the following persons:

- A successful corporate executive with broad experience in computer consulting and directing corporate computer operations
- The chairman of a university computer science department (Memphis State)
- An experienced teacher with an extensive background in computer-aided and computer-managed instruction
- An experienced computer science teacher with government and consulting experience, involved in recent years in building a micro-computer-based computer science program

- A computer consultant with extensive knowledge of computer hardware and medical and library applications

The development of the course was undertaken with the specific expectation that there would be spin-offs in the form of shorter courses, particularly extension courses and teacher workshops. Accordingly, the detailed syllabus for this course may suggest appropriate topics or groups of topics for in-service workshops or individual reading.

The syllabus

The general breakdown of the lectures was as follows:

Topic	Hours	Percent
Hardware	3	7.5
Systems programs	4	10
Introduction to BASIC	4	10
Theoretical computer science	3	7.5
Applications	8	20
Impact on organizations	8	20
Impact on society	9	22.5
Miscellaneous	1	2.5
	40	100

The calendar

Although the calendar naturally varied somewhat from one semester to another, the following was typical:

Week 1. Introduction; Boolean algebra; simple circuits, gates, flip-flops, and adders. *Laboratory:* Use of digital trainers to build flip-flops, half-adders, and simpler circuits.

Week 2. History of computers from 1890 to 1960; a look at artifacts (old core memories, plug-board wiring, modern circuit chips, disks, etc.); brief introduction to machine language. What is an assembler? A compiler? An operating system? *Laboratory:* Introduction to the use of an IBM personal computer; game playing.

Week 3. More about compilers and operating systems; interpreters; first lecture about programming in BASIC. *Laboratory:* Start of programming in BASIC (mainly typing in commands from an instruction sheet to see the result).

Week 4. More lectures on BASIC (mainly built around writing a program to balance a checkbook). Second BASIC laboratory.

Week 5. Examples of scientific programming; discussion of simulating aircraft operation, atmospheric modeling; the concept of structured programming; noting other programming languages. Third BASIC laboratory.

Week 6. Extensive example—how does a business (e.g., a law firm) decide it needs a computer? How does it decide what to buy? What is word processing? How does it relate to data processing? *Laboratory:* Use of a word-processing program.

Week 7. What is artificial intelligence? How do very large programs get written? Top-down programming; management of programming. Second word-processing laboratory.

Week 8. Data base management systems; distributed data bases; computer networking. *Laboratory:* Use of a (small, local) data base management system.

Week 9. Electronic spreadsheet programs for business calculations and forecasting. *Laboratory:* Use of VISICALC.

Week 10. Impact of computers on a business organization; economics of the organization; funding the data-processing operation; internal security of data and equipment. Second electronic spreadsheet laboratory.

Week 11. Life cycle of data processing in the corporation; impact on the organizational structure. *Laboratory:* Use of a personal computer as a terminal to access an on-line, public data bank.

Week 12. Impact of computers on society: new tools, new careers, new businesses. *Laboratory:* Further use of on-line data banks.

Week 13. Computer impacts: privacy problems, computer crime, transborder data flow, displacement of workers. *Laboratory:* Open for work on student projects.

Week 14. Cultural and artistic impact of computers; computer-aided instruction; psychological impact of computers. *Laboratory:* Open for work on student projects.

Credit arrangements

Four semester hours of credit were given for the course, which met for three hours of lecture and three hours of laboratory weekly for fourteen weeks. A brief term paper (at least five pages, prepared on a word processor and requiring output from at least one other program) was also required. The laboratory was available to students for about six hours a week in addition to the scheduled three hours, so that they could use the computers, review slide sets shown in class, or consult with the laboratory assistants. Students enrolled in certain career-oriented programs had the option of undertaking substantially larger projects to bring the total credit up to six hours; some of these projects resulted in significant contributions to the resources available for the course. (One student, through his employer, had access to a Boeing 747 flight simulator!)

Reading list

The textbook (in which we jumped around considerably) was *Computers in Society,* 3d edition, by Donald H. Sanders (New York: McGraw-Hill, 1981). We also used just over half the slide sets included in "The Audio Visual Library of Computer Education" (Prismatron Productions, Inc., Mill Valley, Calif.).

During the development of the course the instructors collected a list of books that could appropriately be read to supplement the text. It included many books that we felt could be read by someone without an extensive technical background but that still had substantial content for the material we were studying. We were less successful than we hoped in getting the students to read extensively in these books but found them very useful in preparing our own lectures.

James L. Adams, *Conceptual Blockbusting* (New York: W. W. Norton & Co., 1980)

Karen Billings and David Moursund, *Are You Computer Literate?* (Forest Grove, Oreg.: Dilithium Press, 1979)

Frederick P. Brooks, Jr., *The Mythical Man-Month: Essays on Software Engineering* (Reading, Mass.: Addison-Wesley Publishing Co., 1975)

H. Dominic Covvey and Neil Harding McAlister, *Computer Consciousness* (Reading, Mass.: Addison-Wesley Publishing Co., 1980)

Tom de Marco, *Concise Notes on Software Engineering* (New York: Yourdon, 1979)

Engineering Concepts Curriculum Project, *Man and His Technology* (New York: McGraw-Hill Book Co., 1973)

Robert Fenichel and Joseph Weizenbaum, Introduction to *Readings from Scientific American: Computers and Computation* (San Francisco: W. H. Freeman & Co., 1971)

Louis E. Frenzel, Jr., *The Howard W. Sams Crash Course in Microcomputers* (Indianapolis: Howard W. Sams & Co., 1980)

Herman R. Goldstine, *The Computer from Pascal to Von Neumann* (Princeton, N.J.: Princeton University Press, 1972)

Frank Herbert with Max Barnard, *Without Me You're Nothing: The Essential Guide to Home Computers* (New York: Simon & Schuster, 1980)

Martin O. Holoien, *Computers and Their Social Impact* (New York: John Wiley & Sons, 1977)

Tracy Kidder, *The Soul of a New Machine* (Boston: Little, Brown & Co., 1981)

Don Lancaster, *The Incredible Secret Money Machine* (Indianapolis: Howard W. Sams & Co., 1978)

Murray Laver, *Computers and Social Change* (New York: Cambridge University Press, 1980)

Blaise W. Liffick, ed., *Program Design* (Peterborough, N.H.: Byte Books, 1978)

James Martin, *The Wired Society* (Englewood Cliffs, N.J.: Prentice-Hall, 1978)

Pamela McCorduck, *Machines Who Think* (San Francisco: W. H. Freeman & Co., 1979)

Glenford J. Myers, *Reliable Software through Composite Design* (New York: Petrocelli/Charter, 1975)

John Nevison, *Executive Computing* (Reading, Mass.: Addison-Wesley Publishing Co., 1980)

———, *The Little Rock of Basic Style* (Reading, Mass.: Addison-Wesley Publishing Co., 1978)

Adam Osborne, *Running Wild: The Next Industrial Revolution* (Berkeley, Calif.: Osborne/McGraw Hill, 1979)

Seymour Papert, *Mindstorms: Children, Computers, and Powerful Ideas* (New York: Basic Books, 1980)

George Penney, *Managing Computers: Data Processing Case Histories* (Rochelle Park, N.J.: Hayden Book Co., 1975)

Robert Persig, *Zen and the Art of Motorcycle Maintenance* (New York: Bantam Books, 1974)

Donald Sanders and Stanley Birkin, *Computers and Management in a Changing Society* (New York: McGraw-Hill Book Co., 1980)

Scientific American, *Microelectronics* (San Francisco: W. H. Freeman & Co., 1977)

Carl Townsend and Merle Miller, *How to Make Money with Your Microcomputer* (Forest Grove, Oreg.: Dilithium Press, 1981)

Dennie Van Tassel, *Program Style, Design, Efficiency, Debugging, and Testing* (Englewood Cliffs, N.J.: Prentice-Hall, 1978)

Mitchell Waite and Michael Pardee, *Microcomputer Primer* (Indianapolis: Howard W. Sams & Co., 1980)

Carl Warren and Merle Miller, *From the Counter to the Bottom Line* (Forest Grove, Oreg.: Dilithium Press, 1979)

Gerald M. Weinberg, *The Psychology of Computer Programming* (New York: Van Nostrand Reinhold Co., 1971)

Thomas Whiteside, *Computer Capers: Tales of Electronic Thievery, Embezzlement, and Fraud* (New York: New American Library, Mentor Books, 1978)

Jerry Willis, *The Peanut Butter and Jelly Guide to Computers* (Forest Grove, Oreg.: Dilithium Press, 1978)

———, *The Techno/Peasant Survival Manual* (New York: Bantam Books, 1980)

Edward Yourdon, *Managing the Structured Techniques* (Englewood Cliffs, N.J.: Prentice-Hall, 1979)

———, *Techniques of Program Structure and Design* (Englewood Cliffs, N.J.: Prentice-Hall, 1975)

Rodnay Zaks, *DON'T (or How to Care for Your Computer)* (Berkeley, Calif.: Sybex, 1981)

6

Mathematics, Computation, and Psychic Intelligence

Edwin E. Moise

IN the next decade, excellence will not prevail in the teaching of school mathematics. The number of underqualified teachers is enormous, and it cannot be reduced soon. In computer science the situation is worse: adequately trained teachers are virtually absent. For this reason, most innovations will be carried out either slowly or badly, and so we had better consider the issues on the basis of first principles.

Mathematics has been brilliantly taught in elementary schools at some times and in some places, but much more prevalently, mathematics in elementary schools has been a disaster. This is where children have gotten the idea that mathematics is the subject in which you go through elaborate procedures that you do not understand and should not even try to understand. This is an almost inevitable response to interminable drill in the algorithms that are used with decimal numerals.

Attitudes are based almost entirely on experiences and hardly at all on preachment. When professional mathematicians use the familiar algorithm to compute (by hand) the product of two positive integers, they know that the problem has a meaning and that the algorithm gives the right answer. But while using the algorithm they do not bother their heads about such matters; this would be a useless distraction and would increase the chance of casual errors. A child can hardly be blamed for taking the same attitude in carrying out the same process. The trouble is that when such processes dominate the child's daily experience of mathematics, the subject is falsified. To reduce a word problem to a well-defined computational problem is mathematical thinking, but to use a familiar algorithm over and over again is drudgery. When this is heavily stressed, the child has a right to conclude that mathematics as a whole is drudgery. Most people form this impression in childhood and never get over it. Very often, when people have asked me what I do for a living, my response has been a conversation stopper, as if I had said I was an embalmer.

Deadly drill in algorithms forms a large part of the child's experience in elementary school. To appreciate the magnitude of the harm that is done, we need to consider the mentality that nearly all children bring with them to the first grade. Normally, children have traits of temperament which in an adult would be called intellectual. They want to know things. And they want to know not just what but also why; that is, they want to understand what they know. Some time between crawling and walking, they address themselves to the formidable task of learning to speak a foreign language. To a baby, all languages are foreign, but every baby learns the language of its parents, including its exact grammar, without the aid of pedagogy. Obviously I have personally observed very few preschool children, but I see good reasons to believe that children in general are inclined to learn, and are able to learn, under unfavorable conditions: if not, they could not learn to talk, but they do. An adult of almost any age can get away with being an old fogy, unreceptive to new ideas, devoted to habits and preconceptions, and reluctant to recognize new situations and problems; but for a little child, this mentality would be a handicap beyond endurance. Thus, in part, the intellectuality of children is a response to practical needs and desires. But the intellectuality of children goes far beyond practical motivations. Their curiosity seems omnivorous. Once they get started on the subject of dinosaurs, for instance, it is hard to get them off it. For the sake of convenience, I shall use the term *psychic intelligence* to describe these traits of temperament. Thus psychic intelligence is an inclination to *use* whatever cognitive intelligence one has—for learning, for adaptive behavior, and for pleasure.

All children have psychic intelligence. The question is how much of it they keep, and for how long. By the age of twenty, as students, most of them are austere utilitarians, continually asking what thus-and-so is good for. Often they want to know whether a particular course, or even a topic within a course, will make a direct contribution to their ability to make more money after they graduate from college. Most of them acquire a monomaniacal obsession with the contemporary, as if the world had been created at approximately the time they were born. But the lower psychic intelligence of most twenty-year-olds is a collection of acquired distastes, and to acquire these takes a long time.

This change can begin in early childhood if the parents do not want to talk to the child, let alone listen to it. Outside the family, children tend to be socialized by their own age group, feeling a need to be exactly like their peers. School routines tend to encourage the idea that knowledge is the ability to conform to the teacher's expectations. All these tendencies are deadly enemies of psychic intelligence, because thoughtful and creative responses are often idiosyncratic, and they need a sympathetic audience. I believe that these considerations largely explain the intellectual advantage of being in some way a foreigner or an outsider: if you have no hope of being exactly like everybody else, then you may as well use your brain for the purpose of thinking, and besides, you may have a child's need to do so.

It is evident that to be an adult intellectual one needs to retain the psychic intelligence of a child. What is less evident, but still true, is that to be highly successful in practical life one needs to retain a certain part of this psychic intelligence and use it in whatever job one is doing. The application of this to the learned professions is obvious, but it applies also in business. An old or young fogy—that is, a creature of habit and conditioned responses—may eke out a living, but people who are very successful in business are continually thinking about the business they are in, reacting to new situations in perceptive and original ways. A striking example of this is the development of new electronic devices in the last fifteen years or so. Plenty of these were developed in people's garages, and some of the owners or renters of the garages became millionaires almost overnight. These extremes of worldly success were due to extremes of psychic intelligence. At the lower end of the spectrum, companies tend to go broke when they are under the control of old fogies. There is a real difference in mentality between people regarded as intellectuals and most of the people who are highly successful in practical life, but the difference is nowhere nearly so great as commonly supposed: it consists mainly in the fact that the practical people have psychic intelligence in a narrower range. Anyone who does a demanding job well must be intelligently interested in that job, though not necessarily in much else.

For these reasons, the preservation of the psychic intelligence of the child is not just an important educational goal; it is an educational imperative, deserving an absolute priority. It is not getting such priority. Any time we convey to a student that knowledge is the ability to give the expected response, we are propagating psychic stupidity. The same thing happens if we assign to the student interminable chores that neither demand nor repay thought.

These ideas imply a policy in the teaching of arithmetic: a child should not be forced to do by hand anything that can be done better and more easily with a pocket calculator. A special form of Occam's razor covers a part of the case: decimal numerals with more than two digits should not be multiplied beyond necessity. It seems likely that children need to know in a pinch how to do the algorithms by hand, just as the owner of a Rolls Royce needs to know how to walk, but this is a practical question, not a question of principle. It may be objected that the use of a pocket calculator teaches the child nothing about the concept of number, or about the meanings of the operations performed on numbers, or about the reasons why the little machine gives the right answers; but this objection is a nullity, because the algorithms are also worthless in all three of these respects.

It is hard to predict the long-range consequences of the use of pocket calculators in elementary schools, but the possibilities that I can see differ only in their degree of excellence. Perhaps the time students save can be used to learn some real mathematics. This may not work for most students, because the intellectual voltage may become too high; but perhaps it will: mathematics will surely become more teachable when the curse is off of it, replaced by a fascinating toy. For years to come, it may be impossible to introduce new mathematical material in elementary schools, since the teachers are barely trained to deal with what they are teaching now. For this reason, we had better go slowly, because when people try to teach mathematics they do not understand, the consequences are terrible. Underqualified teachers cannot tell the difference between a right and a wrong idea; they can tell only the difference between the familiar and the unfamiliar. When unfamiliar insights are ignored as if they were worthless, or actually rejected as wrong, the effect is to discourage students, or corrupt their mentality, or both.

Thus it may be that for quite a while to come the time saved in elementary schools by using calculators to replace algorithmic drill ought to be spent in the study of other subjects. This would be a great improvement. The study of history, literature, and natural science hardly requires justification; but algorithmic drill stands alone in the elementary curriculum: it is the only subject whose study ordinarily damages the mentality of the child.

Similar ideas apply in high schools. Machine computation of any feasible kind ought to replace hand computation. The advantage will probably be less than in elementary schools, because high school mathematics was never a disaster; but it will still be great. Drudgery can be reduced, time can be saved, and problem material no longer needs to inhabit a never-never land in which everything comes out even.

Much of this can be done by rudimentary machine computation with pocket calculators the students already have. If real computer science can be taught, so much the better. Even aside from its scientific and practical importance, it has special virtues in the curriculum. First, students lap it up. Second, society needs for many people to know it. Very few are needed to understand and use the megabuck equipment of physical research, but the theory and practice of computer science require an army, with members ranging from field marshals like von Neumann down to people who have merely been trained in a new profession.

This is not to say that computer science can be a substitute for mathematics, even for a computer scientist, even in high school. In fact, the mathematical ideas that have been superseded by computation are isolated oddities, such as common logarithms, Stirling's formula for the approximate calculation of factorials, and Brigg's already ignored method for the computation of real roots of polynomial equations. Machines do not supersede Simpson's rule for the approximate calculation of definite integrals; on the contrary, they use it. The same is true of Gaussian elimination for solving systems of linear equations. The primary effect of computer science on mathematics has been to make various mathematical ideas *more* important than they were before by making them usable. In fact, computer science owes its existence to a development of this kind. It is based on mathematical logic, which was developed by extremely pure mathematicians with quite a lot of help from philosophers. (Thirty years or so ago I got to see the astonished face of the new dean of arts and sciences at the University of Michigan when he was told that an associate professor in his philosophy department was under contract with the university's Engineering Research Institute.) I believe that the origins of computer science are enough to furnish a utilitarian justification for the salaries of philosophers for many centuries to come. And computer science still uses the sort of abstract mathematics that helped in its invention.

For this reason, computer science and elaborate applications of it ought not to be used in schools to replace any mathematical ideas now taught (except, of course, common logarithms). In the college study of any science—including computer science—a student who can take calculus as a freshman has a great advantage. The college study of mathematics has moved backward, about halfway to the situation of thirty years ago when calculus was not regarded as a freshman subject. The effect of this retrogression has been much worse for science majors than for mathematics majors. A mathematics major who has taken elementary calculus, say, as a sophomore, can catch up by taking courses in parallel in later years. But science departments want the student to know at least some calculus from the beginning, and in this, of course, they are quite right. Computer science departments use the calculus requirement at the start, mainly as a guarantee of a certain degree of mathematical maturity. But the mathematics that would help more directly in their freshman courses would be more abstract than calculus, not less, including, for example, the theory of recursive functions. Therefore nobody at all would benefit from a reduction in the mathematics now taught in schools. The immediate problem, rather, is to work our way back to the standards of about 1970.

So far, I have been discussing the teaching of technology. It remains to discuss the technology of teaching. Computer-assisted Instruction (CAI) is a technical elaboration of Programmed Instruction (PI). (I have spelled the word *programmed* with two *m*s partly because I like it that way and partly because the Skinnerians do not.) There are two fundamental and intractable troubles with CAI and PI. Every conception of pedagogy is based on a concept of knowledge, and CAI and PI are based on a falsified concept: that knowledge is the ability to respond in the expected way. For reasons I discussed earlier, the use of this idea produces cognitive knowledge—at least for the moment—at the price of psychic intelligence. When advocates of CAI or PI are exuberant, they claim that their methods supersede other teaching styles. When challenged, they sometimes retreat to the position that their methods replace various kinds of drill that do not deserve the attention of a human teacher; but these retreats are instances of the Law of the Conservation of Bologna under Thin Slicing. The trouble is that CAI and PI are based on naive misconceptions of the psychology of learning and retention.

Every artificial teaching scheme is predicated on the idea that learning processes work best when they are carefully designed and controlled. This might be true if learning processes were understood, but they are not. The notion that we understand how mental capacities develop well enough to dare to control their development is not just an exaggeration; it is a pack of nonsense, and we rely on it at our students' peril.

It is equally naive to suppose that people understand and remember the things that are explained or told to them clearly. In practice, people understand what they enjoy understanding, and remember what they enjoy knowing. Thus the people who can quote poetry at length are the ones who love poetry, and those who can quote baseball scores and batting averages are the ones who—for reasons that to me are unfathomable—care about such numbers. I have had a social security number for about thirty years. It is written in my appointment book because I have never managed to remember it. But I have not forgotten the telephone number of the woman I was in love with in 1935. Thus all learning processes have an aesthetic and emotional component. When this component is strong, knowledge is retained easily.

I have hopes that the horse I have just been beating is dead, and that the total mechanization of learning, on any significant scale, is merely an eccentric daydream, like the sort of social "progress" that might take us beyond freedom and dignity. In September of 1982 the *New York Times* reported that certain people regarded as educators had developed a computerized cram scheme for coaching students to pass a new test of reasoning ability. The idea of a cram course in reasoning is so ridiculous that the objective of the scheme cannot have been educational; these people must have hoped, more modestly, that they could invalidate a test.

But some very prevalent teaching schemes bear strong resemblances to CAI and PI and have much the same vices. One of their distinguishing features is that they neither require nor produce functional literacy. The literate may skim a paragraph or a page to get its general drift. The question is whether they expect to get more than the general drift. When they do not understand exactly what the paragraph says, do they reexamine it until it comes into sharp focus? If so, they have half of functional literacy (and evidently this half is largely a trait of temperament rather than a purely cognitive skill); the other half is the ability to write exactly what one means.

Any education that does not include functional literacy is deficient. The trouble is that once formal education is over, we have nobody to feed us knowledge out of spoons, and so we must read with care to add to our knowledge or even to preserve it. Moreover, inarticulate knowledge is adequate only for people who work in isolation (if, indeed, for them); and in a highly organized society very few of us do. Important jobs tend to be leadership positions, and since leaders are largely teachers, they need to be able to convey meanings by the use of language.

Nevertheless, most mathematical pedagogy elaborately makes its peace with functional illiteracy. At plenty of colleges, various review material is put on videotapes, which the students look at and listen to in special "laboratories." This scheme is obviously based on the assumption that the student cannot read. I do not question this assumption, but it means to me that the task of teaching students to read is far more important than that of conveying mathematical information to them by illiterate means. The trouble, I believe, is that student illiteracy is encouraged and preserved by daily classroom routines and homework assignments.

The following examples are taken from college mathematics, but it seems unlikely that the demands on literacy are any higher in the schools.

• In calculus courses it is taken for granted that students cannot read the text. At most, they can read the "solved problems" at the end of each section. Even these are treated, not as material to be read and understood, but as behavior patterns to be imitated: given a problem of a certain type, what does one *do*? Students' reactions have convinced me that for them the ostensibly declarative sentences in calculus are construed, not as declarations, calling for assent, but as imperatives, calling for obedience. For example, the declarative sentence: "If $f(x) = x^3$ for each x, then $f'(x) = 3x^2$ for each x" is construed as the imperative: "In a differentiation problem, if $f(x) = x^3$ is given, then you must write $f'(x) = 3x^2$." I believe that for nearly all students, elementary calculus is not a body of knowledge at all; it is a repertory of imitative behavior patterns so that the question of truth hardly arises.

• A few years ago I got a direct confirmation of this in the result of a five-minute quiz. I wrote on the blackboard a statement of the comparison test for the convergence of infinite series, omitting the hypothesis that all terms of both series must be nonnegative. Then I asked the students to tell me whether the statement was true or false. Of course it is false; it "proves" that the series $-1 - 2 - 3 - \ldots$ converges, by comparison with the series $0 + 0 + \ldots$. But in a class of twenty-five, every one of my students said the statement was true. This was not because they did not know how to use the comparison test. I cannot recall even one time that a student has applied this test to a series that did not satisfy the hypothesis. The trouble was that I had asked them to read a sentence carefully enough to tell exactly what it said, and this task was new to them. They called my statement true because at a glance it bore a striking resemblance to familiar printed matter. They thought that a glance was enough.

• In the same course, just before the second hour-test, a worried student asked me if he was going to have to write more sentences. He was dismayed when the answer was yes.

I am afraid that any teacher can furnish from personal experience many examples of this sort of functional illiteracy; the problem is to find examples of the contrary. In the 1980s it is easy to suppose that functional literacy can be achieved only by a tiny intellectual elite, but this is not true. In the late 1930s, in freshman courses in mathematics at Tulane University, students both read and wrote. Part of the classroom routine was blackboard work, in which the students wrote not just solutions of problems but also derivations of general formulas. The derivations were not written as mere strings of formulas; they were written in sentences that explained what was going on. The professor who taught me did some lecturing, but reading the next section of the text with care was a normal part of daily homework. In those days, Tulane was not an "elite" university; the course was not an honors course; and what we studied in the first half of the freshman year was "college algebra" and trigonometry. From this I conclude that average students can achieve literacy if it is taught to them and expected of them.

But this cannot be done quickly. If we believe (as I do) that the study of foreign languages ought to be required, we must still recognize that it would be unreasonable to make a sudden demand that our students be able to read and write French. A sudden demand that they be able to read and write English would also be unreasonable. The liquidation of illiteracy must of necessity be gradual, and it must be done by consensus: no teacher can attack the problem alone in any course taught on a mass basis. But something has got to be done. We are now granting not just high school diplomas but also college degrees to students who do not have an adequate mastery of any language of all; this has got to stop. If one has functional literacy, then one can acquire an immense variety of useful knowledge by examining printed matter with careful attention.

It is for this sort of reason that the practical value of education vastly exceeds that of ostensibly practical training. Most training is out of date in a few years, and its half-life steadily diminishes, because changes in social conditions and the progress of science and technology are steadily accelerating. Thus intellectual education is the only sort of life-adjustment education that will be adequate for the next generation.

Computer technology, when used properly and to greatest advantage, can give teachers the time to encourage, and students the time to develop, the psychic intelligence that is the gift of children and the hope of society.

7

Computer-based Numeration Instruction

Audrey B. Champagne
Joan Rogalska-Saz

TEACHING base-ten numeration is one of the most difficult and important tasks facing elementary school mathematics teachers. Much of the mathematics content taught in the elementary grades assumes a fundamental understanding of our number system. However, many elementary children have little more than a superficial idea of place value. As a result, they learn to perform in a rote fashion without a basic understanding of what they are doing. Developing concepts crucial to mathematical understanding requires more detailed instruction and more opportunities to manipulate objects or pictures that represent number concepts than most elementary mathematics programs currently provide. The computer-based instructional module we describe here uses pictures of physical objects and offers the detailed instruction necessary for developing students' understanding of the base-ten system. (*Note:* The module was programmed to run on a Terak 8210A minicomputer; a commercial distributor for the module is being sought.)

Conventional wisdom and theory suggest that manipulating physical objects helps develop an understanding of place value (Dienes 1959, 1966; Gattegno 1958; Montessori 1961; Williams 1961). However, the literature of mathematics education reveals that even when manipulatives are available, teachers often choose not to use them (Suydam and Osborne 1977) and, further, that when manipulatives are used in mathematics instruction, they are not uniformly effective in improving achievement (Suydam and Higgins 1976).

Current psychological research suggests that if manipulatives are used in certain highly specified ways, they should be effective in producing an understanding of the concept of number (Brown and VanLehn 1980; Hinsley, Hayes, and Simon 1977; Stevens and Collins 1980). Our

Development of the computer module reported here was funded by the National Science Foundation. The theoretical foundation for this development is an outcome of research funded by the National Institute of Education.

computer-based module presents numeration in a way that is consistent with this research and with recent findings on the use of multiple representations in mathematics instruction (Behr, Lesh, and Post 1981; Behr et al. 1980; Lesh, Landau, and Hamilton 1980). It also minimizes the management problems associated with manipulatives. Thus, the module's design exemplifies a principle too often neglected by developers of educational software: the computer is used to instruct when it provides learning experiences not available by more ordinary means.

Content and Instructional Strategies

The module consists of fifteen lessons, each taking thirty to forty minutes and containing an instructional part and a practice part. The practice is set in the context of a simple game that can be played on the computer by one or two children.

The module represents number in three ways: pictorial, verbal, and numerical. The pictorial representation consists of a modified version of Dienes Blocks; the verbal representation presents number words, such as "forty-three," for the pictorial representation; and the numerical representation presents the appropriate arabic numeral (fig. 7.1). We have assumed that pictorial representations are equivalent in information to the physical objects they depict and that manipulating the picture is as instructionally effective as manipulating the physical objects.

REPRESENTATIONS OF NUMBERS

		Examples
Pictorial:	May be any discrete objects	
	1. Dienes Blocks	
	2. Bundle of Sticks	
Verbal:		one hundred twenty three
Symbolic:		123

Fig. 7.1. Three modes of representation in the instructional module

The Instruction

Three important characteristics of our instruction are (1) the pictorial representation we have chosen, (2) the method for teaching the correspondence between the physical representation and the number symbol, and (3) the way the instruction facilitates verbalization of the material being taught.

Pictorial representation

In conventional classroom instruction, Dienes Blocks are often used for the physical representation of number. These blocks, made of wood, consist of small *unit* cubes, *tens* sticks (10 units end to end), and *hundreds* squares (100 units in a 10 × 10 square). We call these "fused" Dienes Blocks. Our module uses a modified version of these blocks. We use the unit cubes, but in place of the standard tens and hundreds blocks, we use long boxes that hold 10 unit cubes and square boxes that hold 100 unit cubes (ten long boxes). We call this the "messy" version of Dienes Blocks. We have argued elsewhere (Champagne and Rogalska-Saz 1982) that this is a better model of the concepts we are attempting to teach. However, they are difficult for students to manipulate physically and often create classroom management problems. The computer solves these problems.

Pictorial displays of unit cubes in tens and hundreds boxes are used in the first four lessons to teach the meaning of the arabic number symbols. In the first lesson the student is given the task illustrated in figure 7.2. She is told that there are some cubes in the bag and that her task is to write the number symbol that tells how many cubes there are. This differs from the usual "how many . . .?" task in that she cannot count the cubes to determine how many there are. Rather, she is given a procedure for grouping them into tens and hundreds. After the student groups all the cubes by tens, she is shown a procedure for generating the number symbol that corresponds to the display. For each kind of group in the display she counts the number of groups and writes a single digit in the appropriate location. The purpose of this task is to teach the correspondence between the kind of group (ones, tens, or hundreds) in the display and the ones, tens, and hundreds places of the numerical symbol.

The completed display and number symbol illustrate several important facts:

1. Ten ungrouped unit cubes can be grouped to form one *ten*.

2. Ten groups of ten cubes can be grouped to form one *hundred*.

3. When a set of objects (fewer than a thousand) is completely grouped by tens, the resulting display may have one or more of these elements:
   a) A set containing fewer than 10 unit cubes
   b) A set containing fewer than ten groups of 10 unit cubes each
   c) A set of fewer than ten groups, each containing ten groups of 10 (or 100) unit cubes

4. A digit from 0 to 9 can be assigned to each set of a particular kind of group by counting the number of that kind of group.

LESSON 1

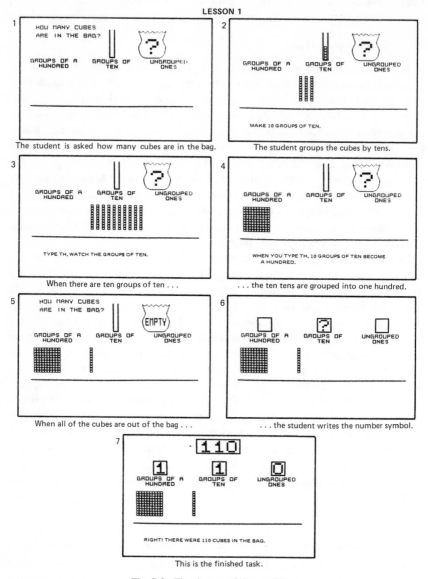

Fig. 7.2. First lesson of the module

In the first lesson, the positions of the hundreds, tens, and units on the screen correspond spatially to the relative positions of the hundreds, tens, and units digits in a number symbol. In the later lessons, the hundreds, tens, and units portions of the physical display appear randomly on the screen to prevent students from associating position rather than type of group with any particular place of a number symbol.

Correspondence

Another feature of our module is that it makes clear the direct correspondence between the physical representation and the number symbol. Evidence that children do not, in fact, link number symbols with other representations of number may be found in Lawler's (1981) study involving early number understanding. Lessons five through eight introduce the concept of regrouping and teach this correspondence between a regrouped display and the number symbol. A lesson in this sequence is illustrated in figure 7.3. This instructional strategy uses pictures of physical objects in a way that psychological theory indicates should be effective in producing understanding. Operations performed on the manipulatives are linked directly to operations performed on the symbols and vice versa. Initially, the student is presented with a pictorial display of more than nine unit cubes (or groups of ten) and asked to write the numeral that tells the number of cubes in the display. This problem is solved by regrouping so that there are nine or fewer cubes (or groups of ten cubes). After regrouping, the student writes the number symbol.

In another part of this same lesson, the student creates a display with a specified number of cubes. She regroups the display to match the verbal description, which specifies that there be more than nine ones or tens (fig. 7.3). For example, she is instructed to create a display of 301 cubes containing eleven ones. When the pictorial display forms on the screen, the numeral 301 also appears. To obtain ten ones, the student must change one *hundred* to ten *tens*. As the picture on the screen changes, the regrouping marks appear on the numeral 301:

To get eleven ones, she changes one ten to ten ones. Once again, the regrouping marks appear on the symbol to show how she has changed the display. Thus the manipulations on the pictorial representation are linked to the equivalent manipulation on the symbolic representation. By alternately performing analogous procedures on the cubes and the symbols, students learn how to (1) represent information contained in pictorial representations with number symbols and (2) interpret regrouped number symbols and demonstrate the regrouping by manipulating the pictorial representations.

Lessons nine through eleven are about numerical equivalence. The student compares the number properties of displays by regrouping the cubes in those displays that contain more than nine ones or nine tens, writing a number symbol for each display, and then comparing the number symbols.

In the last four lessons, the student learns how to interpret regrouping marks and how to write regrouping marks to denote regrouping operations

48 COMPUTERS IN MATHEMATICS EDUCATION

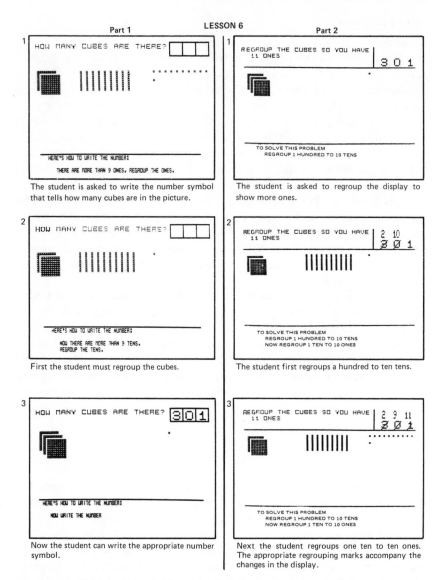

Fig. 7.3. Direct linking of manipulatives and number symbol

that have been applied to pictorial displays. The culminating task is to determine if the value of a number symbol has been maintained through the transformation of regrouping (fig. 7.4). To solve this task, the student creates a pictorial display corresponding to the number and kinds of groups that the regrouped number symbol represents. In the example in figure 7.4, the student builds a display with two groups of one hundred, no groups of ten, and fifteen ones to correspond with the number symbol marked B.

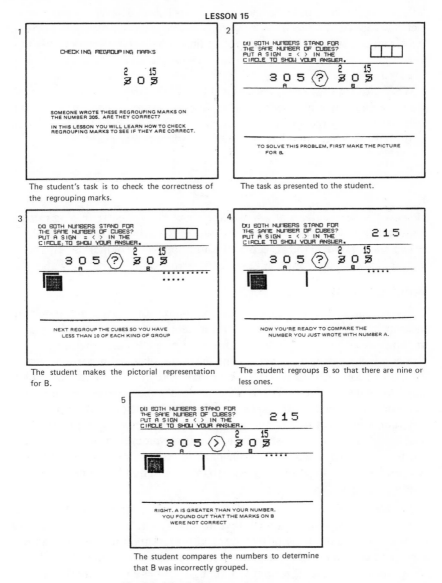

Fig. 7.4. The final lesson of the module

Then she regroups the display so that there are fewer than ten ones and writes (in standard form) a number symbol for the transformed display (215). Finally she compares the newly generated number with the original number to determine whether the original regrouping marks were written correctly.

These examples illustrate how the instructional strategy of the module reflects the psychological theory on which it is based. That is, for physical or pictorial representations of number to facilitate learning, manipulations on these representations must be explicitly linked with the corresponding manipulations on the arabic symbol (Lesh 1979; Resnick 1982; Resnick and Champagne 1980).

When students have not received instruction that explicitly links regrouping on a physical display with regrouping on the corresponding numeral, they often fail to recognize instances in which regrouping has been done incorrectly and the value has not been maintained. For example:

However, when students attempt to carry out the same regrouping using a display of physical objects, the error becomes obvious. The linking of the actions performed on the objects to the notation on the numerals helps them learn to avoid many common regrouping errors of this sort.

Verbalization

Psychological theory suggests that verbalization serves an important mediating function in learning. In this instance, the verbal descriptions of manipulations serve the important function of mediating between the numerical and pictorial representations and thus play an important part in developing concepts (Carroll 1971; Nesher 1976). The instruction emphasizes verbal descriptions (1) of the elements of the pictorial display and (2) of the number symbols. Two aspects of this mathematics module play very different roles in encouraging verbalization—the physical representation itself and a management system that allows two students to work together at one terminal. These two facets of the module provide the students with both the vocabulary and the opportunities to talk about number symbols and the regrouping operation.

The physical representation. The boxes and cubes give students a visible and manipulable system as a context in which to discuss the properties of numbers. For example, with this physical representation, students can observe and talk about the fact that a box (group) containing 100 cubes is composed of ten boxes (groups) containing 10 cubes each. Were the instruction limited to number symbols alone, such properties of the numeration system would be impossible to observe directly and there would be no language available to the student for discussing them.

The physical representation also facilitates verbalizing the processes and results of regrouping because they allow the regrouping operation to be performed as a single-step procedure. For instance, a group of one hundred can be *taken apart* rather than *traded* to obtain ten tens. This simpler procedure eliminates the confusion that some other representations introduce. With the standard Dienes Blocks, for instance, regrouping a hundred to get some ungrouped ones involves two trading procedures: a hundred for ten tens and then a ten for ten ones. This procedure has two disadvantages:

1. It takes several steps and thus does not parallel the steps of the regrouping process as applied to number symbols.
2. It removes some objects from the set under consideration and adds other objects, thus clouding the issue of whether the number is preserved in regrouping.

Regrouping boxes of cubes, however, involves fewer steps and removes no cubes from the display because regrouping a hundred to get some ones is accomplished by simply taking apart a hundred and then taking apart a ten. It is easy to perform and to observe the regrouping as well as to talk about it; it gives the teacher a context for talking with students in concrete terms about the concepts introduced in the module.

The management system. The second aspect of the module that facilitates verbalization is a management system that allows two students to work simultaneously. An option in each program disk can be selected to direct both the instruction and the accompanying problem set to either one or two students. We have incorporated this feature in the module so that a student having trouble with a problem can observe how a more successful student goes about solving it. Students can also help one another overcome difficulties in interacting with the computer itself. Working in pairs encourages students to talk with their partners.

The Role of the Computer

The computer eliminates some problems associated with the use of manipulatives in the classroom. The learner can easily manipulate pictorial displays when the objects themselves are difficult to handle. Our own observation indicates that the manipulation of cubes requires considerable time and attention and often distracts the student from the instructional intent. The student often takes so long placing cubes in boxes or placing them in even rows that the reason for the task is forgotten. Portraying physical representations on the computer allows each child to perform manipulations without these distractions yet does not pose materials management problems for the teacher.

The computer allows for a variety of levels of control over the learner's manipulations of the various representations of number. In the early instruction, the child's interactions with the pictorial and symbolic representations are highly routinized so that object displays are manipulated in instructionally sound ways. Later on, the computer's control is relaxed. This allows the child to explore the alternative forms of number representation and also to explore different methods of solving the problems.

The complexity of learning numeration is such that the instructional time required for all the aspects of the base-ten system to be explicitly developed is approximately fifteen hours. The computer serves as a tireless instructor, presenting the complex interrelationships in a detailed manner that the classroom teacher cannot. Students are free to move at their own pace and can easily repeat parts of lessons if some aspect of the instruction eludes them. In addition, the computer permits students who do not require the detailed instruction to skip the step-by-step instruction and move directly to the practice problems.

We have described an instructional use of the computer which is consistent with current learning theory. The module uses representations in ways that would be difficult to achieve in a regular classroom setting. Because thoughtfuly designed courseware is costly and students' access to a computer is limited, the computer should be used for significant instruction central to the curriculum. In other words, the computer ideally should provide instruction that would be difficult or impossible to present by more conventional means.

REFERENCES

Behr, Merlyn J., Richard Lesh, and Thomas R. Post. "The Role of Manipulative Aids in Learning Rational Number Concepts." Poster session, International Group for Psychology of Mathematics Education. Berkeley, Calif., 1981.

Behr, Merlyn J., Thomas R. Post, Edward A. Silver, and Diane Mierkiewicz. "Theoretical Foundations for Instructional Research on Rational Numbers." In *Proceedings of the Fourth International Conference for the Psychology of Mathematics Education,* edited by R. Karplus. Berkeley, Calif.: The Conference, 1980.

Brown, John Seely, and Kurt VanLehn. "Toward a Generative Theory of Bugs in Procedural Skills." In *Addition and Subtraction: A Developmental Perspective,* edited by T. Carpenter, J. Moser, and T. Romberg. Hillsdale, N.J.: Lawrence Erlbaum Associates, 1980.

Champagne, Audrey B., and Joan Rogalska-Saz. "Cognitive Task Analysis in the Design of Computer-based Mapping Instruction." Paper presented at the Annual Meeting of the American Educational Research Association, 22 March 1982, New York, N.Y.

Carroll, John B. "Learning from Verbal Discourse in Educational Media: A Review of the Literature." *Research Bulletin, 71–61.* Princeton, N.J.: Educational Testing Service, 1971.

Dienes, Zoltan P. "The Growth of Mathematical Concepts in Children through Experience." *Educational Research* 2 (January 1959): 9–28.

———. *Mathematics in the Primary School.* London: Macmillan & Co., 1966.

Gattegno, Caleb. *From Actions to Operations.* New Rochelle, N.Y.: Cuisenaire Co. of America, 1958.

Hinsley, D., J. R. Hayes, and Herbert A. Simon. "From Words to Equations: Meaning and Representation in Algebra and Word Problems." In *Cognitive Processes in Comprehension,* edited by Patricia A. Carpenter and Marcel Adam Just. Hillsdale, N.J.: Lawrence Erlbaum Associates, 1977.

Lawler, R. W. "The Progressive Construction of Mind." *Cognitive Science* 5 (January–March 1981): 1–30.

Lesh, Richard. "Mathematical Learning Disabilities: Considerations for Identification, Diagnosis, Remediation. In *Applied Mathematical Problem Solving,* edited by Richard Lesh, Diane Mierkiewicz, and M. Kantowski. Columbus, Ohio: ERIC/SMEAC, 1979.

Lesh, Richard, Marsha Landau, and Eric Hamilton. "Rational Numbers, Ideas and the Role of Representational Systems." In *Proceedings of the Fourth International Conference for the Psychology of Mathematics Education,* edited by R. Karplus. Berkeley, Calif.: The Conference, 1980.

Montague, William E. "Analysis of Cognitive Processes in the Specification of Interactive Instructional Presentations for Computer-based Instruction." Paper presented at the Annual Meeting of the American Educational Research Association, 22 March 1982, New York, N.Y.

Montessori, Mario M. "Maria Montessori's Contribution to the Cultivation of the Mathematical Mind." *International Review of Education,* vol. 7, no. 2 (1961): 134–41.

Nesher, Paula A. "From Ordinary Language to Arithmetical Language in the Primary Grades (What Does It Mean to Teach '2 + 3 = 5?')" (Doctoral dissertation, Harvard University, 1972.) *Dissertation Abstracts International* 36 (1976): 7918A–7919A (University Microfilms No. 76-10,525).

Resnick, Lauren B. "Syntax and Semantics in Learning to Subtract." In *Addition and Subtraction: A Developmental Approach,* edited by T. Carpenter, J. Moser, and T. Romberg. Hillsdale, N.J.: Lawrence Erlbaum Associates, 1982.

Resnick, Lauren B., and Audrey B. Champagne. "Semantics of Arithmetic: Teaching Understanding and Computational Skill by Computer." Proposal to the National Science Foundation. Pittsburgh, Pa.: University of Pittsburgh, Learning Research and Development Center, 1980.

Stevens, A., and A. Collins. "Multiple Conceptual Models of a Complex System." In *Instruction: Cognitive Process Analysis,* edited by R. Snow, P. Federico, and W. Montague. Hillsdale, N.J.: Lawrence Erlbaum Associates, 1980.

Suydam, Marilyn N., and Jon L. Higgins. "Review and Synthesis of Studies of Activity-based Approaches to Mathematics Teaching." NIE Contract 400-75-0063. Final report. September 1976.

Suydam, Marilyn N., and Alan Osborne. The Status of Pre-College Science Education: 1955– 1975. Volume 2: Mathematics Education. Center for Science and Mathematics Education, Ohio State University, 1977.

Williams, J. D. "Teaching Arithmetic by Concrete Analogy: I. Miming Devices." *Educational Research* 3 (February 1961): 112–25 and (June 1961): 195–213.

8

The Computer as a Learning Center

William H. Kraus

MICROCOMPUTERS can be used effectively in the elementary schools in a variety of ways. In the lower elementary grades, a microcomputer can be particularly effective as a learning center. The experiences recounted here are based on a two-year project funded in part by the National Science Foundation and the National Institute of Education. The project developed and field tested eight instructional computer games in mathematics in grades K–5 in three elementary schools.

Designing a Mathematics Learning Center

Learning centers are places in the classroom where individual students or small groups can pursue learning activities independently—without the teacher's direction. Teachers must consider many things when they design mathematics learning centers for their classroom. The following discussion of some of the more important considerations will give an indication of how effective a microcomputer can be as a learning center.

Instructional objectives

Learning centers are often designed to give students extra practice on mathematical skills. It is relatively easy to program a computer for drill, particularly on computational skills. For example, "Fish Chase," one of the computer games developed in the project, provides practice in addition and multiplication facts (fig. 8.1). A big fish chases a little fish while the student answers addition or multiplication problems. To win the game, the student must correctly answer twenty problems before the big fish catches and eats the little fish.

Learning centers can also provide enrichment experiences. Typically, enrichment activities are more difficult to construct than drill-and-practice

The project discussed here was conducted in part with support of National Science Foundation/National Institute of Education Grant No. SED8012268. Any opinions, findings, conclusions, or recommendations expressed are those of the author and do not necessarily reflect the views of the National Science Foundation or the National Institute of Education.

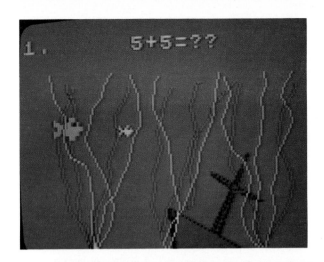

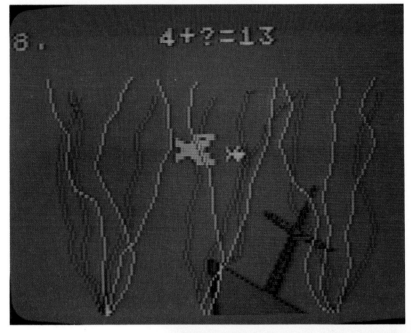

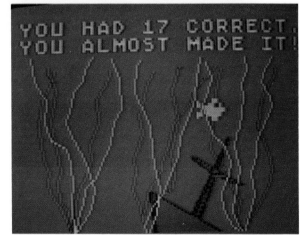

Fig. 8.1. "Fish Chase"

activities. Commercially available computer simulations, such as "Energy Czar" (Atari) and "Three-Mile Island" (MUSE Software), are rich in mathematical applications, but only a few such programs, most notably "Lemonade" (MECC), are appropriate for the lower grades. "The Jar Game" is a nonsimulation game that gives young students experience in probability (see fig. 8.2). In this game the child chooses between two jars, each containing pieces of green and gold candy. After the student selects a jar, a fly enters that jar and buzzes randomly from one piece of candy to another. Each time the student presses the return key, the fly stops momentarily. If it stops on a gold piece, the student scores a point. If it stops on a green piece, the computer scores a point. After each ten turns the student is given a new pair of jars to select from. To win, the student must score fifty points before the computer does. The distribution of green and gold candies in the two jars is different, so in trying to select the jar that gives the better chance of winning, the student is working informally with ratio and probability.

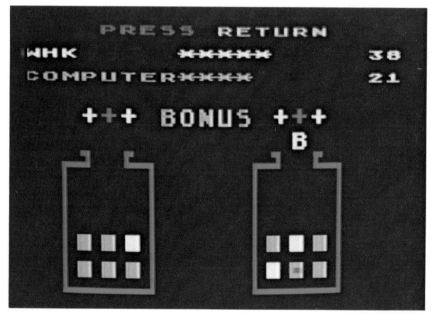

Fig. 8.2. "The Jar Game"

Motivation

When students enjoy activities at the learning center, they are more likely to get involved in the learning process. Computer programs that employ color graphics, animation, and sound are highly motivating. In addition to the intrinsic reward students receive from playing an instructional computer game, they can also be given a motivational message at the end of the game based on their performance. For example, in "The Jar Game" they received two bonus points for selecting the jar that gives the higher probability of winning, and if they make the correct selections throughout the game, the picture in figure 8.3 is displayed on the screen while the computer plays a song.

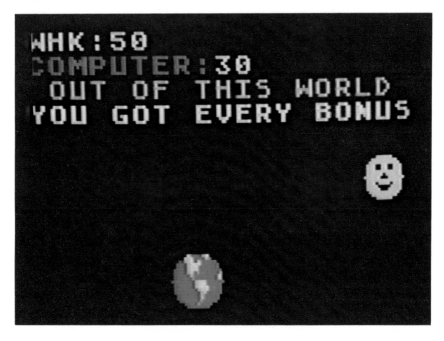

Fig. 8.3. Reward message in "The Jar Game"

Feedback

One of the most difficult tasks in designing a learning center is to arrange for giving immediate feedback or temporarily withholding it, as appropriate. An answer is usually not totally satisfactory since (*a*) the feedback is not immediate, (*b*) once the answer is checked, the student cannot have a second chance at finding the answer, and (*c*) students are often careless in checking their answers. The computer can easily be programmed to give immediate feedback under some circumstances and to withhold it under others. It can give a student any number of chances to answer, and if desired, it can even give clues after an incorrect answer.

Sequencing

If several mathematical ideas or levels of ideas are to be incorporated into a learning center, then the sequencing of these ideas can be very important. Sequencing ideas in a computer program is relatively simple. For example, in

"Golf," students must estimate angles and distances to control their shots on a simulated golf course. The initial holes on the course (fig. 8.4) are relatively easy, whereas later holes (fig. 8.5) demand greater accuracy of estimation. It is also possible to write programs that adjust the instructional sequence based on the responses of the student.

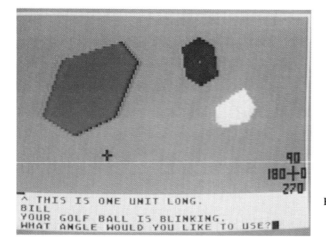

Fig. 8.4. Hole 1 of "Golf"

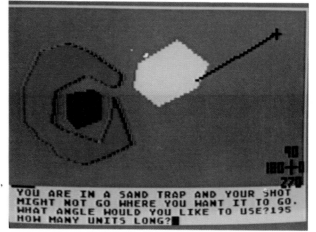

Fig. 8.5. Hole 18 of "Golf"

Time on task

In general, a learning center must be easy to use if students are to use it effectively and independently. It is important that they spend only a small amount of time on the mechanics of using the learning center relative to the time they spend directly involved with the mathematical content of the center.

Figure 8.6 shows the menu of programs from a computer diskette that has been successfully used as early as kindergarten. At the beginning of the school day the teacher turns on the computer and starts the menu program running. Later, when Karl, for instance, wants to use the computer, he only needs to remember the number of the program to be used. When he presses that number on the keyboard, the program is automatically loaded into the computer and begins running. Thus within sixty seconds of sitting down at the computer, Karl has begun working. There are no pencils to sharpen, no papers or other materials to find, and no checking or record-keeping chores to do. Instead, there is immediate and complete involvement in the learning process.

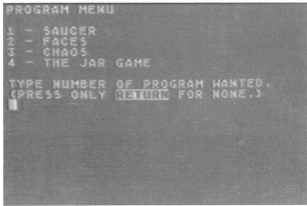

Fig. 8.6. Program menu

Content

Although computational exercises are the easiest to incorporate into a learning center, it is important not to neglect the other areas of the mathematics curriculum. In the project on which this article is based, instructional games were developed in computation, number and numeration, probability, geometry, measurement, spatial relationships, bar graphs, and problem solving. The interactive nature of computers and the graphics capabilities of microcomputers allow almost any mathematical topic to be developed at a level appropriate to elementary school students. In addition, the experience students gain in using computers is important to their developing computer literacy.

Individualization

In designing a learning center, teachers need to include different activities and different levels of activities for different students. For example, in the programs listed in the menu in figure 8.6, "Saucer" (fig. 8.7) is a counting game appropriate for beginning students, whereas "Faces" (fig. 8.8) is a counting game with a variety of levels appropriate for a wide range of students from kindergarten through third grade. It is also possible to write computer programs that automatically adjust the sequence or the level of difficulty of the instruction based on the student's performance on the tasks presented.

Fig. 8.7. "Saucer" encourages children to count by recognizing subsets of 2, 3, or 4 within larger sets.

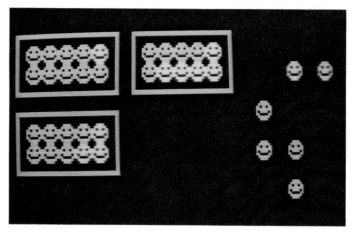

Fig. 8.8. "Faces" focuses children's attention on groups of ten.

Record keeping

The teacher needs to know what activities the students have completed and how well they have done them. For the sake of accuracy, this task should not depend heavily on the students, and for the sake of convenience, it should not require a lot of paperwork from the teacher.

The computer can automatically and unobtrusively keep performance records. In the lower part of figure 8.9 the performance of a student with the initials WHK is displayed. The first time this student played "Fish Chase," he tried the easy addition facts at the slow speed and got nineteen out of a possible twenty problems correct. By examining this record, the teacher can evaluate his progress and plan appropriate further instruction.

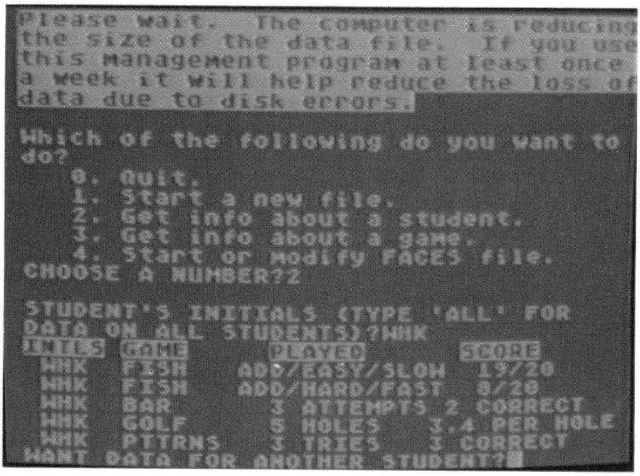

Fig. 8.9. Game management system

Conclusions

The experiences of teachers who have used the instructional games described here have clearly demonstrated the value of using a microcomputer as a mathematics learning center. The teachers uniformly agreed that (a) the computer was easy to use and (b) the students enjoyed and learned from the experience.

Two other observations made by these teachers may prove useful both to other teachers in selecting software and to authors in developing it. First, the combining of sound mathematical instruction with the motivational qualities of a computer game was critical. The use of sound and graphics in the games greatly increased the students' involvement with the mathematical content. (The teachers noted that the sound was not a distraction in the classroom.) Second, time is a critical factor in the elementary classroom. The games used by these teachers were quickly started and allowed students to stop on short notice. The use of disk drives greatly facilitated the use of the games, and teachers who had experience with cassette storage indicated that the disk drive was worth the extra expense because of the time it saved in the classroom.

Used as a learning center, a single microcomputer can have a significant impact in a classroom. In the not-too-distant future it is likely that at least one microcomputer will be found in most elementary school classrooms and that teachers will wonder how they ever got along without them.

9

TABS-Math: A Courseware Development Project

Suzanne K. Damarin

THE Technology and Basic Skills–Mathematics (TABS-Math) project was initially funded in 1980 by the Division of Educational Technology of the U.S. Department of Education to develop innovative technology-based courseware for teaching mathematics in the upper elementary and middle school grades. The charge to the project staff was to develop and test materials for instruction in the basic skills. Attention was directed to four principles:

1. The materials should make exemplary use of "leading edge" technologies.
2. The materials should be mathematically sound.
3. The developers of the materials should be attentive to learning theories and to the results of educational and psychological research.
4. Ultimately, the materials should be accessible to "all children," in the spirit of Public Law 94-142.

The staff was to create materials that were essentially new rather than more polished versions of existing materials.

Planning the Courseware

Initial steps

Given the responsibilities outlined above, the first goals were to provide operational definitions for the terms in the project title: What technologies should be used? Which basic skills should be addressed? Thus the initial tasks were to examine the current state of the art with respect to

The work described in this paper was performed under contract with the U.S. Department of Education, Division of Educational Technology, Office of Libraries and Learning Technologies (Contract No. 300-80-0784). The opinions expressed are those of the author and should not be attributed to the Department of Education.

Preliminary versions of the TABS courseware are currently available for Apple II Plus and Apple IIe. Information on ordering and a price list can be obtained by writing to Suzanne K. Damarin, Ohio State University, College of Education, Arps Hall, Room 273, 1945 N. High St., Columbus, OH 43210.

technology-based mathematics instruction in conjunction with the best available wisdom on basic skills. Principal sources for these analyses were *An Agenda for Action* (NCTM 1980) and its predecessors (NCSM 1977; NIE 1975*a* and 1975*b*) as well as diverse computer literature and software. On the basis of these joint analyses, the project staff made several decisions.

Although the community of mathematics educators was in accord that "appropriate computational skill" is but one of ten basic skills in mathematics, the overwhelming majority of courseware being developed in 1980 was directed toward computational objectives. Moreover, the number of developers working on computationally oriented materials was increasing as textbook publishers and software development houses entered the field. For these reasons, it was assumed that traditional market forces would encourage the development of sound and creative approaches to computation and therefore the TABS project should direct its energies toward other skill areas.

This decision left nine areas from which to choose for technology-based development. An examination of the technology in conjunction with the mathematics education literature indicated four areas for study: geometry, estimation, basic concepts of probability and statistics, and computer literacy (in the sense of studying mathematical relationships through computer-programming approaches to problem solving). The first three of these areas have been the focuses of computer-based development of activities; these materials are discussed in the remaining sections of this paper.

The computer-literacy materials that were developed consist of laboratory booklets, activity cards, reference cards, problem sets, and support materials for teachers. They are designed to be used by children working in a computer environment and have been tested with children in grades 4–8. They are currently being distributed as the *TABS Program Power Pack* (Damarin et al. 1983).

Philosophy

The development of computer-based instructional materials in the areas of geometry, probability, and estimation was guided by a point of view concerning the place and value of computers in the classroom. Key elements of this philosophy include the following:

• Courseware materials should be viewed, not as a curriculum, but as learning activities that can support and enhance the mathematics curriculum as it evolves in our schools.

• Courseware development should be based on an analysis of the educational literature, including both the "common wisdom" concerning children's learning of mathematics and research studies.

• Computer-based experiences can and should help young students understand the relationships between "real world" experience and abstract mathematics.

- Children can and should interact with computers in many ways, but the children should always be in control of the computer rather than vice versa.

- Courseware should be *open* to learners; that is, students should not be limited to interacting with a program while it is running but instead should be able to examine program listings to see how the programmer made it happen. (In actual practice, this was not always feasible, because some programs could not be written well in BASIC. Most TABS courseware consists of BASIC language programs, which call on machine-language routines where necessary. The fundamental structure of a program, branching, looping, and many graphics routines are written in BASIC and can be examined (or changed) by students learning that language.)

- Where possible, courseware should be viewed as utilities for teachers; that is, programs should be designed to have maximum flexibility of use. The materials should lend themselves to integration with other instructional materials according to the plans and style of the teacher and, wherever possible, should be adaptable to local curricula and concerns.

- Finally, the capabilities of the computer, the nature of the mathematical content, and the computer-learner interactions should shape the materials. Rather than beginning with existing materials and asking how they could be adapted to the computer, the project staff should begin with considerations of content and objective and ask how the computer can bring new understanding to this content.

Courseware

Geometry

Geometry was an easy choice for the project staff as an area for development. Computer graphics promised to be an exciting mode in which to work on "motion geometry" as well as processes in geometric reasoning. Moreover, the capability of presenting learners with many diverse examples of geometric concepts rather than the few stereotyped examples that textbooks can offer would afford variety in activities and also incorporate the findings from research on concept learning.

The TABS-Math materials address four broad areas of informal geometry: area and perimeter, triangles, symmetry, and congruence-preserving transformations. In each area there are programs addressed to concept development, practice with the concepts, application, and problem solving.

Area and perimeter disks begin with introductions to these concepts, using carefully constructed graphical illustrations accompanied by as few words as possible. After the concept of area is introduced, students are given problems, such as finding the area of the shape in figure 9.1. The student presses A to indicate a readiness to enter the answer, C to enter "calculator mode" in order to compute the area, or H to request help from the computer. If the student enters the wrong number or asks for help, one of the displays in figure 9.2 (with sides labeled as before) is randomly selected and shown.

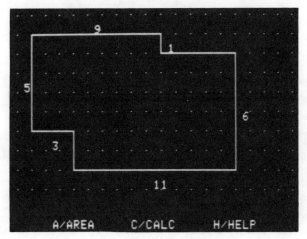

Fig. 9.1

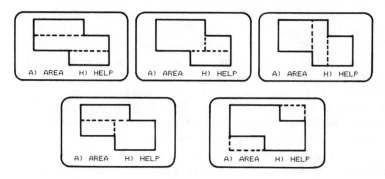

Fig. 9.2

Again there is the opportunity to answer, calculate, or seek help. Successive calls for help in version 1 (fig. 9.2) yield the sequence of displays in figure 9.3; other versions yield similar sequences.

Observing children working with this set of programs, we find that they are challenged by these "difficult" problems; even those who are usually bored and pay no attention to simple applications of the area and perimeter formulas become involved and practice them in this context. After a few examples in which they seek help, children shun this help and seek to reason through to the answer.

What can children learn from a sequence of programs like this? Practice in applying the area formula is one outcome; perhaps more important are

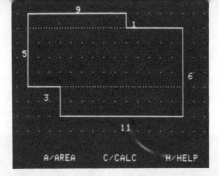

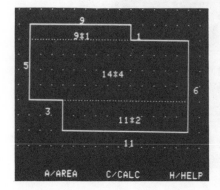
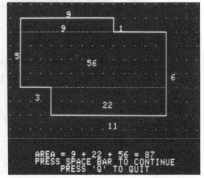

Fig. 9.3

the notions they gain: that there are many ways to solve these problems, that a rectilinear figure can always be dissected into rectangles, that both addition and subtraction strategies are appropriate, and, finally, as one fifth-grade boy put it, "If you think about it, you can solve harder problems than you think you can."

The area-and-perimeter sequence exemplified above is in some ways the least active of the geometry materials developed by the TABS project.

Other gamelike activities are used in teaching other geometric topics, such as symmetry, congruence, and transformations.

Overall, the goal of the geometry courseware created by the Technology and Basic Skills–Mathematics project is to involve young students in activities in which they must visualize and reason geometrically and in which they can cause things to happen.

Probability

The TABS-Math probability materials are designed to support an empirical approach to probability; perhaps more than the other courseware, these activities are designed to extend classroom and other "real world" experiences through simulation of those experiences on the computer. This approach is reflected in most of the TABS probability games and activities; perhaps it is best exemplified by the "Spinner Disk."

Work with the "Spinner Disk" begins with hands-on activities using real spinners in much the way they are traditionally used in elementary classrooms (Hoffer 1978; Shulte 1975). The program "Draw Your Own

Spinner" then allows students to recreate the hands-on spinner (or any other spinner) on the computer screen by using the paddles. The computer spinner can then be used to generate much larger bodies of data than could be collected reliably by hand. Students are led to explore the properties of spinners through a variety of games.

Whereas the initial spinner activities are for data gathering (and generating), "Three Spinners" is essentially a data-analysis activity. In this game (fig. 9.4), the student gathers data in an effort to determine which of three spinners is being "spun" by the computer. As students succeed in this activity, they are promoted to higher positions on the detective force and to problems requiring more discrimination.

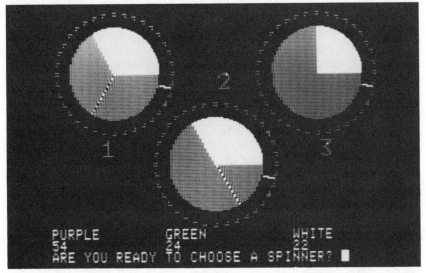

Fig. 9.4

In later games, the student can use spinners of different sizes and shapes both to manipulate the probabilities of game outcomes and to interact with the games. For example, the student can use the spinner to set the probabilities with which the computer will choose rock, scissors, or paper in a computer version of this old game. By experimenting, students learn, for example, that their chances of beating the computer are great if they give the computer a high probability of rock and a low probability of scissors and always play paper themselves. In the two-player "Spin Game," the players move around a randomly colored game board by moving to the next space having the color indicated by a spinner. The catch in this game is that the players must examine the game board and create a spinner that will maximize their own chances of being first around the board.

Other programs in the TABS-Math probability series involve students in games using simulated dice, coins, and color-coded objects. Students are invited to engage in a simulated lottery—and to design their own lotteries within certain constraints—as well as to explore the concept "probability of precipitation" through both simulation and data-gathering activities. The concepts of *randomness, mean, median, mode, expected value,* and *probability* are addressed through experience-based tutorials. Utility programs allow teachers or students to create graphs in any context; these graphs can be produced on the screen or as hard-copy printout.

The overall goals of the probability materials are to deepen students' understandings of the concept of randomness through multiple experiences in diverse settings (Shaughnessy 1981) and to enable them to experience the law of large numbers. Beyond that, the materials are designed to help young students learn how to predict, reason, and test hypotheses within various contexts where random events play an essential role.

Estimation

Estimation was chosen as an area of courseware development for several related reasons. Estimation becomes an increasingly important skill in proportion to society's use of calculators and computers for computational tasks. With the exception of textbook treatments of rounding and a handful of recently developed worksheets (e.g., Hoffer 1978), the teacher has few resources for use in teaching this skill. Moreover, recent research (Levine 1980; Reys et al. 1980) reveals that (*a*) in general, students are rather poor estimators and (*b*) those students who are good at estimating use a variety of strategies, only one of which is rounding. Finally, it seemed to the project staff that the computer was an ideal tool for teaching estimation strategies.

As the staff began work on the courseware, numerous difficulties in the teaching of estimation became apparent. Questions related to how one determines whether an estimate is "good" or not, how students can be given meaningful response without focusing their attention on computation rather than estimation, and how they can be encouraged to learn diverse strategies all needed to be addressed. A consideration of these and related issues led to the decision to focus initially on whole-number multiplication and division and to the identification of four types of courseware for development: prerequisite skills, context-free estimation, estimation in limited context, and multiple related estimates in an "extended context."

Without some understanding of the place-value system in relation to multiplication and division or some knowledge of basic multiplication and division facts, reasonable estimation is impossible. The prerequisite skills courseware is primarily a drill-and-practice package with options for the student to work in specific areas of weakness. Feedback in some sections uses animation to illustrate place-value effects.

In context-free estimation sequences, students are asked to estimate products and quotients of numbers. Various levels of difficulty are available and are defined by the magnitude of the numbers involved and the discrepancy allowed between estimate and computational result. Other programs ask students to compare two numbers (e.g., "which is larger: 80 × 80 or 84 × 76?"). The context-free materials include tutorials using area models and animation as well as drill-and-practice activities. The activities are designed to invite exploration. For example, the "Bull's-Eye" program uses the graphics shown in figure 9.5; a problem is presented (e.g., "Estimate 37 × 54"), and a ring of the display is lighted to indicate the "quality" of the estimate. Students using "Bull's-Eye" are in charge of the quality judgment. Prior to beginning estimation they select from four options: "easy," "medium," "hard," and "set your own difficulty." The first three options set the tolerance for a bull's-eye at 20, 10, and 5 percent, respectively. The fourth option allows the student to assign any percentage error to the bull's-eye and sequentially larger errors to the rings. This option allows students to test many commonly held misconceptions, such as the notion that setting the error tolerance at 100 percent guarantees a bull's-eye every time!

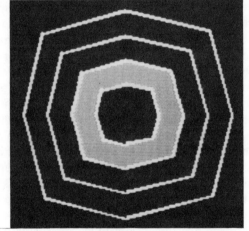

Fig. 9.5

In many senses, the judgment of the quality of an estimate depends as much on the context in which the estimate is made as on the numbers themselves. The limited-context courseware places students in situations such as shopping and racing, where underestimates and overestimates have different consequences. High-speed graphics feedback indicates to the student the effects of an estimate. For example, in an item concerning an automobile race, an underestimate of the distance (from the rate and time that are given) results in the car not completing the race.

Why this courseware enhances learning

A great deal has been written about the usefulness of the microcomputer for enhancing learning. The reasons cited range from capitalizing on children's enthusiasm for video games to providing opportunities for children to invent and experiment with their own mathematics. The TABS project staff has been attentive to all these claims and has tried to create materials with the potential implied by them. In addition, the TABS materials reflect many pedagogical ideas that predate the use of the microcomputer and even time-share computer systems in education.

The "principle of active learning," which asserts that students must be actively involved in their own learning, coupled with the notion that understanding and learning proceed from concrete through semiconcrete to abstract manipulation of mental objects, has guided the development of TABS materials. These same principles have also guided the development of the laboratory approach to mathematics; it is appropriate to view the TABS courseware in the same way one views a math lab, not as a cure-all or a curriculum, but rather as one means of providing experience with the principles that compose mathematics.

The TABS courseware goes beyond traditional laboratory activities because it makes use of some unique capabilities of the computer: random generation, animated graphics, rapid computation. These capabilities enable the developer to add increased validity and new dimensions to the experience base of learners. For example, in traditional laboratory activities involving geometry, the student must both analyze the situation and perform physical manipulations (e.g., transform physical objects, manipulate straightedge and compass, or simply color figures). With the TABS materials, students remain in charge of analysis but they direct the computer to perform the physical manipulation; thus their learning does not depend on psychomotor interests and skills. Similar effects are present in other areas; for example, students' learning of concepts related to data analysis is freed from a dependence on record keeping and computational skills.

Beyond using the computer to do certain types of work in order to focus children's activity on essential parts of learning activities, the materials also use the computer to add new dimensions to learning activities by providing situations and illustrations that were difficult, if not impossible, without the computer. For example, the three-spinners game asks children to make a decision about the source of data, allowing them to gather more data if it is needed. It is hard to imagine a hands-on approach to this activity, since the process of generating data would require a knowledge of its source. Similarly, it is hard to imagine a printed rendition of this activity, since sufficient data would be either present or not; branching to collect more data or to give positive reinforcement would be unrealistic.

Finally, the mathematical topics covered by the TABS courseware are essentially processes or concepts defined in terms of processes. The processes include transformations, geometric constructions, data gathering, probability experiments, and estimation strategies. Such concepts as *symmetry* ("if folded . . ."), *area* ("the number of unit squares needed to cover . . ."), *random event,* and *median* ("arrange the data . . .") are all defined in terms of processes. The TABS-Math courseware gives students the opportunity for involvement with these processes and thus promotes an understanding of them.

Toward the future

Although there is no universally accepted definition of either *mathematics* or *school mathematics,* there does seem to be agreement that what we think of as basic school mathematics will change in response to computers and their extensive use (Davis and Hersch 1981; NCTM 1980; Steen 1981). The TABS-Math courseware is designed with this evolution in mind; although it is grounded in the curriculum of today, it is built on the capabilities of the microcomputer and reaches toward some of the curricular possibilities of tomorrow. Animated graphics, the random generation of data, variable algorithms, the ability to manipulate large quantities of data, and interactive feedback all shape the TABS approach to "the science of quantity and spatial relationships."

REFERENCES

Damarin, Suzanne K. "Technology and Basic Skills–Mathematics." In *Proceedings, Fourth International Learning Technology Congress.* Warrenton, Va.: Society for Applied Learning Technology, 1982.

Damarin, Suzanne K., and others. *TABS Program Power Pack.* Columbus, Ohio: Ohio State University, College of Education, 1983.

Davis, Philip, and Reuben Hersch. *The Mathematical Experience.* Boston: Houghton Mifflin Co., 1981.

Hoffer, Alan. *Didactics and Mathematics: The Art and Science of Learning and Teaching Mathematics.* Palo Alto, Calif.: Creative Publications, 1978.

Levine, Deborah. "Computational Estimation, Ability and the Use of Estimation Strategies Among College Students" (Doctoral dissertation, New York University, 1980). *Dissertation Abstracts International* 41A (1980): 5013.

National Council of Supervisors of Mathematics. "Position Paper on Basic Skills." *Arithmetic Teacher* 25 (October 1977): 19–22.

National Council of Teachers of Mathematics. *An Agenda for Action: Recommendations for School Mathematics of the 1980s.* Reston, Va.: The Council, 1980.

National Institute of Education. *Contributed Position Papers,* vol. 1. Conference on Basic Mathematical Skills and Learning. Washington, D.C.: U.S. Department of Health, Education, and Welfare, 1975.

————. *Working Group Reports,* vol. 2. Conference on Basic Mathematical Skills and Learning, Washington, D.C.: U.S. Department of Health, Education, and Welfare, 1975.

Reys, Robert E., Barbara J. Bestgen, James F. Reybolt, and J. Wendell Wyatt. *Identification and Characterization of Computational Estimation Processes Used by Inschool Pupils and Out-of-School Adults.* Grant 79-0088. Washington, D.C.: National Institute of Education, 1980.

Shaughnessy, J. Michael. "Misconceptions of Probability: From Systematic Errors to Systematic Experiments and Decisions." In *Teaching Statistics and Probability,* 1981 Yearbook, edited by Albert P. Shulte. Reston, Va.: National Council of Teachers of Mathematics, 1981.

Shulte, Albert. *What Are My Chances?* Books A and B. Palo Alto, Calif.: Creative Publications, 1975.

Steen, Lynn A. *Mathematics Tomorrow.* New York: Springer-Verlag, 1981.

10

Technology and Critical Barriers

Glenda Lappan
M. J. Winter

ONE of the applications of mathematics that many students fail to truly understand is the behavior of reflections and mirror images. David Hawkins (1978, p. 3) has called the failure to understand mirror vision one of the "critical barriers to science learning." He defines critical barriers as those "elementary ideas [that] are exceedingly *un*obvious to those who have not yet assimilated them." In this article we propose that technology be used to create "laboratory experiences"—controlled environments in which students can experience the physical and mathematical behaviors of reflections and mirror images. As they experiment, conjecture, and verify, they will have a better chance of discovering and assimilating the principles determining these behaviors.

Teachers can use computers and computer graphics to provide clean, repeatable experimental situations that are not compounded with such factors as poor physical coordination, spin-on balls, or measurements made from inaccurate results or drawings. On a video screen, for example, students can "aim" a ball (or a beam of light) at a spot on a wall and observe the track of its path. Using a ruler and protractor, they can measure distances and angles. They can alter the target spot, repeat the experiment, and compare results.

We describe and illustrate here a sequence of problems for computer experimentation that leads from situations designed to develop basic principles to situations that show applications of these principles.

Both the explanations of these problems and the diagrams illustrating them are displayed on a screen, making this sequence of problems a CAI module. Students are given mirrors, rulers, paper strips, and protractors with which to measure, and perhaps experiment, as they work through the problems.

We begin with a type of optimization problem.

Problem 1.

A pumping station to bring water to towns *A* and *B* is going to be built on the bank of a river. Where should it be located so that the sum of the lengths of the pipes is as small as possible? (See fig. 10.1.)

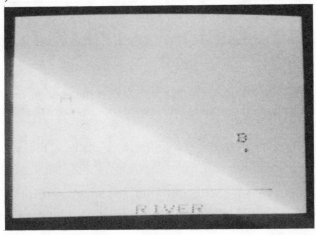

Fig. 10.1

The computer is programmed to display the text of the problem and the diagram of the situation. The student chooses a point on the river, perhaps by touching the screen with a light pen. The computer draws the path from town *A* to the point on the river bank that has been selected, and then to town *B*. Holding a strip of paper to the screen, the student marks off the length of the path on the paper and then measures the paper path to the nearest millimeter. This length is entered into the computer, and the computer checks to see that the measurement of the path is corrected to within a preset tolerance, say two millimeters. When the computer and the student agree on the measure of the first path, the student chooses a second point on the river bank, and the process of measurement is repeated. After three tries the computer display might look like figure 10.2.

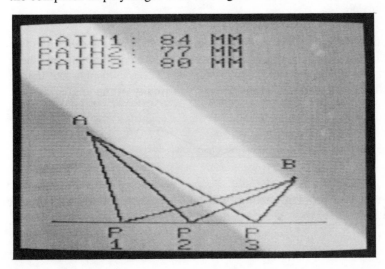

Fig. 10.2

The students' paper strip might look like figure 10.3.

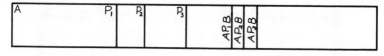

Fig. 10.3

At this stage the computer either agrees that the student has found the shortest path, allows the student three more tries, or gives the best path (fig. 10.4).

The computer then offers a new problem by changing the positions of *A* and *B* and displaying a new diagram for which the student is to find the optimal path.

After several problems of this sort, students should see that if *A* and *B* are the same distance from the river, the point on the river that determines the minimal path is exactly the same distance from *A* as it is from *B* and, in fact, is at the midpoint of the perpendicular projections of *A* and *B* onto the line of the river (fig. 10.5). If *A* and B are not the same distance from the river, then *P* is closer to the point that is nearer the river.

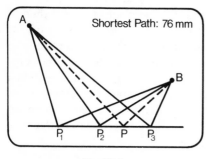

Fig. 10.4

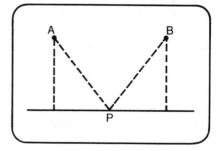

Fig. 10.5

Although angle size may vary from one video display to another, the two angles formed by the river and the minimal path are equal no matter where *A* and *B* are positioned (fig. 10.6). Even with a coarse display like that in figure 10.2, some students will perceive the equality of the angles.

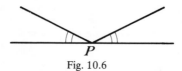

Fig. 10.6

The next two problem settings will help students develop an efficient strategy for finding this optimal path.

Problem 2.

A ball is rolled, without spin, from position B toward a wall (see fig. 10.7). The ball hits the wall at P and bounces off the wall toward a second wall. Where will it hit the second wall?

After the student enters a guess, the computer draws the student's path and then the correct path (fig. 10.8). The computer then presents a new position for B and P, and the student gets to try again.

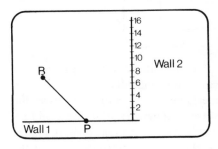
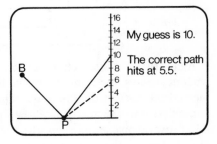

Fig. 10.7   Fig. 10.8

After several such tries, the computer shows a diagram of a path and the angles of incidence and reflection and asks the student to compare them (fig. 10.9).

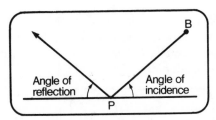

Fig. 10.9

Measure the angle of incidence and the angle of reflection with your protractor.

After the student has correctly entered measurements of several situations, the computer summarizes:

Good, you have discovered the principle that determines the bounce of a ball off a wall:
    The angle of incidence is *equal* to the angle of reflection.
Use this principle to predict the path of the ball in the following situations.

Here the computer returns to similar problems and gives the student a chance to practice applying the newly discovered principle before posing the next kind of problem.

Problem 3.

Imagine that one wall of a room is a mirror. You are standing at point *S*. In what direction would you look to see (in the mirror) an object located at position *O*? (See fig. 10.10.)

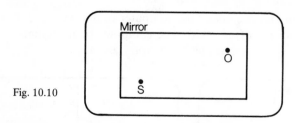

Fig. 10.10

Again there is interaction between the computer and the student. The student guesses; the computer evaluates and responds. If the student has not located the correct direction after three guesses, the computer draws the correct path to the mirror, and then presents a new location for *S* and *O*. After several problems of this sort, the students will, at the very least, realize that looking at the perpendicular projection of *O* onto the surface of the mirror is *not* the correct direction. It is a help to have mirrors in the classroom with which the students can experiment to verify the computer paths.

Once again the computer shows the generalization needed to explain the paths.

When an object is reflected in a mirror; the image appears to be behind (or *in*) the mirror the same distance that the object is from the mirror. For example, the image of an object at position *O* appears to be at position *O'* (fig. 10.11).

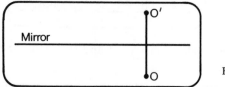

Fig. 10.11

To see the image in the mirror we would look toward *O'*. Notice that the line *OO'* makes a right angle with the mirror.

If you are at *S* and want to see *O* reflected in the mirror, look toward *O'* (fig. 10.12).

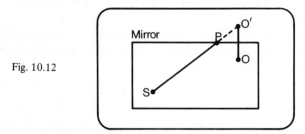

Fig. 10.12

To summarize: Find the reflection of O (O') in the mirror by drawing a line through O that makes a right angle with the mirror. (O' and O are, of course, equidistant from the mirror.) Then draw line SO'. This is the correct direction.

Now try the one in figure 10.13.

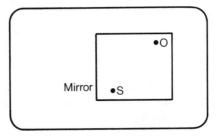

Fig. 10.13

After the student guesses, the computer responds, shows the reflection of O in the mirror, and draws the path (fig. 10.14).

Once a student has been successful with mirror-vision problems, the next step is to establish the connection between the mirror problem and the bouncing ball.

Let's look at the diagram for the angle of incidence and reflection again. If the wall were not there, the ball would continue on a straight path to position A'. Instead, it bounces off the wall to position A (fig. 10.15).

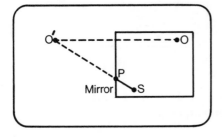

Fig. 10.14

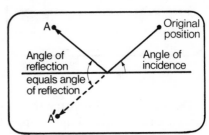

Fig. 10.15

This looks like the problem of the mirror. If the wall were a mirror and we were at the original position, we would see the ball at A by looking toward A'. The technique we used to solve the mirror problems can also be used to solve the bouncing-ball problem.

We look at the reflection of the number rod in the wall (fig. 10.16) and the straight line path tells us that the ball will hit at 4. If you measure the angles marked, you will find that they are equal.

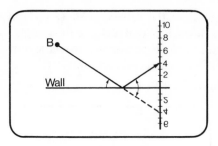

Fig. 10.16

Here students should be allowed to make some mathematical connections for themselves. The computer displays a problem like the first one, which was to connect two towns to the water source (the river) by the shortest pipeline possible (fig. 10.17).

> Can you use the mirror-reflection idea to find the shortest path from *A* to the river to *B*?

The computer can allow the student to try several problems and then give help or reinforcement until the notion of reflecting *A* or *B* in the river is clear (fig. 10.18).

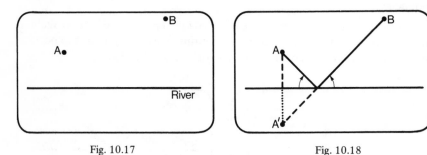

Fig. 10.17   Fig. 10.18

There are many opportunities to use these ideas in sports applications. Here are two simple examples from miniature golf.

Problem 4.

> Your ball is located at *A*, and your opponent's ball is at *B*. You want to bounce your ball off the far cushion (wall) and hit the ball at *B*. At what point on the cushion should you aim?

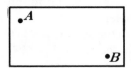

Problem 5.

You are playing miniature golf and you've reached an area like the one shown. Your ball is at A and the hole at H. Where should you aim the ball for it to hit the hole?

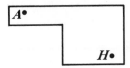

A student who understands the connection between bouncing balls and mirror reflections is ready to learn more complicated applications, which involve predicting the behavior of a ball that bounces against more than one wall.

As an example, consider a miniature golf player whose ball is at B in figure 10.19 and who would like to make a hole in one by hitting the ball so it will bounce off wall 1 (W_1) and then wall 2 (W_2).

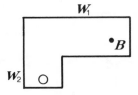

Fig. 10.19

The problem is to decide where to aim the ball so that after a bounce off both walls, the ball will be at the hole. Let's trace the path of the ball. When the ball hits the first wall and goes toward the second, it must be aimed at the reflection of the hole in wall 2. Hence the first bounce, off wall 1, must be aimed at the reflection in wall 1 of the reflection in wall 2 of the hole (fig. 10.20).

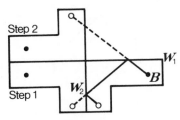

Fig. 10.20

An interactive instruction module might present the problem (draw a figure of the "hole"), and have the user decide where to aim the ball. In the tutorial mode, successive reflections of the hole would be drawn, showing the consequences of the choice. A practice mode might merely graph the entire course of the ball on one hole. The user would choose another impact point, with or without the help of reflected holes.

In three-cushion billiards, the ball, B, must be bounced against three sides of the table before hitting the ball at C (fig. 10.21). If the ball must bounce off sides WZ, ZY, and WX, in that order, how must it be hit?

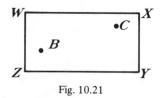

Fig. 10.21

The solution requires reflecting the table about each of the sides in reverse order, as in figure 10.22.

First reflect C in WX to obtain C'.

Then reflect C' in ZY to obtain C''.

Then reflect C'' in WZ (extended) to get C'''.

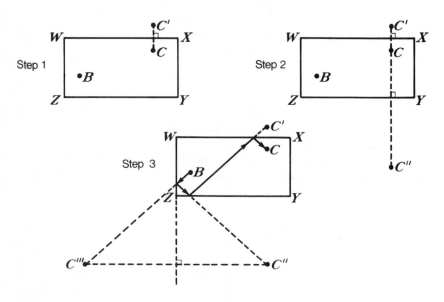

Fig. 10.22

Different bounces could have been called for, although some combinations are clearly impossible.

Here are two additional types of applications that could be included in this CAI module. They are taken from Coxford and Usiskin (1971).

An electron sent from point *A* (fig. 10.23) is to be reflected off lines *l* and *m* in such a way that it passes through point *B*. Find the path of the electron.

Step 1: Reflect *B* in *m* to obtain *B'*.
Step 2: Reflect *B'* in *l* to obtain *B"*.

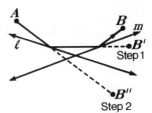

Fig. 10.23

In figure 10.24 a ray of light travels from point *A* and reflects off *p* twice and *q* once before it passes through *B*. Draw the path of the light.

Step 1: Reflect *B* in *p* to obtain *B'*.
Step 2: Reflect *B'* in *q* to obtain *B"*.
Step 3: Reflect *B"* in *p* to obtain *B'''*.

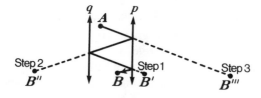

Fig. 10.24

Conclusion

Those who are involved in helping students learn mathematics must continually seek ways to improve instruction. Computers and computer graphics offer new methods to engage students in learning. The mathematics curriculum offers many opportunities for this new technology to allow students to explore problem solutions in an experimental way. We have shown one type of significant application, one that is accessible through computer simulation but very difficult for students to conceptualize otherwise. We hope this article will stimulate many readers to take advantage of other instances where the computer can be beneficially integrated into the teaching and learning of mathematics.

REFERENCES

Coxford, Arthur, and Zalman Usiskin. *Geometry: A Transformational Approach.* River Forest, Ill.: Laidlaw Bros., Publishers, 1971.

Hawkins, David. "Critical Barriers to Science Learning." *Outlook* 29 (Autumn 1978):3–23.

11

Computers: Applications Unlimited

Sharon Dugdale

T HERE were five frogs in the pond. Three frogs jumped out. Does anybody care what fraction of the frogs jumped out of the pond? Probably not.

One problem with mathematics education is that students rarely see any immediate need for much of what they are expected to learn. The "applications" sections of textbooks often contain nothing that students want to figure out and apply to their own world. Instead, books are filled with exercises in which students practice applying textbook mathematics to textbook problems.

There is a growing concern that applications should have a more central role in the school mathematics program, not in the sense of the traditional word problem, but in ways more relevant to the student's interests. Computers offer potential for a wealth of applications and simulations that were not previously possible in the classroom. Let us discuss two such applications and some important considerations in their design and use. The examples presented were created by the author and David Kibbey at the University of Illinois.

Using Math Is Different from *Doing* Math

There is an important difference between *using* mathematics to accomplish some desired goal and *doing* mathematics to satisfy a class assignment. The difference is apparent in the way students approach mathematics, what they try to get out of it, and how they organize what they learn. This difference was highlighted during our first classroom use of "Green Globs," a computer program that provides students a structured environment in which to use, experiment with, and share their knowledge of graphing equations.

In "Green Globs" the student is given coordinate axes with thirteen green

"Green Globs" was created in 1980 with support from the National Science Foundation (NSF-SED80-12449). "Darts" was created in 1973 with support from the National Science Foundation (US NSF C-723). These and related programs are available for use on popular microcomputers. For information contact Sharon Dugdale, 252 Engineering Research Lab, University of Illinois, 103 South Mathews, Urbana, IL 61801.

globs scattered randomly. The goal is to explode all the globs by hitting them with graphs, specified by typing in equations. (See fig. 11.1.) The scoring algorithm encourages students to hit as many globs as they can with each shot.

If a shot misses the expected targets, the graphic feedback (of the display to the student's graph) gives diagnostic information needed for the student to debug his or her ideas about graphs. Perhaps the graph was too wide, or too steep, or upside down.

This activity encourages students of widely varying backgrounds and abilities to participate. It is clearly possible to hit all the globs with linear functions (in fact, with constant functions). However, the more mathematical knowledge students apply, the more globs they are likely to hit with each shot (Dugdale 1982). The game is often played cooperatively by two or more students.

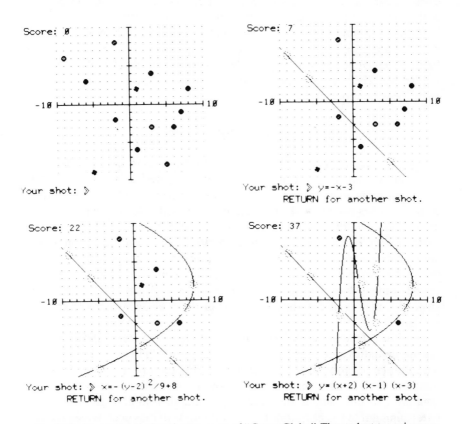

Fig. 11.1. Sequential displays from a game of "Green Globs." The student types in equations, which are graphed by the computer. The green globs explode as they are hit by the graphs. Shown is the initial display of thirteen globs, followed by the student's first three shots.

The top ten scores are kept in a "hall of fame," which displays students' names along with their record-making scores. Each of the top ten games listed in the hall of fame is stored so other students can see what shots and strategies the top players have used. Students frequently replay one or more of the record-making games to gather tools that might be useful to them in future games.

We offered students a selection of several activities, including "Green Globs" and one with a nongame format that guided practice in writing equations for graphs. The items in the practice exercise were carefully sequenced to reveal some general principles about the graphs of equations. Even so, students who had not yet begun to graph equations in "Green Globs" seemed to regard the exercise more as a series of items to work out, without any real reason to distill general principles or collect ideas that might be relevant after leaving the exercise. However, after becoming involved in "Green Globs," students were seen going back to the practice exercise (and sometimes to textbooks), apparently with a new interest in gathering strategies to make graphs behave in particular ways.

Having a compelling environment in which to apply and share what they knew about graphs motivated students to approach the subject in a new light. When it became important to them to be able to manipulate equations and graphs, they saw the need to formulate general strategies and organize their ideas in applicable ways.

Math *Is* Interesting

Hand in hand with providing students opportunities to apply mathematics to situations that they consider important is the desirability of presenting mathematics as inherently interesting. A prominent trend in computerized instruction has been to make mathematics fun, and indeed, computers seem capable of making almost anything fun. Even the old drill-and-practice materials are now dressed up with animated animals on the screen, flashy colorful messages to reinforce correct responses, and peppy tunes from the music synthesizer. Of course, the addition of mathematically irrelevant entertainment does not make the mathematics itself any more or less fun. Instead, it may even shift the focus of the program away from the mathematics.

Providing structured environments that students can manipulate by applying mathematics is very different from "making math fun" by dressing it up with unrelated motivations. The former approach reflects the attitude that mathematics is interesting and useful, whereas the latter implies that mathematics is so unpalatable that it must be diluted with enough superfluous entertainment to be acceptable to the student. Activities like "Green Globs" center students' attention on their own abilities to make interesting uses of mathematics. Programs that rely on the inherently interesting aspects of the topic can grow in interest as the student learns to apply more mathematics, rather than becoming progressively less involving as the student tires of superficial motivation.

A more elementary example, "Darts," has students explore the placement of rational numbers on the number line. (See fig. 11.2.) Balloons are tied to a number line, and the student shoots darts at the balloons by

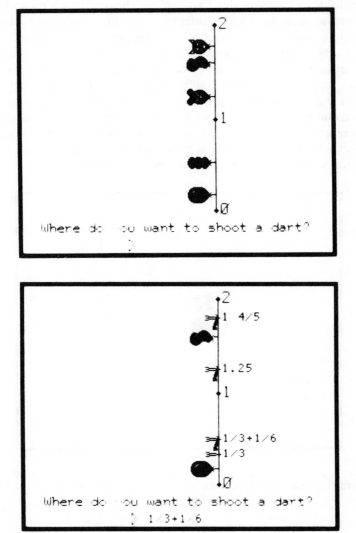

Fig. 11.2. Two screen displays from the lesson "Darts." Balloons are tied to a number line. The student shoots darts by writing a number to tell where on the number line the dart should go. The dart flies across the screen and lodges in the number line, popping a balloon if it hits one. The student may use fractions, decimals, mixed numbers, or expressions. The student's input is shown beside each dart.

estimating their positions on the line. Fractions, decimals, mixed numbers, and expressions using operations are all acceptable input. (This original "Darts" program, created by the author in 1973 using the PLATO system, may differ in some ways from the various versions that have appeared since.)

A critical difference between "Darts" and many other mathematics games that have been written for computers is that "Darts" is actually a mathematical model. When students shoot a dart to hit a baloon, they are learning and using mathematics in a much different sense from those who write the answer to a problem so they can see a clown jump up and down.

In "Darts," both the student's activity and the computer's response revolve around the mathematics. When a dart hits the number line, the students receive immediate visual feedback, learning not just whether the guess was right or wrong but also where the guess lies in relation to the target and previous guesses. For example, figure 11.3 shows a common misconception about negative numbers. The student is assuming that $-1\frac{1}{4}$ is above (i.e., *larger than*) -1. Observation has shown that students frequently enter the lesson with this misconception and then quickly correct it.

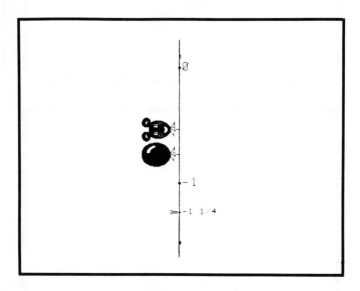

Fig. 11.3. A portion of a screen display from "Darts." The student has just shot a dart at $-1\frac{1}{4}$, expecting to hit the balloon just *above* -1 on the number line. The graphic feedback helps students "debug" their conceptions of rational numbers.

If the student's guess is equivalent to a previous guess, both guesses are recorded, and the equivalence is shown (fig. 11.4). Students are frequently observed to look startled briefly and then say, "Oh, right . . . ." ("Darts" is often used with students who have not yet studied equivalent fractions, so it is reasonable for a student to be thinking in eighths and take a moment to recognize that ⁴/₈ is really another name for ¹/₂.)

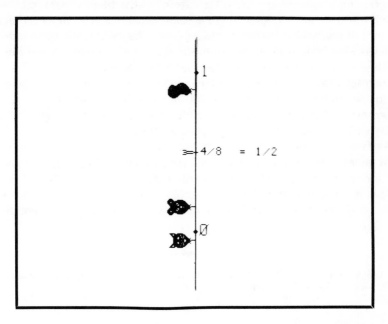

Fig. 11.4. A portion of a screen display from "Darts." The student has just shot a dart at ⁴/₈, only to find that ⁴/₈ is the same as ¹/₂, where he had previously shot a dart. The lesson saves the previous shot and shows its equivalence with the later shot.

The strategies students develop are numerous and varied. It is not uncommon to see a student measure the distance between integers by counting finger widths, then use this same unit to measure the distance to each balloon. This strategy has the interesting feature of having the students frequently using fractions like ¹⁴/₁₉ or ¹⁷/₂₃ with no trouble or confusion at all. One particularly careful student using this method was observed to count 12¹/₂ finger widths between integers. She thought for a moment, then used twenty-fifths, calling each finger width equal to ²/₂₅.

In applying their beginning knowledge of fractions to a mathematically accurate model like "Darts," students who are beginning the study of fractions can discover and figure out ideas well beyond what is traditionally expected. They can also build a comfortable familiarity with rational numbers that will pay off in later work.

Conclusion

Computers in the classroom have opened up a rich new world of potential applications for mathematics—applications that are both motivating and meaningful within the student's world. In addition to applications involving programming, computers can offer carefully structured environments in which students can develop and use mathematical strategies in ways that no amount of textbook calisthenics can achieve. The experience and comfortable working familiarity gained from these computer environments can be invaluable in their later use of mathematical concepts.

Such activities can give a new perspective on the usefulness of mathematics in the student's world, but they do not require a restructuring of the classroom or the curriculum as a whole. They are easily integrated into today's classrooms by today's teachers and students.

As fast-developing technology provides more and more capabilities in affordable classroom computers, we shall have continually increasing potential for sophisticated and varied interaction between students and computers. It is hoped that with these technological advances mathematics will increasingly become something students *use* and decreasingly something they *do*.

REFERENCES

Dugdale, Sharon. "Green Globs: A Microcomputer Application for Graphing of Equations." *Mathematics Teacher* 75 (March 1982):208–14.

12

Teacher-Student-Computer Interaction: An Application That Enhances Teacher Effectiveness

Nira Hativa

Most of the software currently available for computer-assisted instruction in schools has been developed for use by a single student interacting with a single terminal. However, teachers remain the best source for students' learning, irreplaceable by any computer. Therefore, rather than assigning teachers the role of aides to computers, we should use the microcomputer to help teachers provide quality in-class instruction. Computers can be used as a demonstration aid to the teacher in the classroom.

Software programs for this purpose that are already available or that are in the developmental stages take several different forms:

• *Graphic illustrations of concepts.* The teacher illustrates the derivative function, for instance, by using software that plots, point by point, the numerical values of slopes of tangents to the original function and then connects them with a continuous curve.

• *Numerical illustrations of concepts.* The teacher illustrates a limiting process, for instance, by using software that computes quickly and prints the results of each step of the computation.

• *Experimentation.* When teaching the graphing of functions, for example, the teacher can easily demonstrate what happens to the graph of $f(x)$ when a constant is added to the function, as for example $f(x) + 5$, $f(x) - 2$, or the argument, as in the instance $f(x + 5)$, $f(x - 2)$. Similarly, the effect on the graph of multiplying the function or the argument by a constant can also be explored, as in the case $5f(x)$, $\frac{1}{2}f(x)$, $f(5x)$, and $f(\frac{1}{2}x)$.

This article suggests a new use of microcomputer software as an in-class teaching aid, one that will create an environment for three-way interaction: teacher, students, and microcomputer. This kind of software can facilitate teachers' work in lesson preparation, enhance their capabilities in presenting new material, and encourage them to use effective teaching strategies. This mode of teaching is illustrated with a software lesson on parallelograms.

A Lesson: Introduction to Parallelograms

Characteristics and special features of the lesson

This lesson on parallelograms was designed with special attention to effective presentation and to generating student interaction with the visual materials and the teacher. Following are some of its features.

- The program stops often. This enables the teacher to enrich the presentation by asking appropriate questions and leading class discussion. Such questions are either printed on the screen or suggested in a teacher manual. The teacher may stop the discussion to write important points, definitions, theorems, and the derivation of their proofs on the board.

- The lesson presents sequentially all the hierarchical steps necessary for students to understand the new material.

- The software is flexible enough to allow teachers to direct the process in accordance with their own style and their students' rate of learning. They can repeat, skip, or reorder frames, add or replace questions suggested on the screen, and pace the lesson as they wish. They can also give additional illustrations and proofs of theorems. However, teachers are encouraged to use the software in the order given to achieve maximum effectiveness.

- The software is based on an extensive use of color graphics and animation to develop intuition for new concepts and to present practical applications. The accurate and aesthetic illustrations serve also as motivational devices.

- All text and animations are accompanied by sound effects. The sounds are like those used in the popular electronic arcade games and were designed by the programmer of this software—a teenager. It was his idea that the sound effects would make the lesson as attractive to his peers as to himself. However, the teacher has the option of eliminating the sound.

- The program is simple to use and does not require any knowledge of programming.

- The figures and most of the characters in the program are large and can be read easily, even from the back of the classroom. Information specifically for the teacher is the only reading matter printed in small characters.

- Other features include the review of relevant material, framework for future topics, smooth transitions between topics, repetition of key concepts, frequent summaries, elementary problems and questions that each student is able to answer successfully, immediate feedback, and real-life applications that make the topic relevant to students' life experiences.

Using the program

The topic "Introduction to Parallelograms" is developed in four stages; polygons (frame 1), quadrilaterals (frames 2–5), parallelograms (6–10), and real-life applications (11–14). (See fig. 12.1.) Unfortunately, the photographs must be reproduced here in black and white and thus cannot convey the full effect of the colorful program.

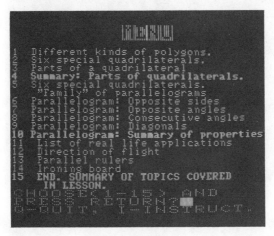

Fig. 12.1

Polygons. When the heading "Polygons" appears on the screen, the teacher may ask the class which polygons they know by name, where in the everyday world they can be found, and how they would define a polygon. When the teacher presses the return key, a few polygons appear on the screen one by one. The program stops after each so the teacher can ask students to name the polygons (triangle, quadrilateral, and pentagon). Finally, the text appears ("This lesson deals with quadrilaterals"), providing a smooth transition from polygons in general to quadrilaterals, one family of polygons.

Quadrilaterals. The teacher and students discuss the names of special quadrilaterals and where they can be found in the everyday world. Next, five special quadrilaterals, in addition to a general quadrilateral, appear on the screen one by one as the teacher touches a key (see fig. 12.2): a trapezoid, a parallelogram, a rectangle, a rhombus, and a square. The teacher has the opportunity to ask students to name each figure before its name appears on the screen.

The next topic is the presentation and definitions of parts of a quadrilateral (fig. 12.3)—vertices, angles, sides (consecutive and opposite), and diagonals. This topic is important to the program because the subject is often overlooked by teachers. They are unaware that many students have to be taught to identify consecutive vertices or opposite angles. Each concept is presented by animation. For example, the text "opposite sides" appears with the symbol "(2)" to hint to students that there are two pairs of opposite sides. Here again the program stops to enable the teacher and the students to

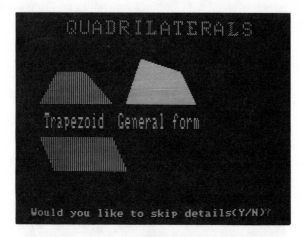

Fig. 12.2

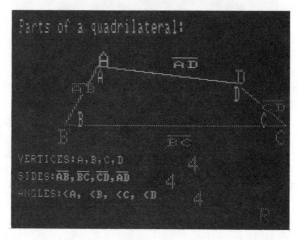

Fig. 12.3

discuss the definition of opposite sides and to name the two pairs. At the beginning, each side of the quadrilateral has a different color. But at this point the teacher presses RETURN and an animated sequence begins: two opposite sides get the same color, flash, and then return to their original colors. This procedure is repeated for the other pair of opposite sides.

To conclude the topic, a summary of all properties and definitions related to quadrilaterals is printed step by step and stops before each step to enable students to state the property before it is printed (fig. 12.4).

For a smooth transition from quadrilaterals in general to parallelograms, the six special quadrilaterals appear again on the screen. This time they appear at once, and the students are asked to identify the number of pairs of

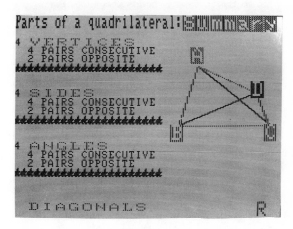

Fig. 12.4

parallel sides in each (0, 1, or 2) (fig. 12.5). When the teacher presses a key, the appropriate number appears inside each quadrilateral. At this point the teacher introduces the definition of a parallelogram (the two pairs of opposite sides are parallel) and shows that this definition holds for the rectangle, rhombus, and square—hence all these are parallelograms—but not for the

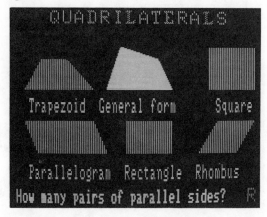

Fig. 12.5

trapezoid. Then, the same six quadrilaterals change their arrangement to a "family tree" (fig. 12.6). This is to show students the relationships among quadrilaterals and prepare them for the next software lesson topic: special parallelograms—rectangle, rhombus, and square.

Parallelograms. Four theorems on parallelograms are introduced. Since the development of each theorem goes through the same four stages, only one—*opposite sides are congruent*—is described below.

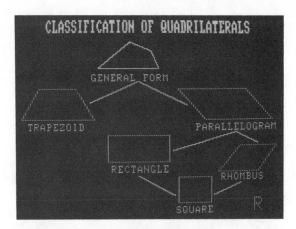

Fig. 12.6

Stage 1. Asking students to guess the theorem. The definition of the parallelogram presented earlier is printed as property number 1.: "Opposite sides are parallel (def.)." Then the numeral 2 is printed with the text: "Opposite sides are . . ." Here the program stops (fig. 12.7), and the students are asked to suggest another property of opposite sides of a parallelogram. A discussion may follow, and whether the students complete the statement of the theorem correctly or not, an animation follows the touch of a key.

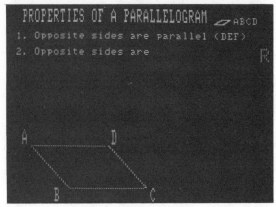

Fig. 12.7

Stage 2. An animation that provides an intuitive justification of the theorem. Two opposite sides become the same color. Then one of these leaves its place and slides along the other two sides of the parallelogram until it covers the opposite side. The process repeats for the other pair of opposite sides. The program stops again, and the students are asked to complete the statement of the theorem. The animation can be repeated until the students offer a correct answer. With the touch of a key, the text of the theorem is completed by the answer "congruent."

Stage 3. An elementary application of the theorem. Text appears that asks the teacher, "Would you like an application? (Y/N)." If the teacher chooses to show the application, a simple one is provided: A statement of the theorem is printed, together with a parallelogram and measures of two adjacent sides. The students are asked to state the measures of the other two sides one by one (fig. 12.8). When a student suggests an answer, the teacher can choose between typing that answer on the keyboard or calling on the student to do it. The typed answer appears on the screen. If it is incorrect, the text says, "Try again." If three incorrect answers are given, the correct one appears.

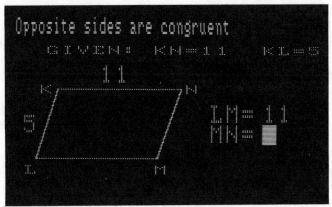

Fig. 12.8

Stage 4: Hints for a formal proof of the theorem. The teacher is asked, "Hints for proof? (Y/N)." If the teacher answers yes, a parallelogram *ABCD* appears on the screen with a statement of the theorem. The teacher goes to the chalkboard, draws a similar parallelogram, and asks the students how to proceed with the proof. If an appropriate answer is not provided by students, the teacher touches a key and one hint appears: the diagonal *AC* is drawn, dividing the parallelogram into two triangles. If a second hint is necessary, it will be that two alternate angles between the parallel sides *AB* and *CD* get the same color. The last hint: The two alternate angles between the parallel sides *AD* and *BC* get the same color. After discovering the proof of the theorem with the class, the teacher with the class's help will write the detailed proof on the board.

Each of the other three theorems about parallelograms is presented in the same four stages. These theorems are (1) "Opposite angles are congruent," (2) "Consecutive angles are supplementary," and (3) "The diagonals bisect each other." Finally, there is a summary of the properties of the parallelogram. Again, the program stops after the beginning of the statement of each property to enable students to complete the theorems before they appear on the screen.

Practical applications. Three applications for parallelograms are suggested: flight direction, parallel rulers used in navigation, and the structure of an ironing board. All three illustrate the properties of parallelograms in real situations. The first application is described as follows:

An airplane is shown flying horizontally when a wind comes up and changes the plane's direction. The program stops and students are asked to suggest what direction the airplane will fly as a result of that wind. The teacher can draw arrows on the board in the direction of the flight and of the wind (with lengths corresponding to the speed of the flight and the wind) and call on a few students to draw an estimate of the final direction. When the teacher presses any key, the *parallelogram of forces* is drawn (two sides of which are the original speed of the airplane and the speed of the wind), and its diagonal is the final speed of the airplane. The teacher may explain in more detail how this works and also provide other examples of the parallelogram of forces.

A list of the topics presented by the software concludes the program.

Most existing software programs for schools are designed for student-computer interaction and require one system (a computer plus a monitor plus software) for every student or every pair of students. A program of the type described here requires only one system for an entire class and makes possible the three-way interaction of student, computer, and teacher. However, the software can be used by individual students as well. This feature would be helpful for those who miss a class, those who could not keep pace, and those who would like to review for a test. I believe that the development of software of this kind for geometry and other mathematical topics would benefit the teaching and learning of mathematics.

The program described here, "Quadrilaterals," runs on any version of the Apple II microcomputer with 48K RAM memory and with the Applesoft language. Diskettes with this and similar programs are available from the following sources:

Reader's Digest Services, Inc.   Chambered Nautilus
Microcomputer Software Division   16 Riverglade Ct.
Pleasantville, NY 10570   Sacramento, CA 95831
Tel. (800) 431-8800   Tel. (916) 393-7533

REFERENCES

Fletcher, T. J. "The Teaching of Geometry: Present Problems and Future Aims." *Educational Studies in Mathematics* 3 (1971): 396–404.
Hoffer, Alan. "Geometry Is More Than Proof." *Mathematics Teacher* 74 (January 1981): 11–18.

13

The Yellow-Light Problem: Computer-based Applied Mathematics

Thomas T. Liao
E. Joseph Piel

$\mathbf{W}$HY are we studying this topic?" This question is often asked, more often silently than aloud. The beginning teacher, as well as the one with much experience, will answer, "Because you will need it later!" The student soon wishes it were later, but so often tomorrow never comes. With the impact of technology on our lives, students should be studying topics today that are related to something that is happening today.

Background and Rationale

The activity described in this paper uses a tool of technology to analyze a situation involving technology and society that most high school students face every day. Very few people who ride in an automobile can say that they have never been in a car that went through an intersection against the red light. The vast majority of people who have done so will tell you that the light was yellow when they entered the intersection but that it turned red before they could get to the other side. Why does this occur? Is the yellow light on for too short a time? Is the intersection too wide? Is the speed limit too low? Does the weather have an effect?

Using a problem like this can motivate students to read graphs, discuss nonlinear relationships, and even take the square root of a number. When used with a computer, the problem can motivate students to analyze mathematical relationships as part of the decision-making process.

In the late 1960s, before inexpensive computers were available in schools, we developed the problem of the yellow light as part of our "Man-Made World" course. Students would discuss the factors that traffic engineers consider as they design intersections and time the traffic lights at those intersections.

97

Response Time

We devised a crude way of measuring response time: having a student catch a ruler dropped by a partner and noting how far it had fallen. Since a body falling from rest follows the equation $d = \frac{1}{2} gt^2$, (where d is the distance the object falls, g is the acceleration due to gravity, and t is the time the object was falling), then if we know d and g, we can calculate t by using the equation $t = \sqrt{(2d)/g}$.

Using graphs of the appropriate equations and a rate of negative acceleration that would provide a comfortable stopping rate, the students were asked to analyze the situation at intersections having a given width and a specific speed limit for different timings of the yellow light. In some cases the parameters, other than the stopping rate, were obtained by actual measurement at local intersections. Students often found that a "dilemma zone" existed between the point beyond which the car could continue through the intersection safely at the given speed limit ("go zone") and the point behind which the car would need to be when the brakes were applied in order to avoid being in the intersection when the light turned red ("stop zone").

Figure 13.1 depicts the situation of a car traveling 30 mph approaching a 3-sec yellow light and decelerating at 13 ft/sec². A car in the dilemma zone could neither stop comfortably nor pass safely through the intersection at the specified speed limit.

The problem was to design an intersection in which there was no dilemma zone. Working with graphs and equations, students soon became discouraged because the chore was tedious. Those who were not discouraged lost sight of the basic questions as they manipulated the various parts of the problem.

Then along came the microcomputer—with graphics! Now we had a means of making the situation much more realistic. A car approaches the intersection, the light changes from green to yellow, and the student decides whether to continue or to stop. Those who decide to continue push the G (gas) key. (Those who decide to stop push the space bar—the brakes.) If the

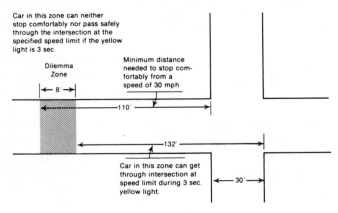

Fig. 13.1

decision to continue is correct, the car passes through safely. If it is wrong, there is a crash with another car coming through at a right angle. After five successful stops, the computer displays the average response time.

Using that response time, the student now designs an intersection by deciding on the speed limit, width, time of yellow light, and stopping rate. By trial and error the student finally eliminates the dilemma zone. He or she is now asked to analyze how each of the factors—reaction time, yellow-light time, speed limit, width of intersection, and deceleration—affects the go zone, stop zone, and dilemma zone.

Teacher's Guide for Microcomputer Courseware Package

This courseware package on the yellow-light problem is one of the units developed under an NSF-sponsored project. Besides the computer program, a teacher's guide provides the information needed to use the courseware effectively. Because of space limitations, only the most relevant sections of the teacher's guide are presented here.

Performance objectives

After completing this courseware package, students should be able to—

1. measure or determine the yellow-light time, response time, speed limit, deceleration, and width of an intersection;
2. explain the meaning of the parameters in (1);
3. explain the meaning of the go, stop, and dilemma zones;
4. determine which of the independent variables in (1) affect which of the dependent variables in (3);
5. graphically determine the mathematical relationships between independent and dependent variables;
6. write a computer program to calculate the go, stop, and dilemma zones;
7. produce a final report based on an analysis of an actual intersection.

Rationale

Students must be given more opportunities to apply mathematics and science concepts to real-world problems. The yellow-light problem can be a meaningful example. By using the mathematics and science applications, they will receive a partial answer to an often-asked question, "Why are we studying these concepts?"

This courseware package also includes investigations that help students learn how independent variables affect dependent variables. They can ask "what if" questions about the relationships among the variables and immediately see the consequences of their manipulations. First, students discover which inputs affect which outputs; then they determine the mathematical equations that describe the behavior of the system. Finally, they use the equations to write their own computer program.

Operation of computer program and sample runs

This program has three primary sections. A menu of options (fig. 13.2) introduces the program. In the first section, students interact with a simulation to measure their response time (see figs. 13.3–13.5). In the second, they collect data about a traffic intersection and use the computer program to determine the go, stop, and dilemma zones. This section also allows students to manipulate the variables and see the results on a summary table (figs. 13.6–13.9). In the third section, students can graphically analyze the effect of inputs on outputs (figs. 13.10–13.13).

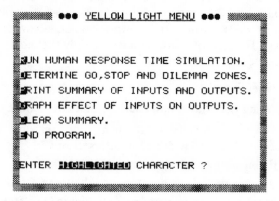

```
●●● YELLOW LIGHT MENU ●●●


RUN HUMAN RESPONSE TIME SIMULATION.
DETERMINE GO,STOP AND DILEMMA ZONES.
PRINT SUMMARY OF INPUTS AND OUTPUTS.
GRAPH EFFECT OF INPUTS ON OUTPUTS.
CLEAR SUMMARY.
END PROGRAM.


ENTER HIGHLIGHTED CHARACTER ?
```

Fig. 13.2. By entering the first letter of the first word, the user can access each option.

Section 1: Response-time simulation. Entering *R* causes a traffic intersection to be displayed and gives instructions for measuring a person's response time (fig. 13.3). If the car is in the go zone when the yellow light comes on and the user pushes the *G* key, a safe trip will result (fig. 13.4). If the car is in the stop zone when the yellow light comes on and the user pushes the *G* key, an accident will result (fig. 13.5). However, if the user pushes the space bar, a response-time measurement will occur.

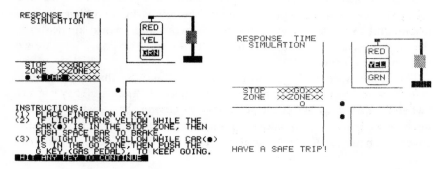

Fig. 13.3   Fig. 13.4

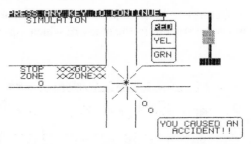

YOU ATTEMPTED TO GO IN THE STOP ZONE.   Fig. 13.5

Section 2: Analysis of traffic intersection. After five measurements of response time, the program indicates the average response time and asks whether the user wants to analyze an intersection. If the user answers yes, he or she is asked to input the appropriate data (fig. 13.6). Based on these inputs, the program produces a scale drawing of the intersection and then asks if the user wants to change one of the variables (fig. 13.7). If the user changes the speed limit from 35 mph to 30 mph, the program will produce the scale drawing shown in figure 13.8.

```
    DATA FOR ANALYSIS OF INTERSECTION

YOUR AVERAGE RESPONSE TIME TO A YELLOW
LIGHT IS .58 SECONDS
WOULD YOU LIKE TO CONTINUE AND
ANALYZE AN INTERSECTION (Y OR N)?  ? Y


RESPONSE TIME (.5-1) SEC              ? .58
SPEED LIMIT (10-55) MPH              ? 30
DECELERATION (10-15) FEET/SEC↑2     ? 12
YELLOW LIGHT DURATION (1-5) SEC     ? 2.5
WIDTH OF INTERSECTION (10-80) FT    ? 28
```

Fig. 13.6

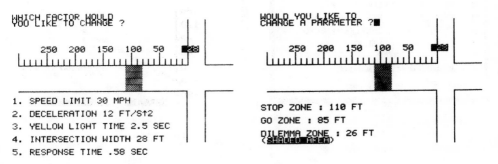

Fig. 13.7   Fig. 13.8

Each of the five factors can be changed to study its impact. A summary table (fig. 13.9) helps the student in the study of which inputs affect which outputs.

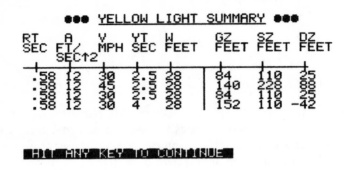

Fig. 13.9

Section 3: Effect of inputs on outputs. The third section of the program helps students to analyze graphically the relationship between the inputs and outputs. A menu describes seven analysis options (fig. 13.10). If option 1 is chosen, the user can vary the velocity and width to obtain a family of straight lines. In figure 13.11, we see two lines of different slopes that have the same y-intercept. If option 5 is chosen, the user can vary the response time and velocity to see how the stop zone is affected (fig. 13.12). If option 7 is chosen, the user can compare the effect of the velocity (V) on both the go zone (GZ) and the stop zone (SZ). Notice that the V-versus-GZ graph is linear and whereas the V-versus-SZ graph is nonlinear (fig. 13.13).

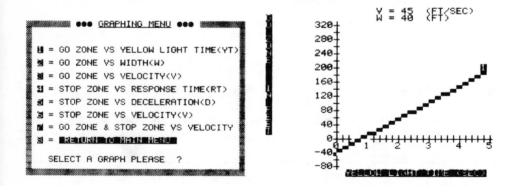

Fig. 13.10   Fig. 13.11

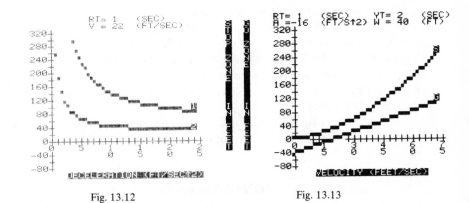

Fig. 13.12 Fig. 13.13

Instruction strategies

To analyze and solve the problems in this courseware package, students must apply concepts of basic algebra and physics. The yellow-light problem involves them in five specific problem-solving activities:

1. Determining human response time and other parameters that affect the go and stop zones at an intersection. This activity involves identifying and collecting relevant data that are needed for solving the problem.

2. Using the computer program to calculate the go, stop, and dilemma zones.

3. Manipulating the input variables to determine which ones affect the go and stop zones.

4. Analyzing graphically the ways that the independent variables (inputs) affect the dependent variables (outputs). Students will be able to discover the answers to two questions:

   a) How do the yellow-light time, speed limit, and width of the intersection affect the go zone?

   b) How do the response time, velocity, and deceleration affect the stop zone?

5. Developing a final report that describes the situation at an actual intersection. This project can include a student-written computer program for calculating the go, stop, and dilemma zones.

Activity 1: *Identifying and collecting of relevant data.* Present the yellow-light problem to students and brainstorm to identify the relevant variables. Since our approach to this problem involves only five easily quantifiable variables, such factors as traffic density and weather conditions are not included in this analysis.

Use Student Worksheet 1 to involve students in measuring their response time for a simple task like catching a falling object. This activity can also be used to introduce or review the concept of uniform acceleration, which will be needed for explaining how a car decelerates.

Point out that the task of noticing the yellow light, making a decision, and moving the foot from the gas pedal to the brake is much more complicated than catching a falling ruler. After using the computer simulation, they can compare those results to the response times obtained when catching a falling object (typical values are 0.2 sec for catching a ruler and 0.6 sec for responding to a yellow light).

Since the yellow-light simulation is only a computer model of the actual situation, ask students how they would modify the simulation to make it

Student Materials

Student Worksheet 1:

Response-Time Activity and Collection of Other Data

A. In order to determine the go, stop, and dilemma zones at a traffic intersection, we need information about human response time; however, that time varies depending on the task to be completed. An example of a simple task is to note the time it takes to catch a falling object, such as a ruler. Students can work in pairs to record times.

Procedure

1. Use a standard 12-inch ruler.
2. Have your partner hold the ruler vertically, letting it hang between your own thumb and index finger, which should be about an inch apart.
3. After your partner has released the ruler, try to catch it as quickly as possible.
4. If using a standard ruler, measure the distance the ruler falls either in feet or meters; then use the formula $t = \sqrt{(2d)/g}$ to determine the time. (Note that $g = 32$ ft/sec^2, or 9.8 m/sec^2. For example, it would take 0.2 sec for a ruler to fall 0.67 ft.)

Since driving a car and responding to a yellow light certainly are not as simple as catching a falling object, you would expect those response times to be longer. You will have an opportunity to use a computer simulation to measure your yellow-light response time.

B. Besides the response time, you must also collect the following information about a traffic intersection in order to determine the go, stop, and dilemma zones. You should complete this task before using the computer program.

Yellow-light time: _____ sec

Speed limit: _____ mph

Width of intersection: _____ ft

Typical values of deceleration are 15 ft/sec^2 (10 mi/hr/sec) to 9 ft/sec^2 (6 mi/hr/sec).

more realistic. As an example, if they were to use foot switches instead of the *G* key and space bar, they would have slightly longer response times.

Remind the students that they should use the bottom of Student Worksheet 1 to collect and record the data they have obtained from observing an actual intersection.

Activity 2: Determining the go, stop, and dilemma zones. The purpose of this part of the computer program is to see how different values of the five inputs (yellow-light time, driver-response time, speed limit, deceleration, and intersection width) result in different scale drawings of the go, stop, and dilemma zones. When students are interacting with this part of the program, encourage them to predict how the scale drawing will change when the input parameters are changed. After a few exploratory runs, students should be guided toward a systematic analysis of the behavior of the system as outlined in activity 3.

Activity 3: Effect of inputs on go and stop zones. To find out which input variables affect the go and stop zones, students should vary one input parameter at a time. After manipulating all five inputs, they should analyze the summary table to determine which inputs affect which outputs; they can also determine whether changing the input makes the go and stop zones increase, decrease, or remain the same. The summary table will also yield information for figuring out how the dilemma zone is ascertained.

Students can use the top half of Student Worksheet 2 to record the data from their manipulation of the variables; they can use the bottom half to record their conclusions based on interaction with the graphical analysis section of the program (activity 4).

Activity 4: Discovery of the mathematical model. The objective of this part of the computer program is to guide students in the discovery of the mathematical model that underlies this problem. For prephysics students, the activity is a good lead-in to the study of kinematics as well as an example of how algebraic relationships can be applied to an actual problem. For physics students, this activity demonstrates how kinematics relationships can be applied to a real-world system.

Activity 5: Project work and report. This activity involves students in collecting data that will be used to analyze and report on the conditions that exist at an actual traffic intersection. This type of project vividly demonstrates to students that the analysis and solution of real-world systems and problems always involves the integration of knowledge from several disciplines.

For further information on these materials, write Thomas Liao, Department of Technology and Society, College of Engineering and Applied Sciences, State University of New York, Stony Brook, NY 11794, or call 516/246-8648.

Student Worksheet 2:

Relationship of Inputs to Outputs

In the yellow-light problem, there are five inputs and three outputs. The computer program includes a summary table of the relationship between the inputs and outputs. Use the following table to record the information that the computer program will provide:

INPUTS					OUTPUTS		
Response time	Decel-eration	Speed limit	Yellow light time	Width of Intersection	Stop zone	Go zone	Dilemma zone

1. Which inputs affect the go zone? _____

   _____

2. Which inputs affect the stop zone? _____

   _____

3. How is the dilemma zone computed? _____

   _____

The last section of the computer program contains graphs that you can generate to help you discover the mathematical relationship between the inputs and outputs. Briefly describe the conclusions based on your manipulation of the variables in the seven graphic routines:

Graph 1: _____

Graph 2: _____

Graph 3: _____

Graph 4: _____

Graph 5: _____

Graph 6: _____

Graph 7: What is the basic difference between the effect of velocity on the go and stop zones? _____

   _____

14

Exploring Data with a Microcomputer

Jim Swift

How often have you looked at a newspaper, magazine, or report and seen some numbers on which the writer has based an opinion? Think, for example, of the arguments presented by the surgeon general of the United States to persuade smokers that they are endangering their health; or the arguments made by the New England states and the Canadian maritime provinces warning of the dangers of acid rain; or the case made by workers for increased wages because of the rise in the consumer price index. What is your reaction, and that of the public, to such arguments? Often, the tendency of the public is to ignore them, perhaps because of the prevalent opinion that statistical arguments are to be distrusted.

But we have an ally in the task of overcoming indifference. Besides generating information, the computer can also help students overcome the attitudes of boredom and irrelevance that so often accompany the study of statistics. Now data that are more interesting to students are as available as the nearest disk drive and the means to ask probing questions no further away than the nearest keyboard. The computer is not just a way of coping with large amounts of data, but even more a way of creating insight through the imaginative use of techniques that have become commonplace among those exploring data for a profession.

This article has been written as a plea to teachers, software writers, and curriculum developers to seize the opportunity presented by the microcomputer and use it to illuminate the art of exploring data, to extract all the information possible from a set of numbers, and to bring our mathematics curriculum into the information age.

What Do We Mean by Exploring Data?

The aim of exploring data is to extract as much information as possible. Therefore, it helps to look at the data in as many ways as we can. Two relatively new methods are the *stem-and-leaf plot* and the *box plot* (see Maher 1981 and Swift 1983).

The stem-and-leaf plot is an improvement of the common bar graph in that the original data is a part of the graph. Here are the heights in centimeters of two samples of students.

107

Sample 1

168 160 163 163 165 160 175 175 168 163 165 163 163 165 168 185 173
170 180 173

Sample 2

165 180 170 175 163 170 168 168 178 170 165 183 175 180 178 175 178
175 163 178

Suppose you made a tally of the heights of the students in sample 1. It might look something like the diagram in figure 14.1(a). This illustration shows us the distribution of the heights in the sample, but it does not make it easy to refer to individual items of the data. John Tukey (1977) devised a method of plotting the data so as to keep the original numbers. In this example, each number is split into two numbers. The units digit is called the *leaf,* and the rest of the number is called the *stem*. Numbers with the same stem are then arranged on the same line. This gives the plot in figure 14.1(b). The second line of the plot

$$(17^* \quad 03355)$$

represents the heights 170 173 173 175 175. The asterisk indicates that the numbers consist of one other digit besides the stem.

180–189	//	18*	05
170–179	/////	17*	03355
160–169	///// /////. ///	16*	0033333555888
	(a)		(b)

Fig. 14.1

The shape of the diagram is quite similar to that of the tally chart, but the stem-and-leaf plot has an advantage: if the plot needs to be altered, it can be done without going back to the numbers in their original form. For example, look at the stem plot of sample 2 put next to that for sample 1:

18*	05	18*	003
17*	03355	17*	00055558888
16*	0033333555888	16*	335588

There is a difference between the two samples, but in these diagrams it seems quite slight. So, instead of arranging for the stems to go up in increments of ten, we can change the stem plot to go up in increments of five. Notice that this is a simple task, even without a computer, when you have the original stem plot to start from. With the computer, it is just a matter of entering INCREMENT ← 5:

18*	5	1			
18*	0	2	18*	003	3
17*	55	4	17*	55558888	(8)

17*	033	7	17*	000	9
16*	555888	(6)	16*	5588	6
16*	0033333	7	16*	33	2

The difference is now more marked with the wider stem plot. We can make the comparison diagram neater by putting the leaves for the two samples on opposite sides of the stem:

	Sample 1			**Sample 2**	
1	5	18*			
2	0	18*	003		3
4	55	17*	55558888		(8)
7	330	17*	000		9
(6)	888555	16*	5588		6
7	3333300	16*	33		2

The numbers to the right and left of the plot are the cumulative frequencies from the least and the greatest heights. The numbers in parentheses indicate the number of leaves in the part of the plot that contains the median. These cumulative frequencies help us find the median and quartiles (needed in the box plot later). There are twenty heights in each sample, so the median lies halfway between the tenth and eleventh heights in order. That is, the median lies between 168 and 165 in sample 1 and between 178 and 178 in sample 2.

The medians of the two samples are not even close:

Sample 1: 166.5   **Sample 2:** 178

But the medians alone do not tell the whole story.

The box plot gives a different perspective. The plot summarises the data, paying attention not only to the median but also to the spread of the data.

The *weights* in kilograms of the students from the same two samples are arranged in ascending order:

Sample 1	51	51	54	55	55	55	57	57	57	58
	58	58	60	60	64	65	68	70	70	73
Sample 2	54	54	54	55	55	59	59	64	66	67
	67	67	68	68	69	69	71	74	75	75

The medians of the two samples are as follows:

Sample 1: 58 kg   **Sample 2:** 67 kg

Now look at the two groups of weights in sample 1 that are above and below the median. The median of the lower group of ten weights is 55 kilograms. This is called the *lower hinge*. The median of the upper group of ten weights is 64.5 kilograms. This is called the *upper hinge*. The *extreme values* in the sample are 51 and 73 kilograms.

These five values are put on a number line (fig. 14.2). A box is drawn between the two hinges and dotted lines extend from the hinges to the extremes. The resulting diagram is called a box plot, or box-and-whisker plot. The box plot for sample 2 is drawn below the same number line.

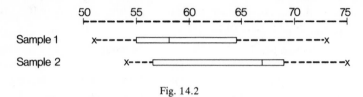

Fig. 14.2

Comparative box plots drawn on the same scale are useful in comparing two sets of data, such as the weights of the students in the two samples. What could explain the differences between the two samples? Sample 1 was taken from the 84 students in the population who where in grades 11 or 12, averaged A or B in their courses, and smoked at least one cigarette a day. Sample 2 was taken from the 148 students in grades 11 or 12 who averaged A or B in their courses and did not smoke! Does this evidence suggest that smoking stunts your growth? The smokers seem to weigh less and be shorter than the nonsmokers! (More will be said about that later.)

Plots such as these are another way of exploring the information contained in a set of data. The exercise of exploration is always fraught with the possibility of meeting the unexpected. But one never knows just when the unexpected will occur. That is what makes this subject so intriguing.

The software package written for the SuperPet contains programs for producing both these plots. Programs in both FORTRAN and APL can be found in McNeil's book *Interactive Data Analysis* (1977), and BASIC and FORTRAN programs can be found in Hoaglin and Velleman's *ABC's of EDA* (1982). The complete set of programs from Hoaglin and Velleman is also available from Conduit in Level 2 BASIC, FORTRAN, and Applesoft BASIC (in ROM) on a 48K Apple II (Conduit #STA 324A).

A Package for Exploring Data on a SuperPet

When the idea for a package for exploring data was first conceived, it was decided to test the feasibility of the concept on a small scale. A Commodore SuperPet was available with a full implementation of APL. This language is particularly suited to statistical work, as demonstrated by the colossal data bases on the I. P. Sharp APL network and by the Statistics Canada Cansim Data Base, also written in APL. The power and productivity of the language make it suitable for feasibility studies such as the one proposed.

A trial data file was written consisting of fictitious data on 1250 students. The data were produced with a random-number generator but contained built-in patterns that had been observed in previous surveys. For each student there were twenty-five items of information (listed later). Functions were written that accessed these data and allowed the user to describe a sample and then collect data from that sample. At first it was thought that an assembler code would be needed if the sample selection was to be accomplished in a reasonable time. So the preliminary specifications put restrictions on the kinds of samples that were allowed. It was, therefore, something of a surprise to find that a sample could be selected and data collected in about eighty seconds at most, and often in less than a minute. So the specifications were changed to allow the samples to be selected more generally by specifying the values of at least three of nine variables.

Although the package is written in APL, the concept can be implemented in any language. The main idea is to have a random access file of data that is used by the master program. Its value will be seen later.

Description of the package

The random access file containing the data was stored on a data disk in drive 1. This disk contained the population, together with the various menus and parameters associated with the population. The randomly generated population has now been replaced by a genuine population. Data were collected from 725 students in Nanaimo, Vancouver, and New Trier Township. The working disk, containing the workspaces, resides in drive 0. The workspaces on this disk consist of the following:

SAMPLER. This workspace allows the user to specify the description of samples from the population and also to collect data from these samples. The data generated for each of the samples is put on the working disk in sequential files named SPL1, SPL2, and so on. The variables from each of the samples are collected together and filed as arrays, one row for each sample. These arrays are labeled V1, V2, . . ., and so on. Thus the data collected by SAMPLER is available for other workspaces on the disk. By the time this article is published, the availability of virtual memory implementations, such as VIZ-APL, may make this provision unnecessary.

ANALYSE. ANALYSE runs immediately after SAMPLER and gives information about the samples stored on the working disk, together with summary statistics for each of the variables.

BOXPLOT. This workspace draws box plots of whatever variables V1, V2, . . . are stored on the working disk.

STEMPLOT. STEMPLOT draws stem-and-leaf plots of whatever variables V1, V2, . . . are stored on the working disk.

Other workspaces in the specifications include those for the creation of scatter plots, contingency tables (including chi-square functions), and the SHARE workspace which is described later.

The use of the workspaces

SAMPLER. A list of the variables available for each student is first displayed as in figure 14.3.

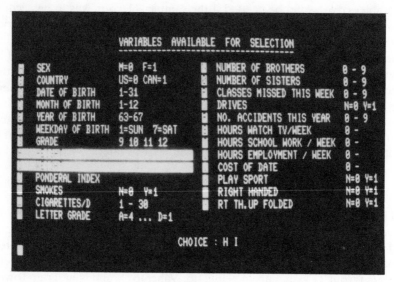

Fig. 14.3

If only one variable is selected, the data will be filed as a vector for each sample. The data for more than one variable will be filed as a matrix with one row for each variable.

To select a sample, the user is first asked to state the number of samples wanted and then to give a description of each of the samples. Several variables from the population are used to specify the characteristics of a sample. The sample selection menu for the student population file appears in figure 14.4. (F, P, J, and S designate *freshman, sophomore, junior,* and *senior.*)

SAMPLE SELECTION

A	SEX		M	F	
B	COUNTRY		USA	CANADA	
G	GRADE	F=9	P=10	J=11	S=12
K	STUDENT SMOKES		N	Y	
M	LETTER GRADE	A	B	C	D
Q	STUDENT DRIVES		N	Y	
W	STUDENT PLAYS SPORT		N	Y	
X	RIGHT HANDED		N	Y	
Y	RT THUMB UP WHEN HANDS FOLDED		N	Y	

Fig. 14.4

At present it is necessary to select at least three variables to describe the
sample in order to avoid filling the workspace. Typical samples might be
Canadian juniors and seniors who smoke, female juniors and seniors who
drive, and even right-handed females who fold their hands with the right
thumb uppermost. The values of each of these nine variables in each record
is coded in a file called CODES. When a sample is described, the list of
matching codes is created and the number of records that fit the description
is calculated. This usually takes up to eighty seconds depending on the
number of variables used in the description. The more variables, the shorter
the time. When the number of students in the population that fit the sample
description is known, then the required size of the sample can be specified.
The sample is selected at random from the list of possibilities and the
variables for the sample filed under SPL1. The procedure is repeated for
SPL2 . . . as required.

The procedure allows the comparison of variables from different samples,
such as the following:

Height and weight	of grade 11–12 smokers	vs. grade 11–12 nonsmokers
Cost of dates	of grade 12 females	vs. grade 10 females
Accidents	of males who smoke	vs. females who don't smoke
Smoking habits	of athletic A students	vs. nonathletic A students

At the conclusion of the sample selection process, a number of options are
available. Two of these options are implemented and examples of their use
are given below for the height and weight of smokers and nonsmokers
among A and B students in grades 11 and 12.

ANALYSIS. The workspace gives a basic set of statistics of the data in the
variables. It is automatically loaded after the samples have been collected.
Alternatively, the student enters DATASUMMARY, and a display similar
to the one in figure 14.5 is given of whatever samples (SPL1, SPL2 . . .) and
variables (V1, V2, . . .) have been filed on the working disk. The picture
given by the table is much less revealing than the more visual image of the
stem-and-leaf plot and box plot.

```
SPL1  —  NONSMOKERS  : GRADES 11 AND 12    : AB STUDENTS
            SAMPLE SIZE   : 20
SPL2  —  SMOKERS      : GRADES 11 AND 12    : AB STUDENTS
            SAMPLE SIZE   : 20
```

VARIABLE V1 HEIGHTS	(in cm)						
SAMPLE	MIN	LOW QTILE	MEDIAN	UPP QTILE	MAX	MID SPREAD	SIZE
1	160	163	166.5	173	185	10	20
2	163	168	175	178	183	10	20

| VARIABLE V2 WEIGHTS (in kg) | | | | | | |
MIN	LOW QTILE	MEDIAN	UPP QTILE	MAX	MID SPREAD	SIZE
SAMPLE						
1	51	55	58	64.5	73	9.5	20
2	54	56.5	67	69	75	12.5	20

Fig. 14.5

BOXPLOT. The workspace BOXPLOT creates comparative box plots of whatever variables (V1, V2, . . .) are on the working disk. The student enters BOXPLOTDATA to obtain displays such as those in figure 14.6. One of the reasons for the lower heights and weights among the smokers is that at these age levels, there are often more smokers among the females than among the males!

```
SPL1  –  NONSMOKERS   : GRADES 11 12   : AB AVERAGES
          SAMPLE SIZE   : 20
SPL2  –  SMOKERS       : GRADES 11 12   : AB AVERAGES
          SAMPLE SIZE   : 20
```

V1 HEIGHTS (CM)

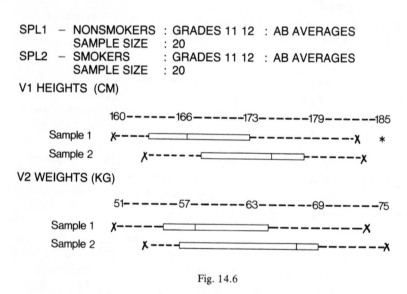

V2 WEIGHTS (KG)

Fig. 14.6

Packaging Data for Exploration

There are some limitations to the package just described if it simply consists of a group of programs accessing a single set of data. Indeed, the effort of developing such a package would hardly be worth the effort. Fortunately, once again, the computer makes it possible to realise the potential of cooperative action. Users of the package will be encouraged to compile files of their own data for circulation and exchange among other users.

The most significant part of the package, therefore, may be the workspace labeled SHARE. This workspace will allow users to create a data file from data compiled in their own locality. The file is put on a disk together with the menus and coding necessary to allow quick and easy access. The process of creating this disk will be done using conversational functions in the SHARE workspace. Once this is accomplished, users can exchange disks of interesting collections of data, all of which will be in a format that can be used by the working disk. So teachers and students with diverse interests can pursue interesting collections of data from such fields as sports, environment, society, history, and demography. Those with an interest in information science can search out and find gems in the vast array of data bases available to users of microcomputers. Furthermore, a convenient forum for the exchange of such data has recently been established in the form of the Statistics Teacher Network, organised by the American Statistical Association/ NCTM Joint Committee on the Curriculum in Statistics and Probability. There are two ways of entering data. If the population is small in size, then manual entry through the keyboard might be feasible. But a preferable way would be to use a card reader such as the Chatsworth or Mountain card reader. The SHARE workspace is being designed to work with such card readers using a standard forty-column card. The data for a single student in the population occupies thirty-nine of the forty columns on a marked card, as shown in fig. 14.7.

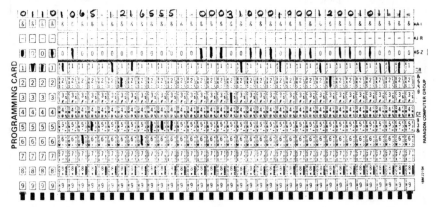

Fig. 14.7

The data on this card were entered from information collected using the student questionnaire in figure 14.8. (*Note:* the P.I. referred to in the questionnaire is the *ponderal index:* $4 \times$ (height)/(cube root of the weight).) This is calculated by the computer, after the card has been read. The day of the week on which a student was born is also checked by the computer. The numbers on the right refer to the columns on the standard forty-column coding card that is readily available. Several commercial data bases, such as DB Master II and the Manager, use similar files in the creation and manipulation of their bases. Users who possess such programs can use their statistical and plotting capabilities to enhance the exploration.

STUDENT DATA QUESTIONNAIRE

Please answer the following questions for a project in a statistics course. DO NOT PUT YOUR NAME ON THE FORM. We not want individual data to be identified. Each response corresponds to a number. For example, in question 1, if you are male, write 0 in the box; if female, then write 1 in the box. Put all your replies as digits in the boxes, ONE DIGIT IN EACH BOX.

1. What is your sex?	male 0	female 1	1	☐
2. In which country do you live?	USA 0	Canada 1	2	
3. When were you born?	day	01-31	3-4	
	month	01-12	5-6	
	year	60-70	7-8	
4. On what day of the week were you born?	sun=1	sat=7	9	☐
5. What grade are you in?	09 -	12	10-11	
6. What is your height in centimeters (to the nearest cm)?	000 - 999		12-14	
7. What is your weight in kilograms (to the nearest kg)?	00 - 99		15-16	
(Leave this line blank)	P.I.		17-18	
8. Do you smoke regularly? More than one cigarette/week?	No 0	Yes 1	19	☐
9. How many cigarettes do you smoke a day (average)?	01-99		20-21	
10. What is your average letter grade in your courses this year?	A B C D 4 3 2 1		22	☐
11. How many brothers do you have?	0 - 9		23	☐
12. How many sisters do you have?	0 - 9		24	☐
13. How many classes (in all subjects) have you missed this week?	00 - 99		25-26	
14. Do you drive a car for any reason more than once a month?	No 0	Yes 1	27	☐
15. How many driving accidents have you been involved in during the last 12 months?	0 - 9		28	☐

On average, how many hours/week do you spend on these activities after school hours, including weekends:

16. Watching television?	00 - 99	29-30	
17. Schoolwork (asignments, etc.)?	00 - 99	31-32	
18. Employment?	00 - 99	33-34	
19. How much do you spend on a date (average), either on yourself or on both of you?	00 - 99	35-36	

20. Do you do any form of exercise REGULARLY (at least once a week)?	No 0	Yes 1	37 ☐
21. Which hand are you using to write this?	Left 0	Right 1	38 ☐
22. When you fold your hands, which thumb is uppermost?	Left 0	Right 1	39 ☐

Fig. 14.8

Conclusion

Stimulating students to want to investigate some data requires at least two vital components: (1) a collection of data in which they are interested, and (2) the means to make that exploration interesting. The second is relatively easy, but the first will continue to be the challenging task that confronts any teacher of this subject. It is clear, though, that in any statistics class a wide range of interests is just waiting to be tapped. The imagination and inventiveness of students who are encouraged not to accept the satisfactory is staggering. They *will* go out of the classroom to collect data, they *are* interested in the ways people behave, and they *are* interested in the world outside the classroom walls. All we, as teachers in the information age, have to do is to recognise this and provide the means of encouraging their interests. You will be surprised at these long-awaited opportunities that the computer is now presenting.

BIBLIOGRAPHY

Hoaglin, D., and P. Velleman. *ABC's of EDA.* North Scituate, Mass.: Duxbury Press, 1982.

Joiner, B. L., B. F. Ryan, and T. A. Ryan. *Minitab Student Handbook.* North Scituate, Mass.: Duxbury Press, 1976.

McNeil, Donald R. *Interactive Data Analysis: A Practical Primer.* New York: John Wiley & Sons, 1976.

Maher, Carolyn Alexander. "Simple Graphical Techniques for Examining Data Generated by Classroom Activities." In *Teaching Statistics and Probability,* 1981 Yearbook of the National Council of Teachers of Mathematics, edited by Albert P. Shulte, pp. 109–117. Reston, Va.: The Council, 1981.

Neffendorf, Hugh. "Statistical Packages for Microcomputers." *Professional Statistician* 1 (June/July 1982): pp. 5–8.

Swift, Jim. "A Statistics Course to Lighten the Information Load." In *The Agenda in Action,* 1983 Yearbook of the National Council of Teachers of Mathematics, edited by Gwen Shufelt, pp. 110–19. Reston, Va.: The Council, 1983.

Travers, K., W. Stout, J. Sextro, and J. H. Swift. *Using Statistics.* Reading, Mass.: Addison-Wesley Publishing Co., forthcoming.

Tukey, John. *Exploratory Data Analysis.* Reading, Mass.: Addison-Wesley Publishing Co., 1977.

15

Programming and Learning: Implications for Mathematics Education

John S. Camp
Gary Marchionini

> In many schools today, the phrase "computer-aided instruction" means the computer teaches the child. One might say the *computer is being used to program* the child. In my vision, *the child programs the computer* and, in doing so, both acquires a sense of mastery over a piece of the most powerful technology and establishes an intimate contact with some of the deepest ideas from science, from mathematics, and from the art of intellectual model building [Papert 1980, p. 5]

PROGRAMMING to promote mathematics learning is not new. The theoretical link comes from research on tutoring, teaching, and practice. In general, tutors learn from tutoring (the basis for cross-age tutoring programs), teachers learn from teaching (ask any teacher), and those who practice learn by practicing. The statement is well known that programming is teaching—teaching a computer—and hence programmers may learn from programming.

What is new, however, are emerging computer-related technologies and associated methodologies. There are now programming languages that can be used with students throughout the grades, and recent work on the format of programming exercises makes programming a viable means for promoting mathematics learning. This essay brings this updated perspective to mathematics educators.

There *is* a role for programming in mathematics education. But as you consider the options, make a clear distinction between the *study* of programming, which belongs to the domain of computer literacy and computer science, and the *use* of programming to achieve learning objectives in mathematics. Programming in mathematics education is defensible to the extent that it helps achieve goals for school mathematics. But if programming is to be a general strategy for mathematics education, then particular attention must be given to format, formality, and methods by which programming is integrated into curriculum and classroom practice.

Format of programming exercises

By definition, computer programming is the process of creating a set of instructions to be executed by a computer. To program requires that one know what instructions the computer understands and how to communicate them so that the program runs correctly. In other words, one must know a computer language and how to use it.

The problem with programming in currently available languages is that it can be a difficult, multistep, time-consuming task. Teachers prefer devoting their time and their students' time to learning mathematics. They recognize that programming in its purest sense can potentially interfere with mathematics learning because it (1) takes too long, and (2) focuses attention on programming rather than on mathematics.

In recent years, various types of programming exercises have been developed to focus the attention on content learning and to reduce the difficulties associated with programming. For our discussion, we shall call these exercises PERCs (for *P*rogramming *E*xercise *R*elated to *C*ontent). PERCs are of general application. They are not restricted to any one language or type of equipment and can be used with young children as well as with older students. One should keep in mind that programs can range from instructions for a treasure hunt or a game designed for young children to instruction sets written in a high-level computer language. The use of *program* in the following types of PERCs should be interpreted broadly:

- Run a program and discuss the results.
- Simulate the execution of a program.
- Annotate a program to explain its features.
- Complete a program by inserting key instructions.
- Predict the output.
- Modify a program to perform a related task.
- Make an inference from an error message.
- Find errors in a program and correct them.
- Compare programs regarding their procedures, efficiency, and output.
- Write and run a program.

PERC *types* give guidance to teachers and authors who want to use programming to promote learning. Whatever the form of the PERC, whether it be "complete key instructions" or "modify the program" to do a similar task, the primary focus of the exercise must be on mathematics rather than programming (although programming skills will be developed over the long run). However, a major benefit is that students will be developing skills with an extremely powerful problem-solving tool. Examples of how PERCs can be written and used to promote the learning of elementary, middle, and high school mathematics topics follow.

Formality of programming languages

Much has been written about computer languages. There certainly are choices. Should the language be BASIC, Logo, or Pascal? How about Ada or Smalltalk?

Consider a developmental point of view. Mathematics education is rich with topics whose instructional development begins with informal readiness activities for the topic and evolves to formal study including applications of the topic in realistic problem situations.

Developmental Sequence for Programming

Stage 1. Present motivational problem situations whose solution requires choosing or following a set of instructions. Developing a treasure hunt, playing "Simon says" using a script, controlling household appliances, and giving directions to get from one location to another are examples of tasks that require "informal programming."

Stage 2. Introduce a subset of standard language and develop mathematics through the use of that language. The subset of Logo known as turtle graphics, for example, can be used with students of all ages. As with the meter and decimeter, the subset will be sufficient for some tasks but not for all.

Stage 3. Study and use a complete high-level language, like BASIC, Logo, or Pascal, and continue to develop mathematics through programming.

The developmental plan for programming ensures that students explore and discover (as in measurement) general concepts about programming (stage 1), develop skill with a standard, relatively easy-to-master set of instructions (stage 2), and then use a high-level language when it is appropriate to enhance the study of mathematical topics (stage 3).

Programming and learning: PERC exercises for K–12 mathematics

The exercises that follow illustrate six of the ten PERC types listed earlier. They were chosen to illustrate the use of programming to develop mathematical content at the elementary, middle, and high school levels. The program listings in the examples are written as generally as possible to run on common implementations of BASIC, Logo, and Pascal. Remarks have been omitted. The reader may wish to add remarks as an example of the annotate type of PERC.

Example 1: Elementary School Arithmetic

PERC types: Simulate the execution/Modify a program

Language level: Informal

Content focus: Counting; inverse operations

Here is the control panel from the Electro Rover, an electronic vehicle that will follow your instructions. The Rover followed these steps to get from its starting point to the finish (marked **X**).

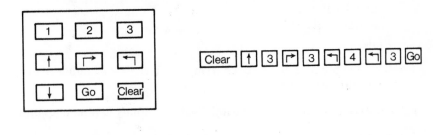

1. Verify that the instructions do take the Electro Rover from START to FINISH. (The vehicle cannot travel on the darkened squares.)
2. Change the instructions so that the Electro Rover can get from start to finish in a different way.
3. Write the instructions that will get the Electro Rover back to start from finish following the original path.

Commentary: Controlling simple electronic devices with a limited vocabulary set can provide the bridge between describing procedures in a natural language and in a symbolic computer language. When students become familiar with the simple vocabulary it takes to describe direction and magnitude, then important concepts, such as looping and branching, can be informally introduced.

Example 2: Elementary School Geometry

PERC type: Find errors and correct/Modify a program

Language level: Formal (Logo)

Content focus: Special polygons

a) The following program is supposed to draw an equilateral triangle. The program contains one error. Correct the program to produce an equilateral triangle.

```
TO TRIANGLE
  RIGHT 90
  FORWARD 100
  LEFT 30
  FORWARD 100
  LEFT 120
  FORWARD 100
END
```

b) Modify the program to trace the triangle in a clockwise rather than a counter-clockwise direction.

c) Modify the program to trace a parallelogram. Modify to trace a square.

Commentary: The turtle graphics subset of the Logo language gives students the opportunity to produce easily a rich variety of graphic images. Describing geometric figures through turtle graphics requires students to specify the angle and distance characteristics of the figure. As students "draw" different figures with Logo, the defining and distinguishing properties of each become explicit. This example could also be a "compare programs" PERC if students were given a corresponding program written with point-to-point (coordinate) specifications and asked to compare the two programs.

Example 3: Middle School Arithmetic

PERC type: Predict the output/Run and discuss

Language level: Formal (Pascal)

Content focus: Order of operations

This program will allow you to enter three numbers. It will combine the numbers using addition, subtraction, multiplication, division, and grouping.

a) Study the program and predict what will be printed for the following values:

```
A = 5     B = 6     C = 2
PROGRAM ORDEROP;
VAR A,B,C  :   INTEGER;
BEGIN
  READ (A, B, C);
  WRITELN (A + B*C);
  WRITELN ((A + B)*C);
  WRITELN (A + B/C);
  WRITELN ((A + B)/C);
END
```

b) Run the program to verify your prediction.

c) Predict the output for A = 3, B = 8, C = 4. Run the program to verify your prediction.

d) Evaluate the following:

1. 8 + 2 × 6   2. 9 + 6/3
3. (8 + 2) × 6   4. (9 + 6)/3

Commentary: PERCs of the "Predict output" or "Run and discuss" type can be used either to reinforce previously learned mathematics or to give students a preview of mathematics to come. This latter application to discovery methods has much potential.

Example 4: Middle School Geometry

PERC type: Complete a program by inserting key instructions.

Language level: Formal (BASIC)

Content focus: Surface area, volume of a cylinder

a) The following program has two incomplete statements. Complete the statements so the program will print the surface area and volume of a cylinder.

```
10 INPUT "HEIGHT "; H
20 INPUT "DIAMETER "; D
30 PI = 3.14159
40 R = D/2
50 PRINT "A CYLINDER WITH RADIUS "; R
60 PRINT "AND HEIGHT "; H;" HAS:"
70 PRINT "VOLUME = "; _____ ; "CUBIC UNITS"
80 PRINT "SURFACE AREA = "; _____ ;
   "SQUARE UNITS"
90 END
```

b) How would deleting line 40 affect your answers?

Commentary: Depending on their programming experience, the example can be modified to require students to enter lines 70 and 80 in their entirety or to rewrite the program to give similar information for other geometric figures.

Example 5: High School Algebra

PERC type: Modify a program

Language level: Formal (Pascal)

Content focus: Slope of a line

The following program asks the user to enter two ordered pairs. It then prints the slope of the line through those two points. Modify the program to check for the special cases *no slope* and *0 slope* and print appropriate messages.

```
PROGRAM SLOPE;
VAR X1, X2, Y1, Y2  :   REAL;
BEGIN
  WRITELN ('ENTER FIRST POINT');
  READ (X1, Y1);
  WRITELN ('ENTER SECOND POINT');
  READ (X2, Y2);
  WRITE ('THE SLOPE IS ');
  WRITELN ((Y2 − Y1)/(X2 − X1));
END.
```

Commentary: Writing a computer program often forces students to consider special cases in detail. Points of inflection, undefined values, or endpoints are often the object of interest in mathematics. (A fall off a building is not what matters but rather the sudden stop at the end!) This PERC activity could be easily modified to be of the *Run and discuss /Make an inference from an error message* type by requiring students to run the program and use the values (3, 5), 3, 7). The resulting error, division by zero, could be used to highlight the special cases.

Example 6: High School Algebra

PERC type: Run and discuss results

Language level: Formal (BASIC)

Content focus: Squaring a binomial

Run this program:

```
10  PRINT "(X + 1)↑2", "X↑2 + 1", "X↑2 + 2 * X + 1"
20  FOR X = −5 TO 5
30  PRINT (X + 1)↑2, X↑2 + 1, X↑2 + 2 * X + 1
40  NEXT X
50  END
```

a) List all your observations about the output.

b) Run the program again for $x \in \{-10, -9, -8, \ldots, 10\}$. How does the output compare?

c) Run it again for $x \in \{-5, -4.5, -4, \ldots, 5\}$. Compare output with results in *a* and *b*.

d) What algebraic identity is suggested by this program and its output?
$(x + 1)^2 = $ _____ .

Commentary: Example 6 shows how programming can be used to help students either discover or verify algebraic identities. However, the exercise is representative of a more general strategy designed to give students the opportunity to *observe* the meaning of *variable* in expressions, equations, and relations. Pencil-and-paper substitutions and calculator computations cannot match the power of computers to display output in a variety of ways that can help students better understand unifying mathematical concepts.

Designing PERCs

In developing learning activities, a teacher must consider not only the content to be learned but also the context in which it is to be presented. For PERCs, programming is the context in which mathematics content is cast. The program should stimulate interest in the content, but more importantly, it should reinforce the meaning and details of the mathematical concepts and skills. Because of the algorithmic nature of programming, its natural handling of numeric data structures, and its increasingly easy way of producing graphic displays, it is a rich context for introducing, developing, reinforcing, and extending mathematics.

There are three general steps in producing a PERC: selecting the program context, writing a program, selecting and writing the PERC.

Step 1: Selecting a program context involves linking the mathematics content and the computer programming. The level of students' programming experience and the choice of language must be considered. Just as arithmetic problems are cast in contexts familiar to students, so should the programming context be familiar.

Step 2: Writing a complete program is necessary in designing a PERC, even if only parts of the program are eventually to be used in the activity. Because many programs can be written for a given task, remarks and variations should be included while the program is under construction because some variations may be deemed more appropriate for some students than for others.

Step 3: Students' programming experience and the way the PERC is to be used will help determine which type should be selected. For example, students with little programming experience would not be expected to write complex original programs or make extensive modifications of programs. Writing the PERC requires artistry and skill—the same ingredients needed to prepare any good mathematical exercise.

Recommendations and Guidelines

Integrating "programming to promote learning" into mathematics teaching and curriculum will be no simple task. First of all, there is the massive problem of teacher education. Teachers not only need to be computer literate but also need to be able to use computers in a variety of ways, including programming, to support instruction. Second is the problem of curriculum development. To date, there are no elementary, middle, or high school mathematics textbook series that truly enhance mathematics learning through computer experiences—*programs to run,* like simulations, tutorial, management, drill and practice, and so forth, or *programming to do,* like the PERCs sequentially developed here. The current state of affairs is that much of the computer material is available principally as optional features to introduce programming rather than to develop mathematics through it.

We should like to present three recommendations for mathematics teachers and authors of computer-enhanced mathematics curricula. The recommendations are derived from the growing body of experiences with computer applications in teaching and learning and from what is known about how to change educational practices.

1. *Computer experiences must be written into mathematics textbooks.* Computer enhancement means that computer experiences, whether they are programs to *run* or programming to *do,* must be a part of the textbooks used by teachers and students. Mathematics teachers usually have neither the time nor the means to collect and sort through resource materials and programs related to computers and mathematics.

2. *The primary purpose of computer enhancement is to develop mathematical concepts and skills through computer-related experiences.* First and foremost, computer-enhanced mathematics curricula must be *mathematics* curricula. As such, the computer becomes a *tool* for teaching and learning mathematics rather than an *object* of instruction. This is the meaning of *instructional computing.*

3. *As much as possible, computer-enhanced curricula should be independent of particular hardware.* Although this general recommendation may seem close to impossible, it is not. Here are some ways hardware independence is possible:

   a) Programs produced to accompany textbooks are produced in multiple versions to run on a variety of computers.

   b) Computer manufacturers agree on standards for programming languages.

   c) PERCs are used as an instructional strategy to promote content and process learning.

Computer enhancement of mathematics will take some time to realize. A truly enhanced curriculum will embody instructional support programs for teachers and students to use as well as programming experiences that focus on mathematics learning. The PERC methodology can be an important component of a comprehensive, timely mathematics program.

REFERENCE

Papert, Seymour. *Mindstorms: Children, Computers and Powerful Ideas.* New York: Basic Books, 1980.

16

Young Children, Programming, and Mathematical Thinking

Richard J. Shumway

REGARDING computers in public education, it is my basic view that as soon as children are in schools they should have opportunities to program computers to solve mathematics problems. I have no special bias about which brand of computer. I would encourage having a variety for breadth of experience and inexpensive ones purchased in quantity to ensure accessibility to all children. BASIC is the most available language and can be used very appropriately. Logo could be the second language.

Why would I advocate that our youngest schoolchildren have opportunities to program computers? Let me begin by illustrating a first lesson on computers that I have used with first graders. We begin with the following program:

```
10   FOR N = 1 TO 12
20   PRINT N, N + N
30   NEXT N
```

Each child is given a copy of the program, and we discuss how the computer sets up an "*N* box" in which the numbers 1, 2, 3, 4, 5, 6, 7, 8, 9, 10, 11, and 12 are placed successively, each new number dumping out the prior number. We discuss how line 30 tells the computer to take the next value of *N,* and how line 20 tells the computer what to print. We simulate the *N* box, write on the board the expected values for *N* from 1 to 6, and write down the expected output. This becomes repetitive and laborious, so I ask if I may quit at 6 and ask the computer to do the work.

Then I type the program on a single machine with TV display for all to see. (Sitting on the floor, twenty-five first graders can get remarkably close to a microcomputer.) I misspell PRINT as PRENT to give the children an opportunity to help me (by spotting the error) and allow me to illustrate

Note: Portions of this article were previously published in the author's article "Computers and Young Children: When Do We Start?" (*Math Lab Matrix,* [Illinois State University Mathematics Department], Spring 1982, pp. 1–4).

"back space" as a way to correct typing errors. Children love the correcting capability because there are no erasing marks; the evidence is gone. (Adults like that feature too.)

I then type RUN and we get the following output:

1	2
2	4
3	6
.	.
.	.
.	.
11	22
12	24

Twelve is a good upper limit because it is not 10 and the complete table can be seen on the screen. It is common for first graders to be very excited with the output and run the program several more times. The two sequences in the table are old friends, since most first graders can count by ones and twos. Children are asked to record the output for the program on their sheets.

The next program I hand them is the following:

```
10   FOR N = 1 TO 12
20   PRINT N, _____
30   NEXT N
```

I tell the children it is their turn and ask what should now be put in the blank in line 20 of the program. Which of the following do you think the students proposed the first time I tried this?

$$N + 1, N - N, N + N + N, N \times N$$

Well, you are wrong, and so was I. They suggested $N + N$. I protested that we should do a different program. (I probably should have gone ahead and done $N + N$.) Now, given we were not going to use $N + N$ again, which of the above would you now guess was suggested?

Wrong again. They suggested $P + P$. I was surprised but interested. The teacher was rolling her eyes and looking embarrassed. My response was to point out that we had not told the computer a number to put in a P box, so the computer would not know what numbers to use for P. (Some computers choose 0; some computers default.) The students seemed to agree that the computer would not know a value for P. Now, I said, what shall we use for the blank?

Another student enthusiastically raised his hand and proudly suggested $K + K$. This time I had help. Several other students immediately pointed out that the computer would not know any values for K, either. Progress! I asked again.

This time the suggestion was $N - N$. I had been hoping for something like $N + N + N$. (I thought $N - N$ would be boring.) We entered the following program:

```
10   FOR N = 1 TO 12
20   PRINT N, N − N, N + N + N
30   NEXT N
```

Before running the program, we again set up an N box and wrote down what the computer was going to do. Because I had not anticipated spacing problems, the actual output was as follows:

```
1        0
3
2        0
6
.        .
.        .
.        .
12       0
36
```

The error was helpful, because it allowed me to illustrate the role of ";" and change a line of a program by retyping the line. (The computer simply uses the last version of a line that has been entered.) So, I typed the following:

$$20 \quad \text{PRINT N}; N - N; N + N + N$$
$$(\text{or } 20 \quad \text{PRINT N}; \text{" "}; N - N; \text{" "}; N + N + N)$$

The output then was this:

```
1        0        3
2        0        6
3        0        9
.        .        .
.        .        .
.        .        .
12       0        36
```

One girl immediately suggested we could have used $3*N$ instead of $N + N + N$. (Even first graders are trying to get ahead of me.)

I left them with the following program:

```
10   FOR N = 1 TO 5
20   PRINT N; _____ ; _____
30   NEXT N
```

Their job was to fill in the blanks and run the program. Also, they were asked to make these changes in the first program and record the results:

10   FOR N = 1 TO 20 STEP 2

or, 20   PRINT N, N*N, 2^N

Some children discover they can make the upper limit on the FOR statement very large (e.g., 10 000).

Now what is going on in an activity such as this for young children? I would make the following observations:

1. Children have been introduced to a very powerful computer program of the general form:

> 10   FOR N = 1 TO B
> 20   PRINT N, _____
> 30   NEXT N

Significant variations in line 20 can produce a whole collection of meaningful programs.

2. Important aspects of the use of variable have been encountered and learned in a natural way.

3. Mathematical ideas equivalent to

$$\sum_{i=1}^{n} 2i$$

have been encountered and explored.

4. Children have discovered that attention to detail and writing careful statements are essential in communication.

My purpose for this extended example is to alert you to the idea that very young children can *write* their own computer programs. I have little patience for computer uses in education where the computer tells the child what to do. The most powerful aspect of computer use is that children can give the orders, see them carried out, and create and discover mathematics on their own. Our job as teachers is to provide the opportunities and help make it happen.

Two years ago, almost all adults were using calculators to do mathematics (Saunders 1980). I have on my desk a powerful computer no larger than the average book (Timex-Sinclair 1000), which—

- uses a TV,
- stores data on tape,
- uses full BASIC,
- costs about $40.

I expect powerful microcomputers of this type to be available for the price of one or two tanks of gas within a year. We must make such devices available to children immediately.

In the last ten years we have seen computation by adults change from old-fashioned paper/pencil algorithms to calculator and sophisticated computer algorithms. What computational skills do today's children need for tomorrow?

> **They most certainly *do not* need paper-and-pencil algorithms such as long division, and they most certainly *do* need to know how to use computers.**

I believe today's mathematics curriculum must show an equal balance of the use of powerful computational devices, such as the computer, with the theoretical mathematics necessary for tomorrow's world.

Here are some suggestions for further work with young children.

1. *Cartesian coordinates* (graphing)

```
 5   INPUT L
10   FOR N = 1 TO L
20   PRINT N
30   NEXT N
```

(The program is designed for the Timex-Sinclair 1000. You can modify it for use with other machines.) Notice we go back to the same basic program, but now we are linking algebra and geometry through the use of the Cartesian plane. This ability to arithmetize geometry is one of the great inventions of mathematics. How wonderful it is to share this invention with young children. Of course, the program above is only a beginning (it draws a diagonal line).

Ask your students to program the computer to draw the other diagonal, the letter N, a square, a rectangle, a triangle, and so on. Try to choose figures that can be efficiently done with FOR-NEXT loops rather than plotting each point separately.

2. *Counting, place value, and big numbers*

```
10   FOR N = 0 TO 40
20   PLOT N,N
30   NEXT N
```

Run the program for different values of $L,$ say 10, 100, 1000 and 10 000. Ask students to time how long it takes for 10 and 100. Now predict the time for the larger values of L. Ask students to watch the numbers change.

Which column changes most frequently? Next most frequently? Next?

What is the relative speed of the change? (Ten times faster?) How long would it take to count to 10 000 000?

Young children need and enjoy the reinforcement of the counting numbers. Encourage them to run this program frequently, but continue to stretch their thinking with additional questions and hypotheses. For example, "When will you get to 1000?" "How far along the way are you?" "Why?" "Are computers slow or fast?" "Why?" Reinforce counting, raise issues about place value, and explore big numbers.

3. *Multiples*

a)
```
10   FOR N = 0 TO 100 STEP 5
20   PRINT N
30   NEXT N
```

b)
```
10   LET N = 0
20   LET N = N + 5
30   PRINT N
40   GOTO 20
```

Program *a* counts by fives to 100 using our same basic program. Program *b* also counts by fives but uses the idea of recursion in doing so. Each next value is computed by adding 5 to the previous value (line 20 LET N = N + 5). Not only does counting by fives prepare for clock and money counting, but the use of variables in a new way in program *b* begins teaching the mathematically powerful idea of recursion. (*Note:* The program may go on and on until it is stopped by a break command.) Suggest that children explore program *b* further by changing line 20. Now try program *c*.

c)
```
10   LET G = 1
20   LET G = G + 5
30   PRINT G
40   GOTO 20
```

Now change line 20:

```
20   LET G = G + G
```

This produces program *d*:

d)

```
10   LET G = 1
20   LET G = G + G
30   PRINT G
40   GOTO 20
```

(For the Timex-Sinclair add line 25 SCROLL.)

Before running program *d,* carefully trace the values of *G* as you go through the program mentally. The program simulates how bacteria grow, or how the thicknesses of paper grow as you cut the paper in half over and over and stack the pieces. There is enough mathematics in this program to intrigue even your brightest students (recursion, exponential growth, large numbers, scientific notation, decimals, and computer overflow, for example). Cut paper and count thicknesses before you run the program. Don't use the fancy words for the mathematics, just let the children experience the ideas and learn with your help.

4. *English*

e)

```
10   INPUT A$
20   PRINT A$, A$ + "S"
30   GOTO 10
```

For a change of pace, program *e* tries to teach the computer how to form the plural of any word we type in after typing RUN. Does it work? See if your children can use it. Can they find words for which the program doesn't work? What goes wrong? Make a list of some words that work and some words that don't work. This activity introduces students to the "ability of the computer to think" and some interesting rules about plurals in the English language.

Summary

Let's summarize what has happened in examples 1–4 at different levels of learning.

Computer literacy

The commands FOR, TO, STEP, NEXT, PRINT, PLOT, INPUT, LET, GOTO, A$, RUN, LIST, and BREAK, were encountered, used, and understood in the context of very short programs that nevertheless, illustrated big, important ideas. None of the programs are silly, and none are just examples to show how commands work. All the programs do real work. Most programs in BASIC use fewer than twenty commands. The children have already used more than half of these. Several limitations of computers have become apparent. Computers do only what they are told to do, they have only a finite number of numbers, they are fast but not *that* fast, and they do not think. The children are well on their way to learning BASIC and becoming computer literate.

Specific mathematics

Such topics as Cartesian coordinates, counting, place value, large numbers, powers of ten, counting by fives, exponential growth, scientific notation, and decimals have been encountered.

General mathematics concepts

Such unifying concepts as variables, sequences, number names, and recursion have been encountered.

Mathematical thinking

Children have dealt with such ideas as the linking of arithmetic and geometry, the power of generalization (for example, writing the program that counts to any number specified instead of just 100), attention to detail (almost any minor change in the program changes the results), the helpfulness of modeling (for example, the counting program or the paper-cutting simulation), and the rules and inconsistencies in the English language.

Problem solving

Although we did not emphasize problem solving, it is clear that as we ask children to write other programs and extend them, they will be engaged in problem solving.

Logical reasoning

It is difficult to make direct claims, but such programming activities as these seem to offer a wealth of logical reasoning experiences for children. In my view, a substantial change in our curriculum can be made as young children have the opportunity to write programs similar to those illustrated. It seems to me we can use programming daily as an integral part of all the mathematics we teach. The richness of the mathematics encountered will be multiplied dramatically; more young children will see mathematics as a dynamic, creative activity; and teaching and learning mathematics will be a lively, active sport indeed.

REFERENCE

Saunders, Hal. "When Are We Ever Gonna Have to Use *This*?" *Mathematics Teacher* 73 (January 1980): 7–16.

17

Microcomputers in the Middle School

Susan Smith

As MORE and more microcomputers find their way into the mathematics classroom, educators must carefully consider the appropriate use of these devices in the curriculum. The current uses of the microcomputer for drill and practice and for programming are not sufficient. If computers are to have a place in the mathematics classroom, then they *should be used as teaching tools when this is appropriate for what is being taught.*

The Student and the Computer

Today's students have grown up in the computer age. They have seen computers used for calculating, retrieving information, managing many aspects of life, and "teaching." They hear about the remarkable capabilities of computers and the predictions of the amazing things computers will do in the future. They wonder about their own future and the necessity of learning facts that can be easily executed by a computer. The following story, written by Nata Lee Smith, eleven, who has had a microcomputer in her home for three years, is an example.

Stara's Computer

It is 2000 years in the future. The world is ruled by computers. Everyone has a computer. Math is not taught or needed.

Stara is sitting at her computer doing her income tax. Her computer breaks down. "Darn," she said. "What a time for it to break down."

Stara couldn't call a repairman, for all the phones were hooked up to the computer. "What am I going to do?" she thought.

Poor Stara was in such a spot. No computer, no income tax. Finally Stara asked her mother what to do.

"I have some old math books up in the attic that belonged to my great-great-grandfather. Perhaps you could study those," she said.

It sounded foolish but she tried it anyway.

Stara learned all about math and never had trouble again.

Students are very accepting of computers. By the time they have reached the seventh grade, many of them have used the computer in the mathematics laboratory and also for drill and practice. The same information and practice problems that students routinely have in their textbooks are now seen on the computer screen. By the time students are in middle school, many are bored with the same drill problems, so they try to outwit the computer by entering all kinds of wrong answers. Their scores on assignments may be low, but because they have experimented with different answers, many have learned a lot about how the computer works and different techniques of programming.

Their reward of course, for getting answers quickly and scoring high on the computer drills is to play one of the educational computer games. These games usually bring more drill and practice. The format is often the same from one grade to another with only the type of problems changed. Compare these games to the ones students play in the video arcades around town. Where is the challenge and the excitement the students experience in the video arcades? Small wonder, then, that these computer-wise kids are not motivated by ten more minutes of computer time.

The Student and the Middle School Curriculum

Look carefully at the seventh- and eighth-grade mathematics curriculum. More importantly, visit the seventh- and eighth-grade classrooms. What's going on? With few exceptions, the textbooks look like the sixth-grade text. The topics covered are essentially review and more practice on the same material covered in grades K–6. The content of seventh- and eighth-grade mathematics programs provides for review, practice, and mastery of all those skills previously taught. True, there are some new topics in the texts and the state guidelines, such as probability, more geometry, an introduction to trigonometry, and a bit of algebra. But then observe the classrooms. What students actually get is drill and practice on computational skills. In fact, sixth-grade teachers often hear, "Oh, I remember we did this last year." Then in seventh grade, students are doing the same thing again and in eighth grade, yet again. Why? There's little doubt that many of our less-prepared students need this practice in basic skills. Students must learn, understand, and be able to compute efficiently and proficiently; they must be well prepared in the basic skills areas.

Educators in a number of states have proposed that all students have training in computer literacy. The definition of computer literacy, however, varies widely from one expert to another. The middle school has been suggested as an appropriate place for this training to take place, and in many schools the responsibility for the instruction is given to the mathematics department. But if computer literacy is added to the typical seventh- and eighth-grade mathematics course, time would dictate that another topic be deleted. Students might learn more about computers, but the mathematics they would be missing is important also.

Instruction in computer programming that is *integrated with the tradition-*

al topics of the seventh- and eighth-grade curriculum can address each of the issues above: basic skills proficiency, the lack of freshness in the middle school curriculum, computer literacy, and time. Being able to write computer programs is a significant component of computer literacy; thus, programming as an integral component of the mathematics instruction necessarily contributes to computer literacy. In the process of writing programs, students explore and develop their own algorithms for solving all kinds of problems. This is an extension of their basic skills. They must also work a number of computational exercises to make sure the computer is giving the answer they want—thus gaining practice. Many facets of the basic skill of problem solving are either taught or practiced in computer programming. *Trial and error,* an important problem-solving technique, is seldom used by students with conventional textbook problems, but it is very effective in the computer solution of certain problems. *Thinking ahead* is another problem-solving competency used in computer programming. Students must ask themselves at each step, "What will happen if I do this?" Once a program is written, they can be encouraged to ask, "What will happen if I change this?" The latter question is the *looking back* step in problem solving.

If programming is integrated with the mathematics curriculum, then the extra time spent learning to program is minimal. For example, programming can be incorporated into, and enhance the learning of, new concepts and skills. The following is one of many models. The teacher introduces a new skill, the students work a number of problems until they think they can tell the computer how to do them, and finally the students program the computer and test their program. This programming activity gives students additional practice on the concept, tests their understanding of the concept, increases their programming skills, and gives them a better understanding of computers.

In the preceding model for integrating mathematics and computer programming, the focus was on the learning of new mathematics, but the integration can also be achieved when the focus is on the learning of programming. The following section offers some suggestions for how this might be accomplished.

Introducing Computer Programming

You can begin by introducing a complete program to students. This is probably more effective and certainly less time-consuming than teaching programming one step at a time. (The listing below is a suitable program.)

```
10  INPUT N                    60  END
20  FOR J = 2 TO N             70  PRINT J
30  F = N/J                    80  N = F
40  IF F = INT(F) THEN 70      90  GO TO 20
50  NEXT J
```

Discuss with the class how the computer processes the program in a manner similar to the following discourse.

> After the program is typed in, you need to type RUN. At this point a "?" appears on the screen. The computer is waiting for a value for N from line 10. Suppose you choose 18 for N. The computer will execute the program for 18 in the following manner:

Computer Program	Execution
10 INPUT N	Type in 18. N then is equal to 18.
20 FOR J = 2 TO N	The first J is 2.
30 F = N/J	F = 18/2 = 9
40 IF F = INT(F) THEN 70	Since F is an integer, go to line 70.
70 PRINT J	2 appears on the screen.
80 N = F	N now becomes 9.
90 GO TO 20	Go back to line 20.
20 FOR J = 2 TO N	J is still 2.
30 F = N/J	F = 9/2 = 4.5
40 IF F = INT(F) THEN 70	F is not an integer, so go to the next line.
50 NEXT J	J changes to 3 and this step leads back to line 20.
20 FOR J = 2 to N	Since J is not larger than N = 9, continue.
30 F = N/J	F = 9/3 = 3
40 IF F = INT(F) THEN 70	F is an integer, so go to line 70.
70 PRINT J	3 appears on the screen.
80 N = F	N = 3
90 GO TO 20	To line 20
20 FOR J = 2 TO N	J = 3
30 F = N/J	F = 3/3 = 1
40 IF F = INT(F) THEN 70	F is an integer.
70 PRINT J	3 appears on the screen.
80 N = F	N = 1
90 GO TO 20	To line 20
20 FOR J = 2 TO N	Since N is 1, J cannot be between 2 and 1, and this leads to line 60.
60 END	The program ends.

The teacher should then ask the students to play computer by taking a number and following the program carefully one step at a time to determine the output. This tests the students' understanding of the program. On comparing the numbers entered with their output, students should discover the purpose of the program: it finds the prime factors of any whole number N. For $N = 18$, the numbers shown on the screen are 2, 3, and 3.

Other sample programs should be used as necessary to ensure that students have some understanding of how a computer program is executed. Students might be asked to follow the steps of this next program to determine the output and purpose of the program. Two new concepts should be pointed out. In line 10, two numbers, A and B, are entered. The $*$ in line 70 means to multiply the numbers together.

```
10   INPUT A, B                90   END
20   L = 1                     100  G = B / J
30   FOR J = 2 TO A            110  IF G = INT(G) THEN 130
40   F = A / J                 120  GO TO 60
50   IF F = INT(F) THEN 100    130  L = J * L
60   NEXT J                    140  A = F
70   L = A * B * L             150  B = G
80   PRINT L                   160  GO TO 30
```

The program given will find the least common multiple of two numbers, *A* and *B*.

As a follow-up activity, have students write and test a program that will find the greatest common factor of two whole numbers. For those who have difficulties, give them this hint: The program can be very similar to the previous one. In fact, if one line is eliminated from that program, the number that appears on the screen will be the GCF.

Neither these programs nor the programs students are asked to write include the output of verbal information. Although nicely formatted output is easier to read and interpret, this is not a goal of the early introduction to programming; the goals are to teach the logic of a program and mathematical problem solving. Further, excluding complicated PRINT statements cricumvents, somewhat, the middle school student's lack of keyboard skills.

With this type of introduction to programming, and patience and guidance on the part of the teacher, students will soon be able to write a vareity of programs.

The Computer and Problem Solving

The computer can and should be used as a tool in problem solving. A number of problems that are solved in later years by algebraic means can be solved at this age by looking at a simpler problem, generating charts and tables, and looking for a pattern. Two such problems are given.

Problem 1: A popular airline has seats for 125 to 150 passengers, depending on the aircraft scheduled. On the flight from El Paso to Austin, there is one empty seat for every eleven passengers. How many passengers are on this flight?

From the chart generated below, two answers are possible: 121 or 132 passengers.

```
10      PRINT "EMPTY", "PEOPLE", "SEATS"
               "
20      A = 0
30         PRINT
40      A = A + 1
50      B = 11 * A
60      C = A + B
```

```
70      IF C > 150 THEN 200
80      PRINT A,B,C
90      GOTO 30
200     END
```

```
]RUN
```

EMPTY	PEOPLE	SEATS
1	11	12
2	22	24
3	33	36
4	44	48
5	55	60
6	66	72
7	77	84
8	88	96
9	99	108
10	110	120
11	121	132
12	132	144

Problem 2: Tickets to a basketball game are $0.75 for students and $1.25 for adults. If 195 tickets were sold, producing receipts of $201.25, how many of each type were sold?

The program given below illustrates a trial-and-error strategy. Ideally, the student would make a better-educated guess each time.

```
LIST
        PRINT "ENTER A NUMBER FOR YOU
        R GUESS ON THE NUMBER OF STU
        DENT TICKETS SOLD"
10      INPUT N
20      A = 195 - N
30      S = .75 * N
40      P = 1.25 * A
50      T = S + P
51      PRINT "STUDENT",N,S
52      PRINT "ADULT",A,P
53      PRINT "TOTAL",195,T
54      PRINT
60      IF T = 201.25 THEN 90
70      PRINT "GUESS AGAIN"
80      GOTO 10
90      PRINT "THAT'S CORRECT"
100     END
```

```
RUN
ENTER A NUMBER FOR YOUR GUESS ON THE NUMBER OF STUDENT
    TICKETS SOLD
60
STUDENT         60          45
ADULT           135         168.75
TOTAL           195         213.75
GUESS AGAIN
ENTER A NUMBER FOR YOUR GUESS ON THE NUMBER OF STUDENT
    TICKETS SOLD
70
STUDENT         70          52.5
ADULT           125         156.25
TOTAL           195         208.75
GUESS AGAIN
```

ENTER A NUMBER FOR YOUR GUESS ON THE NUMBER OF STUDENT
  TICKETS SOLD
75

STUDENT	75	56.25
ADULT	120	150
TOTAL	195	206.25

GUESS AGAIN
ENTER A NUMBER FOR YOUR GUESS ON THE NUMBER OF STUDENT
  TICKETS SOLD
80

STUDENT	80	60
ADULT	115	143.75
TOTAL	195	203.75

GUESS AGAIN
ENTER A NUMBER FOR YOUR GUESS ON THE NUMBER OF STUDENT
  TICKETS SOLD
85

STUDENT	85	63.75
ADULT	110	137.5
TOTAL	195	201.25

THAT'S CORRECT

These two programs represent two fairly simple strategies that the middle
school student might choose to use in solving problems. Both strategies
incorporate a trial-and-error problem-solving technique. In the airplane
program, the computer makes the guesses and the student must sort out
which are erroneous and which are correct. In the basketball game program,
the student supplies the trials.

Practice and Extension of Basic Computational Skills

The practice and extension of basic computational skills is an important
facet of integrating mathematics learning and computer programming. It is
illustrated by the following sample student assignment:

> Write and test a computer program to multiply two fractional
> numbers.

Complete the following exercises before writing the program, to determine
what you want the computer to do.

1. Calculate the product

$$\frac{2}{3} \times \frac{5}{7}.$$

2. What did you do to find the numerator of the product? _____

   What did you do to find the denominator of the product? _____

3. Suppose you were given this piece of the program for calculating

$$\frac{2}{3} \times \frac{5}{7}.$$

```
10   P  = 2
20   Q  = 3
30   R  = 5
40   S  = 7
```

If you use *N* for *numerator,* what would you write in the program to find the numerator of the product

$$\frac{2}{3} \times \frac{5}{7}?$$ _____

If you use *D* for *denominator,* what would you write in the program to find the denominator of the product? _____

4. Complete the program and have your answer appear in the form *N/D* (for example, 4/5 instead of $\frac{4}{5}$).

5. Change the program so you can enter any group of numbers you wish for the numerators and the denominators of the numbers whose product you wish to find.

6. Change your program so that if the product is an improper fraction, it will rename the fraction as a mixed numeral. Give your answer in the form *W N/D* where *W* is the whole number part of the mixed numeral, for example, the 2 in 2 3/4.

Challenge for Champions

7. Revise your program so it will give the product in lowest terms.

The following programs for this assignment were run on an Apple II Plus.

Exercise 5

```
10      PRINT "E  = ";: INPUT E
20      PRINT "F  = ";: INPUT F
30      PRINT "G  = ";: INPUT G
40      PRINT "H  = ";: INPUT H
50   N = E * G
51   D = F * H
52      IF D = 0 GOTO 10
90      PRINT E;"/";F;" * ";G;"/";H;"
           = ";N;"/";D
100     END
]RUN
E = ?8
F = ?3
G = ?9
H = ?4
8/3 * 9/4 = 72/12
]RUN
E = ?5
F = ?8
G = ?2
H = ?15
5/8 * 2/15 = 10/120
]RUN
E = ?8
F = ?3
```

```
G = ?9
H = ?15
8/3 * 9/15 = 72/45
```

Exercise 6

```
10      PRINT "E = ";: INPUT E
20      PRINT "F = ";: INPUT F
30      PRINT "G = ";: INPUT G
40      PRINT "H = ";: INPUT H
50      N = E * G
51      D = F * H
52      IF D = 0 GOTO 10
80      IF N < D GOTO 90
81      Q = N / D
82      IF Q < > INT (Q) GOTO 85
83      PRINT E;"/";F;" * ";G;"/";H;"
        = ";Q
84      GOTO 100
85      W = INT (Q)
86      N = N – W * D
87      PRINT E;"/";F;" * ";G;"/";H;"
        = ";W;" ";N;"/"D
88      GOTO 100
90      PRINT E;"/";F;" * ";G;"/";H;"
        = ";N;"/"D
100     END
```

If the result is a whole number, the quotient is N + D.

The whole number part of the mixed numeral is the integer part of N + D. Subtract the product of the whole number and the denominator from the numerator to get the new numerator.

```
]RUN
E = ?8
F = ?3
G = ?9
H = ?4
8/3 * 9/4 = 6

]RUN
E = ?5
F = ?8
G = ?2
H = ?15
5/8 * 2/15 = 10/120

]RUN
E = ?8
F = ?3
G = ?9
H = ?15
8/3 * 9/15 = 1 27/45
```

Exercise 7

```
10      PRINT "E = ";: INPUT E
20      PRINT "F = ";: INPUT F
30      PRINT "G = ";: INPUT G
40      PRINT "H = ";: INPUT H
50      N = E * G
51      D = F * H
52      IF D = 0 GOTO 10
60      IF N<> D GOTO 64
62      Q = 1
63      GOTO 83
64      IF N < D GOTO 67
65      I = D
66      GOTO 68
67      I = N
```

If the numerator and denominator are equal, the product of the two fractions is 1.

To reduce the fraction to lowest terms, the greatest number one has to check for a common factor of the numerator and denominator is the smaller of the two numbers.

```
68      FOR Z = I TO 2 STEP - 1
69      IF N / Z = INT (N / Z) GOTO      ]  Numbers are checked in decreasing
71                                          order for being common factors. The
70      NEXT Z                              first common factor found is the greatest
71      IF D / Z = INT (D / Z) GOTO         common factor.
73
72      NEXT Z
73    N = N / Z                           ]  Reduce to lowest terms.
74    D = D / Z
80      IF N < D GOTO 90
81    Q = N / D
82      IF Q < > INT (Q) GOTO 85
83      PRINT E;"/" ;F;" * " ;G;"/" ;H;"
         = ";Q
84      GOTO 100
85    W = INT (Q)
86    N = N - W * D
87      PRINT E;"/" ;F;" * " ;G;"/" ;H;"
         = ";W;" ";N;"/" D
88      GOTO 100
89      PRINT Q
90      PRINT E;"/" ;F;" * " ;G;"/" ;H;"
         = ";N;"/" D
100     END

]RUN
E = ?8
F = ?3
G = ?9
H = ?4
8/3 * 9/4 = 6

]RUN
E = ?5
F = ?8
G = ?2
H = ?15
5/8 * 2/15 = 1/12

]RUN
E = ?8
F = ?3
G = ?9
H = ?15
8/3 * 8/15 = 1 3/5
```

Programming assignments on adding fractions, performing operations with exponents, and writing the expanded form of a decimal numeral are additional activities that give practice on basic computational skills, highlight basic concepts such as *denominators of zero are not allowed,* and reinforce students' knowledge of the process.

Another feature of computer programming assignments that this example illustrates is the provision for individual differences. Exercise 7 is most likely suitable only for students of high ability, whereas exercise 5 can be completed by almost all students.

Introducing a New Topic: The Fibonacci Sequence

The model described earlier for introducing a new topic with programming can easily be implemented with Fibonacci sequences. The teaching sequence might be as follows: A Fibonacci sequence is defined by the teacher, the students create several such sequences on paper, and finally, when the students think they can tell the computer how to create a sequence, they program the computer and test their program. The program is quite straightforward, but it does require the problem-solving strategy of thinking ahead and an understanding of recursion. Considerable computation is also needed to check the program. The program listing below is for a sequence having 1 and 1 as its two initial terms, but it can easily be changed to accept any two first terms.

```
10   A = 1
20   B = 1
30   PRINT A
40   PRINT B
50   C = A + B
60   PRINT C
70   A = B
80   B = C
90   IF C < 100 THEN 50
200  END
```

Output: Mathematical Learning

Computer programming can help students acquire a deeper understanding of the concepts developed in the middle school mathematics curriculum. For the slower ones, it will provide needed practice, both from doing their own assignments and from checking the programs of classmates. For the gifted, it results in many opportunities for creativity by exploring and using computer capabilities. For the teacher, such an approach brings the reward of seeing the output: mathematics learning taking place.

18

Euclid: A Graphics Language for Plane Geometry

Newcomb Greenleaf

FIVE years ago, computer graphics was possible only on large computers. Now many popular microcomputers can be adapted to support graphics capabilities, and graphics software for the classroom is beginning to appear. The best-known developments center on the Logo language and are highly innovative. At Sigma Design we are developing a graphics language and system called Euclid for the plane geometry classroom. The Euclid language owes a great deal to Logo, but the subject matter is traditional Euclidean geometry.

Computer graphics can make plane geometry a vital and interesting subject. But it is perhaps equally important that geometry is an ideal setting for learning to program. Further, the Euclid system, with its simple push-button menu, makes introductory geometry available to much younger students.

Friendly, accessible microcomputers are now everywhere, and we have discovered something that would have seemed quite startling a mere ten years ago: children take very easily to programming, provided they are presented with reasonable software and hardware and sufficient access to a terminal. Some do much better than others, but all children can learn to program. The great success story in this area is Logo, the language of "turtle geometry." Logo is, among other things, an interactive graphics language in which the student draws on the display screen by issuing commands to a "turtle" cursor. Further, Logo makes it extremely easy to create new higher-order commands or procedures out of the simple Logo primitives. The student is soon writing programs, even quite large programs. Versions of Logo are now available for many popular microcomputers. (For more information about Logo, see Abelson [1982], Harvey [1982], and *Byte* [1982].)

With Euclid, as with Logo, the computer's role in the mathematics classroom can become learning to program rather than programmed learning. We would subscribe to much of the Logo philosophy as expounded by Seymour Papert (1980). It was summarized in Harvey (1982) as follows:

LOGO is a language for learning. That sentence, one of the slogans of the LOGO movement, contains a subtle pun. The obvious meaning is that LOGO is a language for learning programming: it is designed to make computer programming as easy as possible to understand. But LOGO is also a language for learning in general. To put it somewhat grandly, LOGO is a language for learning how to think. Its history is rooted strongly in computer-science research, especially in artificial intelligence. But it is also rooted in Jean Piaget's research into how children develop thinking skills.

A similar idea was put forth with more brevity by Carole Greenes (1981, p. 589):

> The act of developing an algorithm to solve a particular problem, programming it, testing it, and refining it is itself problem solving.

Euclid builds on two specific aspects of Logo's success:

1. A small, core vocabulary of primitive commands that cause immediate visual output.
2. A simple framework for creating higher-order commands or procedures (i.e., for writing programs).

But Euclid differs from Logo in being more conservative with regard to subject matter. Whereas Logo introduces new (and valuable) elements to the curriculum, the language Euclid attempts to bring new life to the most venerable of all subjects, the plane geometry of Euclid. This is a particularly natural subject because the language of straightedge-and-compass constructions is already close to being a graphics programming language.

The Euclid Graphics System

Computer graphics today covers a wide area, from animation to engineering drafting. A good survey of many aspects of computer graphics hardware and software can be found in Foley and Van Dam (1982). When engineers or architects use a graphics system, they interact with the machine (and its software) to produce various geometric patterns on the display screen, and the resulting drawings are then plotted automatically. The systems sold to engineers and architects, which feature high speed and large memory, have only recently begun to sell for less than $100 000 (see fig. 18.1). Graphics systems adequate for classroom needs, however, can now be added to most microcomputers for a modest sum.

In the Euclid classroom, each desk incorporates a simple graphics workstation. We shall briefly describe the system in terms of the input and output devices it uses (see fig. 18.2). The input devices are as follows:

1. A keyboard, which is the standard input device.
2. A simple push-button menu, also a keyboard type of device (to be described in considerable detail), which allows for quick learning and effi-

Fig. 18.1. A graphics workstation marketed to architects and engineers. The computer is in the cabinet under the table. On the table are a plasma device for prompts and error messages, a keyboard incorporating a joystick, and a large push-button menu. To the left of the CRT is a printer that can also make copies of the picture on the display screen. To the right of the CRT is an eight-pen plotter than can produce drawings up to 24 inches by 36 inches. Photo courtesy of Sigma Design, Inc.

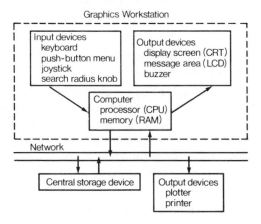

Fig. 18.2. Schematic of Euclid workstation showing connections to network

cient use of the basic Euclid commands. It replaces the keyboard for very young students and supplements it for all users.

3. A joystick and search radius knob, which control a cross hair on the screen. They are incorporated into the menu.

The output devices are these:

1. A graphics display screen (CRT), preferably a color screen for interest, aesthetics, and clarity.

2. A liquid crystal display (LCD), which is the plasma device in figure 18.1, for prompts and error messages and a buzzer to warn when they appear. The LCD is also incorporated into the menu unit.

3. Two hard-copy devices, a plotter to make accurate copies (in color) of the drawing on the CRT and a printer to provide listings of programs. With the stations connected in a network, each hard-copy device can serve a large number of students.

The network connection has other uses. There is a central storage device, which allows students to store their drawings (graphics data bases) and their programs between classes. The network also allows the teacher to communicate with individual students and, when desired, students to communicate with each other.

Controlling the Graphics Display

In Euclid, computer control is achieved by the use of either the Euclid menu keyboard or by programming. Students first become familiar with the Euclid language by using the menu board (fig. 18.3). The menu board is divided into four areas: Point, Line and Circle, Control, and Programmable. Note that Euclid is completely geometric. Unlike Logo, it makes no use of numbers in its initial formulation, though they can be introduced later.

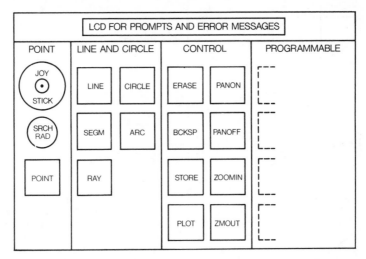

Fig. 18.3. The Euclid menu board

All points are entered by "pointing" with the cross hairs (which are controlled by the joystick) and then pushing the POINT button. We shall refer to points entered in this way, as well as the intersection points of lines and circles, as *special* points. Points are most often entered in response to prompts from other commands, such as LINE or CIRCLE.

The operation of POINT is complicated by the fact that there are three different possible intentions in pointing. When we position the cross hairs, we may intend—

1. to indicate a special point already entered in the drawing;
2. to indicate a nonspecial point on a line or circle of the drawing;
3. to indicate a new point not yet in the drawing.

To allow us to fulfill any of these intentions, the cross hairs contain a circle (fig. 18.4) whose size is controlled by the Search Radius knob. When POINT is pushed, the computer first looks for a special point inside the circle. If it finds one, the closest special point to the center of the cross hairs is chosen. If there is no special point inside the circle, the computer next searches for a line or circle of the drawing and takes the closest point to the center of the cross hairs if any are found. If no points of the drawing lie inside the circle, then a new point is entered at the center of the cross hairs. See figure 18.4 for examples of all these possibilities.

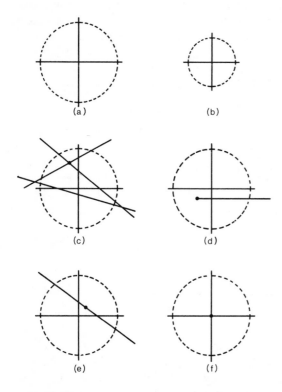

(a)

(b)

(c)

(d)

(e)

(f)

Fig. 18.4. The on-screen cross hairs. The size of the circle is controlled by the Search Radius knob in (a) and (b). When POINT is pushed, the computer searches within the circle for the nearest special point, (c) and (d). Failing to find such a special point, the computer searches for the nearest point on a line or circle (e). If no points of the drawing lie within the circle, the computer chooses the point at the center of the cross hairs (f).

The buttons in the Line and Circle area of the menu allow us to enter (extended) lines, line segments, rays, circles, and arcs. Push any of these buttons and we are prompted to enter the necessary points. If we push LINE, we will be prompted to enter two points to determine the line. (If we enter the same point twice, we will receive the error message "Points must be distinct" and asked again for the second point.)

The operation of the CIRCLE button is based on the use of the compass. Push CIRCLE and we are asked in turn for the center, the first measurement point, and the second measurement point. The system then draws a circle whose radius equals the distance between the two measurement points. The operation of the SEGMENT, RAY, and ARC buttons is similar.

As a drawing is created, the sequence of buttons pushed is listed in a panel at the side of the screen. This list is very helpful to students when they write a program to create automatically what has been done "by hand."

The operation of the buttons in the Control area is fairly self-evident. PLOT sends the drawing to the printer, and STORE sends the drawing (more correctly, the associated graphics data base) to the central storage device. ERASE first provokes the prompt "Push ERASE again to erase drawing." When that is done, the screen is cleared and the data base is deleted from memory, allowing the operator to start with a clean slate. BACKSPACE deletes the last item entered from the drawing (and from the list of operations). It can be pushed repeatedly to delete several items.

The viewing area is controlled by the four buttons PANON, PANOFF, ZOOMIN, and ZOOMOUT. PANON deletes the cross hair from the screen and sets the joystick in control of translating the viewing area. This allows the student to locate intersection points that are "off screen." PANOFF restores joystick control of the cross hair. ZOOMIN first issues the prompt "Enter lower left corner." When that is supplied, the image is magnified twofold with the viewing window lower left at the indicated point. ZOOM-OUT reverses this process, shrinking the scene in the view window and placing it in the center of the screen. The Control area of the menu also contains buttons (not shown in fig. 18.3) for setting the color.

The Euclid language, like Logo, allows students to begin writing their own programs almost immediately. It then allows them to assign some of these programs to the buttons in the Programmable area of the menu board. This is done from the keyboard.

Using the Euclid Menu Board

Beginners and young students should learn to use the menu to "sketch." It is an easy exercise to draw a triangle, and much more challenging to draw a house. Artistic students could draw faces or landscapes.

To see how the menu can be used in the traditional curriculum, consider the problem of drawing the perpendicular bisector to the line segment $P1P2$, shown in figure 18.5. This can be accomplished by the following sequence of operations:

Button	Cross hairs positioned at—
CIRCLE	
POINT	$P1$ (center point)
POINT	$P1$ (first measurement point)
POINT	$P2$ (second measurement point)

CIRCLE
    POINT $P2$ (center point)
    POINT $P2$ (first measurement point)
    POINT $P1$ (second measurement point)

LINE
    POINT $Q1$ (first point)
    POINT $Q2$ (second point)

As the student executes this sequence, or a similar one, the sequence of button pushes appears on the screen along with the drawing of figure 18.5. However, the names for the special points are given here for explanatory purposes only. Variable names are not used with the Euclid menu but become necessary when the student starts to write programs.

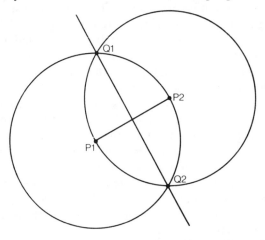

Fig. 18.5. The Euclid construction of a perpendicular bisector. The point labels are not entered when the construction is made from the menu, but they are used in the BISECT program. When the construction is made from the menu, the sequence of buttons pushed appears in a column at the left of the screen and is plotted when PLOT is pushed.

The problem of constructing the perpendicular bisector has three principal phases. Once students can do this construction from the Euclid menu, they have completed the first phase. In the second phase, which will be described in the next section, the student writes a program or procedure incorporating this sequence of operations so that the perpendicular bisector is drawn automatically once the points $P1$ and $P2$ are entered. This is done from the keyboard and requires the student to learn further aspects of the Euclid language. We shall define a BISECT procedure below.

The third phase is one of verification. How do we know that our program actually does construct the perpendicular bisector? Here traditional proofs enter the picture, but their role has been redefined. A proof allows us to know that our program actually does what we want it to do. We can think of

no better way of motivating students to understand proofs. They need proofs
to defend their programs against criticism.

Once a BISECT program has been written, debugged, polished, and
verified, it can be assigned to a programmable button. This will prove very
useful when it comes to solving the problem of drawing a circle through three
noncollinear points.

Programming in Euclid

There is not space here to describe the Euclid programming language in
detail. Those familiar with Logo will see right away how it should go. We
shall content ourselves with describing the construction and operation of the
BISECT procedure.

To construct the procedure, simply type in the following seven lines (the
line numbers are not part of the program but only for our explanations):

1. TO BISECT P1 P2
2. MAKE C1 CIRCLE P1 P1 P2
3. MAKE C2 CIRCLE P2 P2 P1
4. MAKE Q1 FIRST MEET C1 C2
5. MAKE Q2 SECOND MEET C1 C2
6. OUTPUT LINE Q1 Q2
7. END

The word TO in line 1 tells the computer that we are defining a procedure
called BISECT. The other two entries in line 1, P1 and P2, denote variables.
If they have not been previously assigned to points when the procedure is
run, the operator will be prompted to enter them.

The word MAKE tells the computer that the next word in the line is being
defined as equal to the term following it. Hence, line 2 says that C1 is the
circle centered at P1 whose radius is measured from P1 to P2. Line 3 is
similar.

MEET C1 C2 is a "list" consisting of those points in the intersection of C1
and C2 (if that intersection were infinite, the procedure would halt with an
error message). FIRST picks out the first element of that list (if the intersection were empty, the procedure would halt with an error message). Hence,
line 4 defines Q1 to be the first element in the list and line 5 defines Q2 to be
the second (if the intersection contained a single point, the procedure would
halt at line 5 with an error message).

OUTPUT causes the indicated line to be drawn on the display screen (if
Q1 and Q2 were the same point, an error message would result). Finally,
END means what it says.

To run BISECT, simply type in BISECT P1 P2 (where P1 and P2 may be
replaced by other names). If P1 and P2 have already been defined, then the
program will run. If P1 and P2 have not been defined as existing points in
the drawing, we will be prompted to enter them with the cross hairs. When

the program runs, the circles $C1$ and $C2$ will be computed and entered in the graphics data base as nondisplay items, since they are not connected with an output statement.

This is not an ultimate BISECT program. Error trapping should be added. If the points $P1$ and $P2$ are the same, the computer should reject them and request changed input.

The option of running Euclid's procedures in the DEBUG mode is also available. When DEBUG is turned on, the procedure executes slowly, with each program line displayed on the LCD as it runs. All items (including nondisplay items) are shown on the display screen. In the DEBUG mode, Euclid presents a great opportunity for learning to program and debug. As students watch their program being executed, they can see exactly where its operation deviates from their expectations.

From Euclid to Descartes

How should numbers be introduced to the Euclid system? We need only turn to (the original) Euclid's *Elements* for the answer. He presents a purely geometric construction for measuring the length of one line segment in terms of another, the "unit." When this method is taught in a traditional plane geometry class, it generally seems completely pointless, because obviously no one would try to measure length in such a complicated way. But his (Euclid's) algorithm for measuring turns into a perfectly lovely program, Measure, which students can write. This can be done as a class project in which all students would work on programming the procedures necessary to create Measure.

The operation of Measure would be very simple. Type in MEASURE, and you will be asked to supply the UNIT, a nondegenerate segment, in terms of its endpoints and to supply the SEGMENT to be measured. The procedure will then produce a number, the length of SEGMENT in UNITs.

Once lengths have been introduced, it is natural to begin the transition to analytic geometry. This is accomplished by adding to the Euclid language new commands to deal with coordinates. Perhaps the expanded language should be called Descartes!

REFERENCES

Abelson, H. "A Beginner's Guide to Logo." *Byte* 7 (August 1982): 88.

Byte editors. "Logo for the Apple II, TI-99/4A, and the TRS-80 Color Computer." *Byte* 7 (August 1982): 230.

Foley, J. D., and A. Van Dam. *Fundamentals of Interactive Computer Graphics*. Reading, Mass.: Addison-Wesley Publishing Co., 1982.

Greenes, Carole. "The Computer in Mathematics Education." *Mathematics Teacher* 74 (November 1981): 588–89.

Harvey, B. "Why Logo?" *Byte* 7 (August 1982): 163.

Papert, Seymour. *Mindstorms: Children, Computers, and Powerful Ideas*. New York: Basic Books, 1980.

19

Computers Need Math!

Lois B. Whitman

MOST college students take at least one course involving the operation of computers. Students specializing in computer science, or related fields, complete several such courses. Even in secondary schools, the majority of students study computer programming. How can elementary and secondary mathematics teachers lay the foundation for this work?

First, we can explore some of the thinking styles and teaching strategies that have evolved in computer science courses and find fresh approaches to standard mathematical topics. Second, we can reevaluate our mathematics curricula—from basic skills to recently abandoned components of the new math to ancient mathematics—with the intent of selecting those concepts and skills that provide tools for computer courses.

Computing Strategies
for Mathematics Instruction

Several techniques developed in computer courses provide new strategies for teaching mathematics. These techniques require no special equipment, since the ideas and thinking styles stand alone. They have been influenced by the characteristics of computers.

The electronic speed of computers contributes to their tremendous power. They operate quickly, progressing through a long sequence of simple, logical steps in a fraction of a second. Computer scientists describe such a sequence as an *algorithm:* a series of steps to find the solution to a problem. When an algorithm includes looping for repetition, a few lines can represent a great many steps in a calculation.

For example, to find the sum of the even numbers from 10 to 200, the algorithm outlined below is sufficient:

1. Initialize the sum to 0 and the number to 10.

2. Repeat the following steps until the number exceeds 200:
    a) Set the sum to the old sum plus the number.
    b) Set the number to the old number plus 2.

3. The sum is complete.

155

A streamlined representation of this algorithm appears in the diagram in figure 19.1, called a *flow block*.

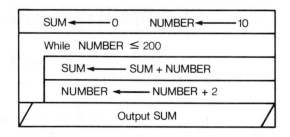

Fig. 19.1

In structured programming, a flow-block diagram describes an algorithm more conveniently than a flowchart. In mathematics classes, the strategy of flow-block diagramming can be used to teach, for example, the concept of inverse function. To illustrate, consider the function for temperature conversion defined by the equation $F = \frac{9}{5} C + 32$. The diagram for this function (fig. 19.2(a)) shows the series of steps performed on an input, C, to attain the

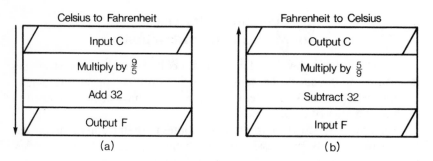

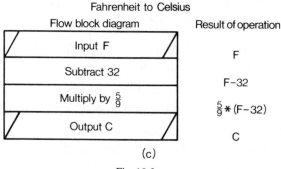

Fig. 19.2

output F. The flow-block diagram for the inverse function, that is, entering F for an output of C, can be developed by reading the first diagram from bottom to top and performing the inverse of each of the steps in the original sequence. This is shown in figure 19.2(b). Since it is conventional to read flow-block diagrams from top to bottom, the diagram in figure 19.2(b) is redrawn as shown in figure 19.2(c).

In most computer languages, asterisks are used to designate multiplication, as in the expression 5/9 * (F − 32). This, too, is a computer science feature that should be borrowed for mathematics instruction. The use of this notation in elementary schools could eliminate any need to introduce the multiplication sign (×), which is superfluous, even troublesome, in algebra.

Data-flow diagrams are another device that can be used in teaching mathematics. These diagrams simply show data flow, indicating the input and output of an algorithm, without any other details. The diagrams in figure 19.3 show the data flow for three geometry problems about the right triangle pictured, where two sides are known and the required information is indicated by a question mark.

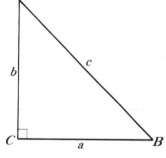

The use of data-flow diagrams might help students review problem solving. The flow-block and data-flow diagrams in figure 19.4 illustrate the use of these strategies for a trigonometry problem in which two sides and one angle of an oblique triangle are known. Additional drawings could make an effective summary of a chapter while exposing students to a technique used by computer programmers.

Variables in flow diagrams (fig. 19.5) can illustrate an elementary operation, such as the process of finding a quotient, Q, and the remainder, R, by successive subtractions of the divisor, D. A slight modification finds the integral logarithm, L to the base B, of a positive number, N, using successive divisions.

To determine $\log_2 64$, the second algorithm counts the number of times 64 must be divided by 2 to leave the loop. Calculating logarithms by this method can illuminate their meaning.

Mathematical Concepts Needed for Computing

A mathematics curriculum that prepares students for computer science courses must emphasize logarithms, truncating numbers, and powers of 2, particularly the binary place-value system.

Place value lies at the heart of our methods of calculation with decimal numerals and forms the basis of the binary representation used in computers. Carefully sequenced presentations in different number bases can

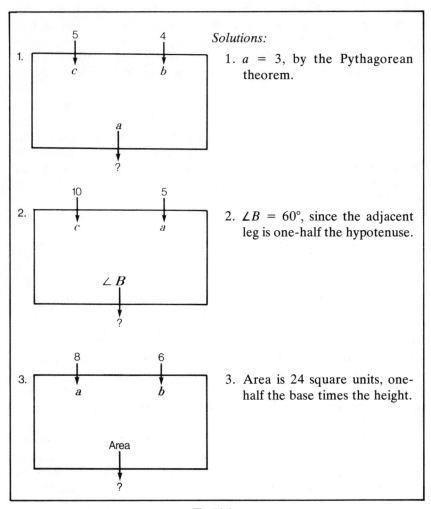

Solutions:

1. $a = 3$, by the Pythagorean theorem.

2. $\angle B = 60°$, since the adjacent leg is one-half the hypotenuse.

3. Area is 24 square units, one-half the base times the height.

Fig. 19.3

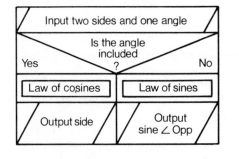

Fig. 19.4

The Division Algorithm

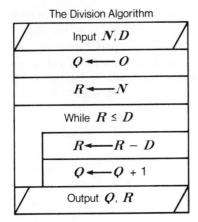

The Logarithm Algorithm

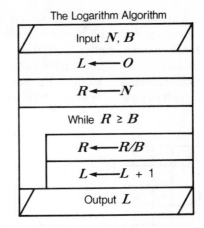

Fig. 19.5

increase students' understanding and teach them skills that are useful in communicating with computers.

Binary, octal, and hexadecimal notations predominate in computer science materials. Base four can be taught to younger students using multibase blocks. Conversion between base ten and other bases can be achieved by rearranging the blocks or by using cardboard grids or graph paper to show the new groupings. Base systems can be compared by direct reference to a counting chart, with different bases in parallel columns:

Decimal	Binary	Hexadecimal	Octal
00	000000	00	00
01	000001	01	01
02	000010	02	02
03	000011	03	03
04	000100	04	04
05	000101	05	05
06	000110	06	06
07	000111	07	07
08	001000	08	10
09	001001	09	11
10	001010	0A	12
11	001011	0B	13
12	001100	0C	14
13	001101	0D	15
14	001110	0E	16
15	001111	0F	17
16	010000	10	20

Extending the list should lead to the discovery of some relationships that can be verified with blocks or grids. For example, in figure 19.6, the blocks for the binary number 110110 are composed of one group of thirty-two, one of sixteen, one of four, and one of two. However, it can be seen in figure 19.7 that the same blocks can be used to show 66_{octal} as well. Using the same display of blocks (or grids) shows the hexadecimal representation to be 36_{hex}.

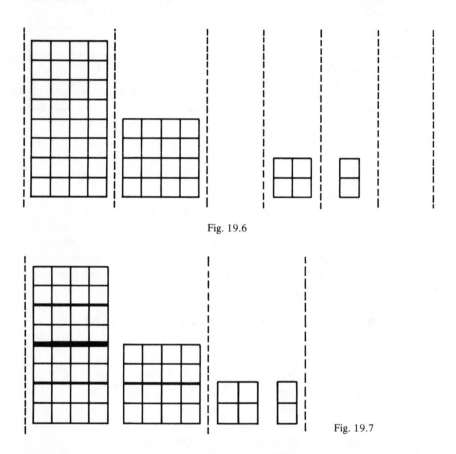

Fig. 19.6

Fig. 19.7

When we group decimal digits in triplets in order to read numbers like 24 358 (twenty-four thousand three hundred fifty-eight), we rely on an implied base of one thousand embedded in our decimal system. Each triplet of binary digits can be translated directly into one octal digit in a similar manner. Consider the binary numeral 110101. If the digits are grouped into periods of three, the translation to octal can be performed as follows:

$$110\ 101_{two} = 110_{two} * 1000_{two} + 101_{two}$$
$$= 6_{eight} * 10_{eight} + 5_{eight}$$
$$= 65_{eight}$$

The fact that four bits (binary digits) can be translated into each hexadecimal digit can be seen with multibase blocks or by the proof

36_{hex} means 3 times sixteen plus 6 times one,

which can be written in binary numerals as follows:

$$36_{hex} = 3_{hex} * 10_{hex} + 6$$
$$= 11_{two} * 10000_{two} + 110_{two}$$
$$= 110110$$

(Written as a full byte, this is 00110110.)

It is evident that the procedure applies to any two-digit hexadecimal numeral and can be extended to more digits. In most systems, a group of eight bits is called a byte and half a byte is called a nibble.

The study of number theory, including results about prime numbers and Fibonacci numbers, offers abundant opportunities to investigate loops. For example, a well-known property of square numbers states that the sum of the first n odd numbers is n^2. This suggests the algorithm in figure 19.8 for finding square roots.

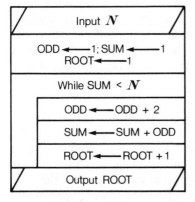

Trace

ODD	1	3	5 . . .
SUM	1	4	9 . . .
ROOT	1	2	3 . . .

(This table is a "trace" of the variables as the algorithm loops.)

Fig. 19.8

Other topics relevant to computer programming from the new mathematics curricula are sets, logic, matrices, and probability, among others. Scientific, or exponential, notation is widely used, as are random variables, the greatest integer function, and mathematical induction. Not only is increased attention to these topics needed as preparation for computing, but computing can also serve as the motivation for their study.

Although teachers are finding fascinating uses for microcomputers in their classrooms, hardware use is but one aspect of the alliance of computer science with mathematics education. Alternative approaches to problem solving and particular thinking styles can bring new methods to our instruction. In addition, we have the obligation to present material within regular mathematics courses that can help our students in their future work with computers.

20

Programming to Learn Problem Solving

Robert S. Roberts
Margaret L. Moore

WRITING a computer program is problem solving. This article presents a variety of mathematics problems that high school students can solve with the aid of a microcomputer. The goal is to demonstrate how the computer can affect mathematics content by augmenting traditional topics and providing easy access to some nontraditional content areas such as number theory, probability, and statistics. Our examples have been chosen to stimulate thought and discussion about how the mathematics curriculum can be enhanced through the use of microcomputers. The problems have all been field tested with secondary school students in summer institutes conducted over the past ten years.

Problems for Computer Solution

Each of the following problems illustrates a different reason for using programming as an aid in mathematics problem solving. Each problem is annotated with a few comments and a short program listing. (All the programs were written for the TRS-80, but we have tried to keep the BASIC code as generic as possible. One exception is the RND(x) function. Apple and PET micros have an RND (1) function, which returns a random number between zero and one but will not respond to RND(365) as TRS 80 BASIC will; RND(365) can be replaced by INT(365*RND(1)) + 1, which will generate a random integer in the range from 1 to 365.) Program listings are included with each of the problems to illustrate how short programs in BASIC can be used to aid in solving difficult mathematics problems.

Richard and Josephine Andree have conducted summer workshops for high school students at the University of Oklahoma every summer for more than ten years. Support for these workshops has been provided by NSF grants, a variety of grants from the university, and the Andrees' donated time and money. Many of the problems given here come from their text *Exploring Computing with the TRS-80 (and Common Sense)* (1982). We thank the Andrees for their suggestions and permission to use these examples.

Problem 1

$4x^3 - 8x^2 - 29x - 13 = 0$; find three roots between -10 and $+10$
(Andree and Andree 1982, p. 45).

To solve the problem with a computer, a very short program can be written to evaluate the expression on the left-hand side of the equation for different values of x. The student can plot y versus x or make a table of y versus x and search for values of x for which $f(x) = 0$. Because the function in this problem is a third-order polynomial, there must be at least one root and maybe three roots. The information about the suggested domain for x and the number of roots is given as a hint and need not be included.

Students can easily investigate the function and quickly pin down roots by using a very short computer program such as the one in figure 20.1. A whole range of similar problems have been used to explore polynomials and other functions that are usually beyond the scope of traditional high school algebra. With the computer, much of the tedious detail of evaluating functions is removed, and students can focus on the features of the function and the search strategy.

```
100 PRINT "GIVE A STARTING VALUE AND STEP SIZE"
110 INPUT X1,ST
120 FOR X=X1 TO X1+10*ST STEP ST
130 Y= 4*X*X*X − 8*X*X − 29*X − 13
140 PRINT X,Y
150 NEXT X
160 GOTO 100
```

Fig. 20.1

Using the computer to evaluate functions for tables or plotting is so generally useful that it is worthwhile to encourage some of the better students to write general-purpose programs for function evaluation and plotting. They could also be encouraged to try to write programs that will incorporate some search strategy to locate roots automatically.

Problem 2

Find all of the 4-digit integers which are perfect squares and in which all of the digits are even. Your final program should run in less than 3 seconds (TRS-80 Model III). If your program takes longer, do some additional analysis and try again (Andree and Andree 1982, p. 204).

There are many ways to write a program that searches combinations of four-digit numbers for solutions. The program is reasonably short, but without a bit of thinking it runs much longer than necessary. For example, one could try to look at all possible four-digit numbers with even digits and then determine which are perfect squares; another approach would be to look at all the numbers that, when squared, would be four digits in length, and then determine which of these squares have only even digits. In the first instance the program would need to examine 500 numbers; in the second instance the program would search through only 33 numbers. The programs in figs. 20.2 and 20.3 illustrate the two strategies. The first program takes about one minute, but the second program can list all of the numbers in about three seconds on a TRS-80 Model III.

```
100  DEFINT N,Y
110  FOR N1 = 2 TO 8 STEP 2
120    FOR N2 = 0 TO 8 STEP 2
130      FOR N3 = 0 TO 8 STEP 2
140        FOR N4 = 0 TO 8 STEP 2
150          Y=N1*1000 + N2*100 + N3*10 +N4
160          X=SQR(Y) : REM SQR IS SLOW!
170          IF ABS( X − INT(X) )<.0001 THEN PRINT Y;
180  NEXT N4,N3,N2,N1
```

Fig. 20.2

```
100  DEFINT A-Z : REM INTEGER CALCULATIONS ARE FASTER
110  REM SQR(1000)= 31.XX & SQR(9999) = 99.99
120  FOR X=32 TO 98 STEP 2
130    Y= X*X
140    N1=Y/1000: REM REMEMBER ALL NUMBERS ARE INTEGERS!
150    IF N1/2 <> INT(N1/2) THEN 210 : REM IF NOT EVEN, THEN MOVE TO
       NEXT VALUE
160    N2=Y/100 − 10*N1
170    IF N2/2 <> INT (N2/2) THEN 210
180    N3=Y/10 − 100*N1 − 10*N2
190    IF N3/2 <> INT(N3/2) THEN 210
200    PRINT Y; '
210  NEXT X
220  END
```

Fig. 20.3

In the faster program, x is an integer than ranges from approximately the square root of 1000 to the square root of 9999. Notice that we have included only those instances for which x is even, since the square of an odd number would be odd and thus would not satisfy one of the conditions of the problem. The variables $N1$, $N2$, and $N3$ are the first three digits of the number from left to right; the fourth digit need not be checked, since only even numbers are squared and thus the last digit will be even. In general, the first digit of a four-digit number y is found by taking INT $(y/1000)$, but since $N1$ is defined as an integer, it is only necessary to use "$N1 = y/1000$" (and the integer arithmetic is faster). By contrast, taking the square root of y in the first program (line 160) helps slow the program because taking the root requires the computer to perform many internal calculations. Further, to test whether x is an integer is not as easy as "if int$(x) = x$ then . . .," because when the computer takes a square root it may find 4.999 . . . instead of 5! There is more than one way to get around this particular problem, and in our sample program it has been avoided by looking for a very close fit between int(x) and x instead of a match (line 170). However, this program still runs much more slowly than the other one.

Notice how much mathematics is used in the design of this efficient program! Programming efficiency is often a real-world constraint, and students should be encouraged to compare strategies and try to find an efficient strategy. The major improvements in running time are achieved through looking at the mathematics of the problem. However, be sure that programming tricks and shortcuts to improve efficiency do not lead to excessively complex and unreadable programs. There are many books and articles that discuss programming style (Leuhrmann 1983; Nevison 1979; and Jaquiss 1979) so we have avoided any lengthy discussion about that here.

Problem 3

A *Cryptarithm:* KISS × KISS = PASSION. This multiplication problem is coded; each letter stands for a single digit. Break the code and find the number that each letter represents.

Some students might like to solve such problems with pencil and paper, but a few lines of computer code will allow them to check quickly the many combinations of numbers that are possible. As in problem 2, the running time and efficiency of such programs will vary greatly, depending on how much thinking is done before the program is written. For example, can S be 0, 1, 5, or 6? (No, because when numbers that end in 0, 1, 5, or 6 are squared, the answer also ends in 0, 1, 5, or 6.) Students can compare strategy and running time to evaluate programming efficiency. The program in figure 20.4 is a typical solution to this problem.

```
100  DEFINT A-X: DEFDBL Y
110  FOR S = 2 TO 9
120    IF (S=5) OR (S=6) THEN 230
130    FOR I = 0 TO 9
140      FOR K = 1 TO 9
150        X = K*1000 + I*100 +S*10 +S
160        Y = X*X
170        Y$=STR$(Y)
180        LN=LEN(Y$)
190        IF VAL (MID$(Y$, LN-2,1)) <> I THEN 220
200        IF VAL(MID$(Y$,LN-4,2)) <> S*11 THEN 220
210        PRINT X,Y : REM POSSIBLE SOLUTION!
220      NEXT K,I
230  NEXT S
```

Fig. 20.4

In this program, there is a systematic search through possible values for K, I, and S. The square of KISS is formed in line 160. In lines 170 through 200, ascending sequential functions (string functions) are used to manipulate the product of KISS times KISS (y) to find which products have the same values for I and S as they would appear in the word *paSSIon*. Any solution is printed out by line 210. For this particular problem there is only one solution.

Problem 4

Write a program to simulate the toss of a penny. Two persons, X and Y, start with five pennies. Each tosses a coin. If the coins match, X gets both pennies; if they don't, Y gets both. Have the computer show the total number of pennies both X and Y have after each toss. The game ends when one person runs out of pennies. (Adapted from Andree and Andree [1982, p. 145].)

The program in figure 20.5 explores this problem.

```
100  X=5 : Y=5
105  PRINT X,Y
110  IF RND(0)<.5 THEN X=X+1:Y=Y-1 ELSE X=X-1:Y=Y+1
120  PRINT X,Y
130  IF X=0 OR Y=0 THEN 150
140  GOTO 110
150  END
```

Fig. 20.5

As extensions to this problem, students could modify their programs to repeat the entire experiment twenty or even fifty times. Students should also investigate what happens when the starting amounts are not equal. For example, what happens when X starts with three pennies and Y with five? Whoever starts with the smaller number is at a disadvantage. In fact, it can be shown that the probability that X will win all the money is given by $x/(x+y)$. This problem can be found in many probability texts as the "gambler's ruin" (Freund 1962, p. 94).

What does the computer add to the classroom in this problem? The students could toss coins, but the computer can simulate such an experiment much faster. It is thus possible to get more data very easily (a computer could be left to continue the simulation overnight if necessary), and there will be time to conduct more experiments on variations of the basic problem. This problem demonstrates how the computer can serve as a mathematics laboratory where students use simulation and experimentation to explore important concepts in probability and statistics.

Problem 5

The Eight Queens Problem. The problem of placing eight queens on a chess board so that no queen can attack any other queen is an old one. (Queens can attack any piece they can reach by moving in a straight line vertically, horizontally, or on either diagonal.). . . .

Write a program to solve the eight queens problem if you wish or ask your instructor for a program listing of a solution. See if you can figure out how the program works and why it produces all 92 possible solutions. *Note:* the program your instructor will give you may run as long as 30 minutes to find all 92 solutions. (Andree and Andree 1982, p. 217).

This is a difficult problem but has been repeatedly solved by secondary school students. This problem demonstrates two important points. First, computer-aided problem solving can greatly extend the type and complexity of problems that students can solve. Second, this problem is often used to teach backtracking, a problem-solving strategy that is peculiar to computer problem solving. The eight queens problem and many types of combinatoric puzzles can be solved using the computer and backtracking strategies. Other commonly used examples are the "Towers of Hanoi" and the "instant insanity puzzle." A good discussion of the backtrack strategy can be found in Nievergelt, Farrar, and Reingold (1974).

It is not always necessary for students to devise original solutions to programming problems. Figuring out someone else's program is a learning experience. Any program can be improved, and frequently improvements can be made to decrease the running-time required. Note that of the ninety-two solutions there is some duplication if symmetrical solutions, alike except for a rotation or a flip, are considered. As a challenge, students can be asked to write a program that would check the list of solutions for the rotational and mirror-image duplicates or to write a program that finds all the solutions but prints only those that are unique.

In the program in figure 20.6, we assume that the eight queens are in eight different columns on the chess board. If any two were in the same column, then there would be a conflict.

```
100 REM   EIGHT QUEENS
110 DIM X(8) :REM ROW POSITION IN EACH COLUMN
120 J=1: X(J)=1:REM PUT A QUEEN IN COL, ROW: 1,1
130 REM TAKE OUT "REM" ON NEXT LINE TO SEE THE PROGRAM WORK
140 REM FOR N=1TOJ:PRINT N;" -";X(N);:NEXT N:PRINT
150 FLAG=1 :  REM CHECK FOR CONFLICTS WITH OTHER QUEENS
160 IF J=1 GOTO 220
170 FOR K=1 TO J-1
180    IF X(J)=X(K) THEN FLAG=0: REM   FLAG = 1 MEANS 'GOOD' POSI-
       TION
190    IF X(J)-X(K) = J-K THEN FLAG=0
200    IF X(J)-X(K) = K-J THEN FLAG=0
210 NEXT K
220 IF FLAG = 1 THEN 300 ELSE 400
300 REM GOOD MOVE - GO TO NEXT COLUMN OR PRINT SOLUTION
310 IF J=8 THEN GOTO 500 : REM FOUND SOLUTION
320 J=J+1 : X(J)=1
330 GOTO 140
400 REM TRY NEXT POSITION OR BACKTRACK (BACKUP)
```

```
410  IF X(J)=8 THEN J=J−1: GOTO 410
420  X(J)=X(J)+1  :REM TRY NEXT MOVE
430  IF J=0 THEN END
440  GOTO 140
500  REM PRINT OUT A SOLUTION
510  FOR M=1 TO 8: LPRINT X(M);:NEXTM:LPRINT
520  GOTO 400
```

Fig. 20.6

The position (row) for each queen is stored in the array $X(1) \ldots X(8)$. For example, $X(3) = 8$ would place a queen in column three, row eight. (See fig. 20.7.) The program begins by putting a queen in column one, position (row) one (line 120). After each move or change in the chess board, it is necessary to check if there is another queen on the same row or on a diagonal from the new queen (lines 150–210). If there is only one queen on the board, then there is no need to check for conflict and the position is safe (line 160). If the position is safe, then the program goes on to put a queen in the next column. If the position is not safe, then the program tries the next position for that queen; if there are no more positions (rows) to try, then this must be a dead-end situation and the program must back up (backtrack) to find a different safe position for the previous queens. Once a solution has been found, it is printed.

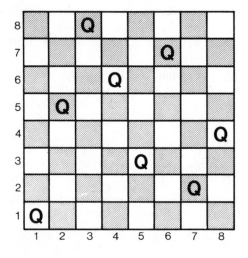

$X(1)=1$
$X(2)=5$
$X(3)=8$
$X(4)=6$
$X(5)=3$
$X(6)=7$
$X(7)=2$
$X(8)=4$

Fig. 20.7. A solution to the Eight Queens Problem as represented on a chess board and as represented in the computer.

Trying this by hand with a chess board will demonstrate that this is a very simple, but lengthy, strategy requiring days, if not weeks. The computer can do the search without error in a short time. Changing line 140 by removing the letters REM will slow the program down, but it will show each of the combinations of positions through which the program is searching and will allow the student to watch the computer search and backtrack.

Problem 6

A *"micro-research problem."* A theorem from number theory states that every integer N is expressible in the form

$$N = X^2 + Y^2 - Z^2$$

where X, Y, and Z are integers.

a) Write a program that will accept a value of N from -100 to $+100$ and print out N, X, Y, and Z.

b) Modify your program to test all integers from -100 to $+100$.

c) Can you speed up your program enough so that it could reasonably work for -5000 to $+5000$?
(Andree and Andree 1982, p. 203)

The program listing in figure 20.8 is a typical try at a solution. It may not represent the best solution strategy, but it would get someone started.

```
100  DEFINT A-Z
110  REM  FINDING SOLUTIONS FOR N = X*X + Y*Y - Z*Z
120  REM     A FIRST TRY - - - ( -20 to + 20 )
130  FOR N = -20 TO 20
140    X=1
150      FOR Y=0 TO X : REM ASSUME Y IS LESS THAN OR EQUAL TO X
160        B = X*X + Y*Y - N
170        IF B < 0 THEN 200
180        Z = SQR(B) : REM REMEMBER Z IS AN INTEGER!
190        IF Z*Z = B THEN PRINT N;X;Y;Z: GOTO 220
200      NEXT Y
210    X = X+1 : GOTO 150
220  NEXT N
```

Fig. 20.8

Andree (1982) has used the term "micro-research problems" because these problems do not always have known solutions, and although they are usually easy to understand, they are difficult to attack. For motivated and talented students, micro-research problems, which are usually taken from number theory or recreational mathematics, can challenge both mathematical and programming skills.

Summary

The problems and solutions discussed here demonstrate that microcomputers can facilitate several types of change in the mathematics curriculum.

First, the ability of computers to perform quick and accurate computations can increase the number and complexity of problems that students can investigate and solve. Second, computer-aided problem solving can extend the content of secondary school mathematics by enabling students to explore topics that are not normally included in the secondary curriculum, such as number theory, probability, and statistics. Third, computer-aided problem solving introduces students to new programming and problem-solving concepts and techniques such as recursion, backtracking, nesting loops, and so on. And finally, when computers are available in the mathematics classroom, teaching methods can change significantly. For example, some mathematics courses may adopt the format and methods of laboratory science classes; by programming the computer, students can perform "experiments," such as verifying the effects of particular parameters on the shape of a function's graph or estimating the probability of a particular event by simulation techniques.

There are a number of good sources for more problems and sample solutions that would be quite suitable for secondary school mathematics classes. Books by Andree and Andree (1982) and Spencer (1982) are excellent to start with, since they include instruction in BASIC and a number of example program listings. Ahl's (1979) collection of articles on computer applications for mathematics classes is an excellent source and includes a large number of good problems to solve with a computer. Several authors (McGettrick and Smith 1983; Rogowski 1979; Spencer 1977) have also published collections of problems for computer solution.

REFERENCES

Ahl, David H., ed. *Computers in Mathematics: A Sourcebook of Ideas.* Morristown, N.J.: Creative Computing Press, 1979.

Andree, Richard V., and Josephine P. Andree. *Exploring Computing with the TRS-80 (and Common Sense).* Englewood Cliffs, N.J.: Prentice Hall, 1982.

Freund, John E. *Mathematical Statistics.* Englewood Cliffs, N.J.: Prentice Hall, 1962.

Jaquiss, Robert S., Sr. "How to Hide Your BASIC Program—Round 2." In *Computers in Mathematics: A Sourcebook of Ideas,* edited by David H. Ahl, pp. 172–74. Morristown, N.J.: Creative Computing Press, 1979.

Leuhrmann, Arthur. "Slicing through Spaghetti Code." *Computing Teacher* 10 (April 1983).

McGettrick, Andrew D., and Peter D. Smith. *Graded Problems in Computer Science.* Reading, Mass.: Addison-Wesley Publishing Co., 1983.

Nevison, John M. "How to Hide Your BASIC Program." In *Computers in Mathematics: A Sourcebook of Ideas,* edited by David H. Ahl, pp. 170–72. Morristown, N.J.: Creative Computing Press, 1979.

Nievergelt, Jurg, J. Craig Farrar, and Edward M. Reingold. *Computer Approaches to Mathematical Problems.* Englewood Cliffs, N.J.: Prentice Hall, 1974.

Rogowski, Stephen J. *Problems for Computer Solution.* Student and teacher eds. Morristown, N.J.: Creative Computing Press, 1979.

Spencer, Donald D. *Problems for Computer Solution.* Rochelle Park, N.J.: Hayden Book Co., 1977.

———. *Computers in Number Theory.* Rockville, Md.: Computer Science Press, 1982.

21

Computer Methods for Problem Solving in Secondary School Mathematics

Dwayne E. Channell
Christian R. Hirsch

Two of the most challenging tasks facing teachers of secondary school mathematics are those of motivation and the development of student facility in problem solving. Almost two decades ago, Morris Kline (1966) recommended that "by utilizing real problems chosen from the world in which the student lives and involving phenomena which he himself experiences we may be able to motivate the study of mathematics" (p. 329). To date, Kline's recommendation has had little impact on secondary school mathematics curricula or its teaching. This is not surprising, since traditional methods for solving real-world problems typically involve extensive computations or a knowledge of linear algebra, calculus, probability theory, or other advanced mathematics. Today, however, the availability of computers in mathematics classrooms provides a unique opportunity not only to take advantage of the motivational effects of real-life problems but also to develop useful methods for attacking such problems within the mainstream of secondary school mathematics.

In this article we illustrate how a computer can be used as a tool to help pupils solve realistic mathematical problems while simultaneously reinforcing their understanding of problem-solving *processes*. Three different problem situations are presented. For each situation, a four-stage problem-solving model à la Polya is given: Problem Statement, Analysis, Computer Program, and Looking Back/Looking Ahead.

The article is divided into two sections: "Problem Solving Using Algorithmic Methods" and "Problem Solving Using Simulation Methods." The first section treats two problems whose solutions result from straightforward numerical computation. The solution process involves designing a computer algorithm for carrying out computations that would be tedious to perform by hand or even with a calculator. In the first example, the method involves constructing an algorithm specific to the situation; in the second example, the method simply involves modifying the formula for the volume of a right circular cylinder. The results of computing do not provide the solution to the problems but rather tabular data to be analyzed and acted on by the student.

The second section is devoted to a problem representing situations for which there is no known mathematical algorithm for solution or for which the algorithm is so complicated that requiring its use would make the solutions inaccessible to all but advanced high school students. Rather than ignoring such problems, students can be guided to simulate the actual physical situation. That is, they can formulate a mathematical model that may be used to represent or imitate the actual physical phenomena. Once the model has been constructed, a computer program can be developed or supplied to investigate the model over time or under varying conditions. Problems that involve randomness can be solved by special simulation techniques known as Monte Carlo methods. Simulations of this type use random numbers as elements in the mathematical model.

Problem Solving Using Algorithmic Methods

Problem 1. The Magical Mystery of Mathematics

Once upon a time, a group of students had the pleasure of attending a performance by Math E. Magic, a mathematically inclined magician. He involved them in several interesting mathematical magic tricks, the final one of which we want to share with you. He asked each member of the audience to choose a natural number and follow these instructions in order:

1. Write the number.
2. If your number is 1, stop.
3. If your number is even, divide it by 2 and then return to instruction 1 and follow through the sequence of steps with this new number.
4. If your number is odd, multiply it by 3, add 1, and then carry out instruction 1 with this new number.

When everyone had finished, he boasted that no matter what number is chosen, his instructions will always produce a 1. No one in the audience could find a counterexample to the magician's claim. Can you?

Analysis

Students should be reminded, if necessary, what a natural number is and then asked to test the claim for a number of their choice. It will be helpful if they actually write the sequence of results. For example, if the choice is 6, then the sequence of results is

6, 3, 10, 5, 16, 8, 4, 2, 1   (stop).

Once students understand the instructions and their repetitive nature, they can be guided to translate the sequence of instructions into a BASIC program.

Program

The BASIC program in figure 21.1 follows directly from the given instructions. Therefore it can provide a nice introduction to the use of *conditional* branches (lines 70 and 80) and *unconditional* branches (lines 100 and 120) in programming. The program permits the user to easily test the claim for many numbers, including large ones.

```
10  REM        PROGRAM TO TEST
20  REM        MAGICIAN'S CLAIM
30  REM
40  PRINT "ENTER A NATURAL NUMBER";
50  INPUT N
60  PRINT N;",";
70  If N = 1 THEN 130
80  IF N/2 = INT (N/2) THEN 110
90  LET N = 3*N + 1
100 GOTO 60
110 LET N = N/2
120 GOTO 60
130 END

RUN

ENTER A NATURAL NUMBER ?10
  10 , 5 , 16 , 8 , 4 , 2 , 1 ,

ENTER A NATURAL NUMBER ?13
  13 , 40 , 20 , 10 , 5 , 16 , 8 , 4 , 2 , 1 ,

ENTER A NATURAL NUMBER ?50
  50 , 25 , 76 , 38 , 19 , 58 , 29 , 88 , 44 , 22 , 11 , 34 , 17 , 52 , 26 , 13 , 40 , 20 , 10 , 5 , 16 , 8 , 4 ,
  2 , 1 ,
```

Fig. 21.1

Looking Back/Looking Ahead

The results of our runs provide support for the magician's claim, but do not confirm (prove) it. In fact, the question of whether this algorithm always produces a 1 (i.e., terminates) remains an unsolved problem, despite the efforts of some of the best number theorists in the country. Nievergelt, Farrar, and Reingold (1974) report that the magician's claim has been shown to be true for all natural numbers $n \leq 10^{40}$. However, no one has provided a proof for the claim, nor has anyone found a counterexample. Perhaps one of your precocious students might find a solution and be recorded in history. Below are some related questions and problems on which all your students can work:

1. Explain how a computer could be used to *prove* the magician's claim for all natural numbers less than or equal to 100. Modify the program to produce such a proof.

2. Let us define the *length* of a sequence as the number of terms in the sequence. The first run of the program produced a sequence of length 7. Can you find two consecutive natural numbers for which the magician's trick will produce sequences of the same length? Can you find three consecutive natural numbers that will yield sequences of the same length?

3. Is there a power of 2 that is most frequently generated first?

4. Explain how a computer might be used to *disprove* the magician's claim.

5. If the magician's claim were false, we could run into an endless cycle in our program. If you are observing the output as it is being printed, what would be the signal that the program was not going to terminate? Modify the program so that it will automatically terminate if the magician's claim is false.

6. For variety, the magician is considering replacing instruction 4 with the following statement:

   If your number is odd, multiply by 3, subtract 1, and then carry out instruction 1 with this new number.

   Modify the program to test whether the magician will be able to make the same claim if his trick is altered as described.

7. Investigate what would happen if instruction 4 was modified to "Multiply by 5 and add 1" or "Multiply by 5 and subtract 1."

Problem 2: Optimization and Container Design

A container-manufacturing company has been contracted to design and manufacture cylindrical cans for 2-cycle lawn mower motor oil. The volume of each can is to be 0.236 liters. In order to minimize production costs, the company wishes to design a can that requires the smallest amount of metal possible. What should the dimensions of the can be?

Analysis

To ensure that all students understand the problem, take a piece of tagboard and illustrate the process by which the cans are made (fig. 21.2). Review the formula for the volume, V, of a right circular cylinder ($V = \pi r^2 h$) and derive, if necessary, a formula for the surface area, S:

$$S = 2\pi r \times h + 2\pi r^2$$
$$= 2\pi r(h + r)$$

These formulas can then be used to approximate the volume of the resulting tagboard can.

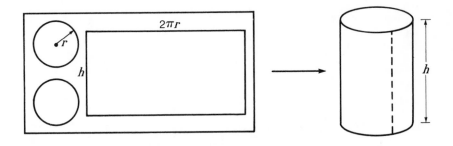

Fig. 21.2

With this background, students can be guided to a solution of the original problem. Initially they should ignore the thickness of the metal as well as the metal wasted when the parts are punched from the metal sheet. Since the completed can is to hold 0.236 liters, or 236 ml, of oil and since 1 ml = 1 cm³, the dimensions of the can can be most easily expressed in terms of centimeters. Substituting 236 ml for the volume, we have

$$236 = \pi r^2 h,$$

or equivalently

$$h = \frac{236}{(3.14159)r^2},$$

and thus the height can be found once a value for r is determined. For practical purposes we shall assume $h \geq 1$, and thus $r \leq 9$.

Program

The ideas above can be easily translated into a BASIC program that initializes and then increments the length of the radius and at each step computes and prints the corresponding height and surface area of the can. The sample run shows the results for a radius with initial length and increments of 0.5. (See fig. 21.3.)

```
10   REM     MINIMIZING SURFACE AREA
20   REM           OF A CLOSED CAN
30   REM
40   PRINT "ENTER INITIAL LENGTH OF RADIUS"
50   INPUT R1
60   PRINT
70   PRINT "RADIUS", "HEIGHT", "SURFACE AREA"
80   FOR I = 1 TO 40
90   PRINT "-";
100  NEXT I
110  PRINT
120  REM     THIS LOOP ADJUSTS THE DIMENSIONS
130  REM         AND COMPUTES THE SURFACE AREA
140  REM
150  FOR R = R1 TO 9 STEP R1
160  LET H = 236/(3.14159*R ^2)
170  LET A = 2*3.14159*R*(H + R)
180  PRINT R,H,A
190  NEXT R
200  END
```

RUN

ENTER INITIAL LENGTH OF RADIUS
?.5

RADIUS	HEIGHT	SURFACE AREA
0.5	300.485	945.571
1	75.1212	478.283
1.5	33.3872	328.904
2	18.7803	261.133
2.5	12.0194	228.07
3	8.3468	213.882
3.5	6.13234	211.826
4	4.69507	218.531
4.5	3.70969	232.123
5	3.00485	251.48
5.5	2.48335	275.884
6	2.0867	304.861
6.5	1.77802	338.08
7	1.53309	375.304
7.5	1.33549	416.362
8	1.17377	461.124
8.5	1.03974	509.489
9.5	0.927422	561.382
9		

Fig. 21.3

Looking Back/Looking Ahead

An analysis of the output will suggest that the optimal length for the radius is between 3 cm and 4 cm. To approximate this length to the nearest 0.1 cm (which is more than adequate), students can modify the program as follows:

1. Delete lines 40 and 50.
2. Replace line 150 with

150 FOR R = 3 TO 4 STEP .1.

A run of the modified program will indicate that the optimal dimensions for the oil can are $r = 3.3$ cm and $h = 6.9$ cm. Students might visit a hardware or lawn-and-garden store to check how closely the dimensions of the cans actually sold compare to those of their "ideal" can. In some cases they will be pleasantly surprised. You may wish to indicate that advanced mathematics (e.g., the arithmetic-geometric mean inequality or calculus) can show that the surface area is minimal when $h = 2r$.

Depending on the level of your students, you may wish to have them pursue one or more of these related activities:

1. Modify the original program so that it can be used to help find the optimal dimensions for a can of automotive motor oil ($V = 0.946$ L).

2. Modify the original program so that the user can enter the volume of the can whose surface area is to be minimized.

3. Write a program that will help determine the dimensions of a cylindrical can that will yield the greatest possible volume for 354 cm^2 of metal (surface area).

4. Suppose the container-manufacturing company has been supplied with 36 cm × 20 cm sheets of tin from which to manufacture open-top rectangular storage bins for small machine parts. The bins are to be made by cutting squares of the same size from each corner of a sheet and then bending up the tabs and spot-welding (fig. 21.4). If the company is to manufacture bins with the largest possible volume, what should the dimensions of the bins be?

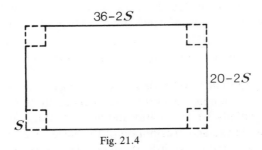

Fig. 21.4

5. Suppose the tin sheets supplied in exercise 4 were 24 cm × 30 cm. Note that these new sheets have the same area as the old ones. Modify the program for exercise 4 to use these new dimensions and compare the tabular results.

Additional minimization and maximization problems such as those discussed here can be found in any standard calculus book. This example suggests that these topics can be investigated much earlier in the mathematics curriculum if students have access to a computer and have been introduced to computer approaches to problem solving.

Problem Solving Using Simulation Methods

Problem 3. Resource Management

In 1830, there were 40 million buffalo in the western United States. By 1887 only 200 buffalo remained because of a lack of policy for resource management in this country. Today, there are approximately 26 000 buffalo, distributed as follows:

adult males	10 400	male calves	3 380
adult females	9 100	female calves	3 120

Assume the Department of the Interior is considering implementing a controlled harvesting program on these animals. They first need to formulate a policy on how many buffalo can be taken each year. It has been decided that no calves or adult females may be harvested. The department is considering allowing the harvesting of 1 000 adult males annually. What will be the effect of this policy on herd size over the next ten years?

Analysis

To solve this problem, we must first develop a model of population growth for the buffalo herd. Recent studies provide the following facts:

1. Calves are considered adult animals at two years of age.
2. For every 100 adult females at the beginning of a year, 90 calves are born during the year, of which 48 are male and 42 are female.
3. Only 50 percent of the calves reach one year of age, and of these, 60 percent reach maturity. The survival rate for adults is 0.90.

Elementary algebra can now be used to construct a mathematical model. Let us use M and F to denote the current numbers of adult males and females respectively. Initially $M = 10 400$ and $F = 9 100$. Without additional information about the age distribution of the calves, we shall assume two-thirds of the males and two-thirds of the females are newborns and denote these numbers by M1 and F1 respectively. Thus, $M1 = 2/3 \times 3 380$ and $F1 = 2/3 \times 3 120$. We shall assume the remaining calves are one year of age and denote the numbers of these males and females by M2 and F2. At the *beginning* of the period one year from now, the buffalo population can be described as follows:

1. New male calves (M1): .48F
2. New female calves (F1): .42F
3. One-year-old male calves (M2): .5M1
4. One-year-old female calves (F2): .5F1
5. Adult males (M): .90M + .6M2 − 1 000
6. Adult females (F): .90F + .6F2

This yields a herd size of M + F + M1 + F1 + M2 + F2.

Program

Now that we have a mathematical model for describing the buffalo population, we can write a BASIC program that uses the model to simulate
changes in the herd size over time—in our example, over the next ten years.
Initially one might think that the replacements for the variables suggested
above could be directly translated into BASIC statements. However, the
computer executes assignments sequentially, one by one, rather than simultaneously. As soon as the replacement suggested in (1) is executed, the old
value of M1 is lost. But it is needed for the replacement suggested in (3).
Note that replacements (3) and (4) cannot be executed first, since the old
values of M2 and F2 would not be available for use in (5) and (6). To
eliminate this problem, we make copies of the values M, F, M1, F1, M2, and
F2 using the variables T1, T2, T3, T4, T5, and T6 respectively.

The program in figure 21.5 prints a table of the distribution of the buffalo
population for the next ten years, beginning with the present population.

```
10   REM    SIMULATION PROGRAM FOR
20   REM       BUFFALO POPULATION
30   REM
40   PRINT "ENTER NUMBER OF ADULT MALES";
50   INPUT M
60   PRINT
70   PRINT "ENTER NUMBER OF ADULT FEMALES";
80   INPUT F
90   PRINT
100  PRINT "ENTER NUMBER OF MALE CALVES";
110  INPUT C1
120  PRINT
130  PRINT "ENTER NUMBER OF FEMALE CALVES";
140  INPUT C2
150  REM MODEL ASSUMES TWO-THIRDS THE CALVES
160  REM ARE NEWBORN AND THE OTHERS ARE 1 YEAR OLD
170  REM
180  LET M1 = (2/3)*C1
190  LET M2 = C1 − M1
200  LET F1 = (2/3)*C2
210  LET F2 = C2 − F1
220  PRINT
230  PRINT "            BUFFALO POPULATION DISTRIBUTION"
240  PRINT "HERD", "ADULT", "ADULT", "MALE", "FEMALE"
250  PRINT "SIZE", "MALES", "FEMALES", "CALVES", "CALVES"
```

```
260  FOR I = 1 TO 65
270  PRINT "-";
280  NEXT I
290  PRINT
300  FOR Y = 1 TO 11
310  LET S = M + F + M1 + F1 + M2 + F2
320  PRINT S,M,F,M1 + M2,F1 + F2
330  LET T1 = M
340  LET T2 = F
350  LET T3 = M1
360  LET T4 = F1
370  LET T5 = M2
380  LET T6 = F2
390  LET M = .9*T1 + .6*T5 − 1000
400  LET F = .9*T2 + .6*T6
410  LET M1 = .48*T2
420  LET F1 = .42*T2
430  LET M2 = .5*T3
440  LET F2 = .5*T4
450  NEXT Y
460  END


RUN


ENTER NUMBER OF ADULT MALES ?10400
ENTER NUMBER OF ADULT FEMALES ?9100
ENTER NUMBER OF MALE CALVES ?3380
ENTER NUMBER OF FEMALE CALVES ?3120
```

	BUFFALO POPULATION DISTRIBUTION			
HERD SIZE	ADULT MALES	ADULT FEMALES	MALE CALVES	FEMALE CALVES
26000	10400	9100	3380	3120
28206.7	9036	8814	5494.67	4862.
28392.6	7808.4	8556.6	6414.72	5612.88
27852.7	7337.96	8847.54	6222.53	5444.71
27760.	6873.38	9073.35	6300.4	5512.85
27809.7	6418.19	9244.15	6478.62	5668.79
27887.7	6050.42	9434.52	6614.79	5787.95
28037.2	5751.94	9634.31	6747.17	5903.77
28260.	5507.9	9835.64	6888.76	6027.66
28544.	5315.68	10040.8	7033.34	6154.18
28884.9	5171.46	10250.7	7180.15	6282.63

Fig. 21.5

Looking back/looking ahead

The results of our simulation indicate the effects of the proposed harvesting policy over the next ten years. This particular harvesting policy would permit the herd to continue to grow in size. The obvious advantage of simulations is that we can examine the effects of harvesting policies without actually endangering the buffalo population. The results of the simulations can be used to make logical resource-management decisions.

Related activities and problems that students might investigate include the following:

1. Could one avoid the use of the temporary variables T1–T6 by sequencing the replacements as follows: 5, 6, 3, 4, 1, 2? Explain.

2. Recall that INT(X) computes the greatest integer less than or equal to X. Using the INT function, modify the program so that the values printed are rounded to the nearest integer.

3. Modify the program so the user can enter the size of the adult male harvest and then investigate the effects of differing harvest sizes on the herd size over a ten-year period.

4. Modify the program in exercise 3 so that it also permits the harvesting of adult females and examine the effects of this new policy on herd size over a period of years.

5. Try to find a constant harvesting policy for adult males and females that will maintain the herd at its present level over the next five years.

6. *a)* Consult Johnson (1979) for information on the birth and survival rates of deer. Using this information, construct a mathematical model and simulation program for a deer population. Investigate the effects of various harvesting policies on this important resource.

   b) Read "Life or Death for the Harp Seal" in the January 1976 issue of *National Geographic.* Will this valuable marine resource survive present levels of harvesting, or will it become extinct? Write to the Canadian Minister of Fisheries for appropriate data from which you can develop a mathematical model and simulation program for investigating harvesting policies that will save the seals.

Suggestions for additional modeling activities of this sort that are ideally suited to computer simulation can be found in *The Man-Made World,* developed by the Engineering Concepts Curriculum Project (1971).

Monte Carlo Methods

Many interesting problems involving randomness can be solved using Monte Carlo methods. You might like to challenge your students with some of those that follow. Before attempting to write a simulation program, the students should develop a mathematical model that describes the situation and involves the generation of random numbers. If possible, the procedure specified by the model should first be carried out using dice, coins, or random number tables. Finally, the procedure can be translated into a BASIC program that performs several trials and summarizes the results in an appropriate form.

1. Experience indicates that 5 percent of the light bulbs produced in a certain factory are defective. If you purchase six of the bulbs, what is the probability of getting two or more defective bulbs?

2. Assume you take a ten-item true/false test by guessing at each answer. What are your chances of getting seven or more answers correct?

3. A recreational diversion consists of two towers built of three and seven blocks respectively (fig. 21.6). A tower is chosen at random—say, by the flip of a coin—and a block is removed from this tower and placed on top of the other tower. The procedure is repeated until all the blocks have been removed from one of the towers to the other. On the average, how many moves are required to move the blocks from one tower to the other?

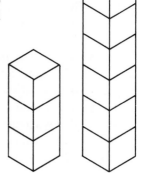

Fig. 21.6

4. In the game of craps, a pair of dice is rolled and the sum of the spots is observed. The player wins with a 7 or 11 and loses with a 2, 3, or 12 on the first roll. If any other number comes up, it becomes the player's "point" and the player continues to roll the dice. If the player's point comes up again before a 7 is thrown, the player wins; otherwise, the player loses. What is the probability of winning a single game of craps?

5. The graph of the ellipse $x^2/4 + y^2 = 1$ can be enclosed in a 2 × 4 rectangular region (fig. 21.7). If several ordered pairs are randomly generated within the rectangular region, some will fall within the ellipse and some will not. For a large number of points, the ratio of the number of points falling within the ellipse to the total number of generated points should approximate the ratio of the area of the ellipse to the area of the rectangle. Use the technique suggested here to approximate the area of the ellipse.

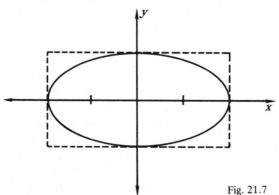

Fig. 21.7

Additional examples of problems suitable for solution by Monte Carlo methods can be found in *Teaching Statistics and Probability* (NCTM 1981).

Conclusion

The problem situations discussed in this article can be adapted for secondary school mathematics classes with students of differing levels of computer-programming ability. Variations of the programs can be written by students themselves, or the sample programs presented here can be supplied for their use after the problem has been analyzed. In either event, experiences with the roles computers can play in solving mathematical problems should increase students' understanding of computer methods as well as problem-solving processes.

Problem solving is probably the most significant learning we can direct. The increasing availability of computers, particularly low-cost microcomputers, would suggest that *all* secondary mathematics students be exposed to computer methods for attacking problems. These experiences should include opportunities to formulate mathematical models for real-life problems, design computer programs based on such models, interpret computer results, and formulate and further test conjectures based on computations.

REFERENCES

Channell, Dwayne, Carol Cody, and Christian Hirsch. "Computer Methods for Problem Solving." In *Computers in the Mathematics Classroom,* Monograph No. 17 of the Michigan Council of Teachers of Mathemtics, pp. 65–107. Lansing, Mich.: The Michigan Council, 1982.

Engineering Concepts Curriculum Project. *The Man-Made World.* New York: McGraw-Hill Book Co., 1971.

Johnson, David C. "Wildlife, Unemployment, and Insects: Mathematical Modeling in Elementary Algebra." In *Applications in School Mathematics,* 1979 Yearbook of the National Council of Teachers of Mathematics, edited by Sidney Sharron, pp. 137–48. Reston, Va.: The Council, 1979.

Kline, Morris. "A Proposal for the High School Mathematics Curriculum." *Mathematics Teacher* 59 (April 1966): 322–30.

Nievergelt, Jurg, J. Craig Farrar, and Edward M. Reingold. *Computer Approaches to Mathematical Problems.* Englewood Cliffs, N.J.: Prentice-Hall, 1974.

National Council of Teachers of Mathematics. *Teaching Statistics and Probability.* 1981 Yearbook, edited by Albert P. Schulte. Reston, Va.: The Council, 1981.

22

Mathematical Applications of an Electronic Spreadsheet

Deane E. Arganbright

THE electronic spreadsheet, with VisiCalc being the best-known version, is one of the most popular items of microcomputer software. (VisiCalc is a trademark of VisiCorp.) Its visual format and its ability to implement a user's "What if . . .?" questions in an interactive manner make it a powerful tool for economic modeling, business forecasting, and similar applications. These applications, which provide dynamic illustrations of interesting and practical uses of mathematics, by themselves make the electronic spreadsheet a useful and exciting tool for the mathematics classroom.

However, the electronic spreadsheet can also be used effectively and creatively in mathematics itself. Algorithms that are recursive, iterative, or suitable for tabular format can be implemented easily and naturally on a spreadsheet in a way that allows a user to change initial values, step sizes, and other parameters and instantly see the result. Moreover, many mathematical word problems can be set up, analyzed, and solved on a spreadsheet. Thus, the electronic spreadsheet can be used for teaching mathematical modeling and problem solving as well as for the study and implementation of algorithms. This paper presents some of the basic features of the electronic spreadsheet and shows how it can be employed in many areas of mathematics. Although the particular electronic spreadsheet illustrated here is Visi-Calc, other versions are essentially the same.

A Spreadsheet Example

Suppose that an individual wishes to make a budget projection for the coming year by constructing a model based on the following assumptions:

- Monthly income will start at $1500 and increase by 10 percent in April.
- The rate of inflation will be 1 percent a month throughout the year.
- A savings account will pay 6 percent interest compounded monthly.
- Food and automobile expenses will vary with the inflation rate.
- Mortgage expense will be constant; insurance payments will vary.

184

- Some income will be set aside for contributions (10 percent) and investment (5 percent).
- The initial savings-account balance will be $1000; surpluses will go into the account, and deficits will be made up from the account.

After making a large number of calculations based on these assumptions, the individual could construct the table, or spreadsheet, shown in figure 22.1.

Financial Model

	Jan	Feb	Mar	Apr
Income	1500	1500	1500	1650
Savings Int.	6%	6%	6%	6%
Inflation	1%	1%	1%	1%
Food	400.00	404.00	408.04	412.12
House	400.00	400.00	400.00	400.00
Auto	200.00	202.00	204.02	206.06
Invest	75.00	75.00	75.00	82.50
Contrib.	150.00	150.00	150.00	165.00
Insurance	200.00	0.00	400.00	0.00
Expenses	1425.00	1231.00	1637.06	1265.68
Savings	1080.00	1354.40	1224.11	1614.55

Fig. 22.1

After completing all the required calculations, the individual may then want to question certain of the assumptions: for example, What if the initial income is cut to $1400? What if the inflation rate drops to 0.5 percent in March? What if food expenses can be reduced by 10 percent? In order to see the effects produced by various combinations of such possible changes, it would be necessary to recalculate much of the table continually. The spreadsheet program VisiCalc was developed in the late 1970s by Bricklin and Frankston to handle efficiently similar calculations in a variety of like economic models.

A spreadsheet program uses a large matrix whose rows are identified by positive integers and columns by letters. Locations, or cells, in the matrix are identified by column and row (e.g., E3 in fig. 22.2).

Each cell can contain a descriptive label, a number, or an algebraic expression that refers to other cells in the spreadsheet. The program calculates values for the expressions in the spreadsheet using the values of the cells to which the expressions refer and displays the evaluated spreadsheet on the computer screen. A user can change the content of a particular cell by positioning the screen's cursor on that cell and entering a new value or expression. When this is done, the value of each cell in the spreadsheet is immediately recalculated, and the screen display is updated (all examples in this paper assume that calculations are carried out row by row). A user can also cause the spreadsheet to be recalculated by typing the "!" key. (This "recalculate" command will be used later.)

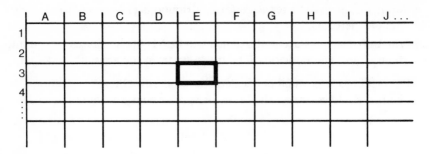

Fig. 22.2

Figure 22.3 contains a spreadsheet that incorporates the assumptions of the initial example of a budget projection and generates a display similar to figure 22.1. Note that only a few numbers are entered directly into the spreadsheet. Instead, most of the cells contain algebraic expressions that receive their values from cells they reference. For example, the food expense for March (D6) is the product, +D4*C6, of the current inflation rate (D4) and the food expense for the previous month (C6); April's income (E2) is 10 percent above March's (D2); and the total expense for January (B13) is found by using the built-in function @SUM. As a result, if any one of the entries in figure 22.3 is changed to reflect a change of the model's hypotheses, the screen display is updated instantly as the value of each cell is recalculated. For instance, if B2 is changed to 1400, the value of B10 becomes 140 and the value of E2 becomes 1540. Finally, in the construction of the spreadsheet, only a few of the expressions in figure 22.3 need be entered directly. Most (those in italics) can be entered by replicating (or repeating) expressions, a technique that greatly simplifies the construction of a large spreadsheet. The replication feature is discussed in a later section.

Financial Spreadsheet

	A	B	C	D	E
1		JAN	FEB	MAR	APR
2	INCOME	1500	+B2	+C2	1.1*D2
3	SAV INT	1.005	+B3	+C3	+D3
4	INFLAT	1.01	+B4	+C4	+D4
5					
6	FOOD	400	+C4*B6	+D4*C6	+E4*D6
7	HOUSE	400	+B7	+C7	+D7
8	AUTO	200	+C4*B8	+D4*C8	+E4*D8
9	INVEST	.05*B2	.05*C2	.05*D2	.05*E2
10	CONTRIB	.1*B2	.1*C2	.1*D2	.1*E2
11	INSURE	200		400	
12					
13	EXP	@SUM(B6...B11)	@SUM(C6...C11)	@SUM(D6...D11)	@SUM(E6...E11)
14	SAVE				
15	1000	+B3*A15+B2−B13	+C3*B15+C2−C13	+D3*C15+D2−D13	+E3*D15+E2−E13

Fig. 22.3

Thus, the electronic spreadsheet not only provides a graphic way to model the original set of assumptions of the example but also furnishes a way for the individual to obtain rapid answers to a variety of "What if . . .?" questions as the original model is modified. Similar models can be created for school or business budgets, income tax forms, enrollment projections, inventories, and sales forecasts.

Word Problems

Electronic spreadsheets can be used to supplement the study of word problems in algebra, trigonometry, and calculus. These problems can be formulated on a spreadsheet using formats commonly adopted to derive algebraic solutions. The spreadsheet's "What if . . .?" capabilities encourage trial-and-error experimentation, both in arriving at solutions and in examining the effects that changes in parameters have on the solutions. Example 1 illustrates this point.

Example 1—mixture problem: Find the mixture of two kinds of coffee, one costing $2.00 a pound and the other $3.40 a pound, which gives a blend costing $2.60 a pound.

The spreadsheet in figure 22.4 is set up so that a user enters into cell B2 a trial value for the percentage of Coffee I. The cost of the corresponding blend is calculated in C5, the component costs in B4 and C4. By varying the entry in B2, a user can observe the effect that increasing the percentage of Coffee I has on the blend's cost and ultimately discover the correct proportion. It is also possible to use the problem's algebraic solution to design a spreadsheet in which coffee costs (B3,C3) are parameters, so that the relationship between these costs and the proportions in the final blend can be studied.

Mixture Problem

	Spreadsheet				Screen Display		
	A	B	C		A	B	C
1		COFFEE I	COFFEE II	1		COFFEE I	COFFEE II
2	%--->	.2	1−B2	2	%--->	.2	.8
3	$/LB	2.00	3.40	3	$/LB	2.00	3.40
4	COST	+B2*B3	+C2*C3	4	COST	.40	2.72
5		BLEND-->	+B4+C4	5		BLEND-->	3.12

Fig. 22.4

Algorithms

The electronic spreadsheet is an excellent tool for executing mathematical algorithms. It permits a user to implement algorithms on a computer in a natural, concrete manner—essentially as they are presented in a mathematics class or text—and to be able to vary parameters easily. This section contains several representative examples as well as a description of replication.

As an illustration of the replication command, consider the spreadsheet in figure 22.5(a). (In this section the values of algebraic expressions that appear on the screen are shown in brackets.) A user can replicate the expression in cell A2 by placing the cursor on that cell and typing the command to replicate (/R in VisiCalc), followed by A2 . . . A2:A3 . . . A5, indicating that the expression in A2 is to be copied into each cell in column A from A3 to A5. A prompt then asks the user whether the location A1 in the expression $1+A1$ is to be treated as a constant, or no-change (N), location or as a relative (R) location. If N is entered, the expression $1+A1$ is copied down column A with no changes, generating the spreadsheet shown in figure 22.5(b). If R is entered, A1 is treated as a relative location, or as "the cell immediately above the current cell" (since the formula involving A1 is in cell A2), and the spreadsheet in figure 22.5(c) results.

Replicate A2...A2:A3...A5			$1+A1$ − N(o Change)			$1+A1$ − R(elative)		
	A			A			A	
1	1	[1]	1	1	[1]	1	1	[1]
2	$1+A1$	[2]	2	$1+A1$	[2]	2	$1+A1$	[2]
3			3	$1+A1$	[2]	3	$1+A2$	[3]
4			4	$1+A1$	[2]	4	$1+A3$	[4]
5			5	$1+A1$	[2]	5	$1+A4$	[5]
	(a)			(b)			(c)	

Fig. 22.5

Recursively defined sequences can be generated readily on an electronic spreadsheet. Examples of these sequences include factorials, binomial coefficients, figurate numbers, interest formulas, and terms in Euclid's algorithm for the greatest common divisor. Examples 2 and 3 illustrate such sequences.

Example 2—Fibonacci numbers: The sequence of Fibonacci numbers is defined recursively by

$$a(1)=1 \; ; \; a(2)=1 \; ; \; a(i)=a(i-1)+a(i-2) \text{ for } i>2.$$

In figure 22.6(a) the first two terms of the sequence are entered into cells A2 and A3, and the expression for the third term, $+A2+A3$, is entered into cell A4. This expression is then replicated down column A, treating A2 and A3 as relative locations. Column B contains the ratio of successive terms of the sequence and is constructed similarly. If the value of either of the first two terms is changed, a new sequence is generated (e.g., A2=1, A3=3 gives the Lucas numbers), and the spreadsheet is updated, although the limit of the sequence in column B (the golden ratio, $[1 + \sqrt{5}]/2$) remains unchanged.

Fibonacci Numbers

	A		B	
1	FIB NO		RATIO	
2	1	[1]		
3	1	[1]	+A3/A2	[1]
4	+A2+A3	[2]	+A4/A3	[2]
5	+A3+A4	[3]	+A5/A4	[1.5]
6	+A4+A5	[5]	+A6/A5	[1.667]
7	+A5+A6	[8]	+A7/A6	[1.6]
:				
19	+A17+A18	[2584]	+A19/A18	[1.618]
20	+A18+A19	[4181]	+A20/A19	[1.618]

(a)

Factorials

	A		B	
1	N		N!	
2	1	[1]	+A2	[1]
3	1+A2	[2]	+A3*B2	[2]
4	1+A3	[3]	+A4*B3	[6]
5	1+A4	[4]	+A5*B4	[24]
6	1+A5	[5]	+A6*B5	[120]

(b)

Fig. 22.6

Example 3—factorials: For a positive integer n, $n!$ is defined recursively by

$$1! = 1 \; ; \; n! = n*(n-1)! \text{ for } n>1.$$

Figure 22.6(b) describes a spreadsheet that produces $n!$. Both column A and column B are generated by replicating the expressions in row 3.

Models of exponential growth also give rise to recursive sequences (e.g., an 8 percent annual growth rate is described by $a(n+1)=1.08a(n)$ and related algebraic formulas. Example 4 allows the user to compare different rates of growth.

Example 4—compound interest: The value A of a principal P invested at an annual compound rate of $R\times100$ percent for Y years is given by $A = P(1+R)^Y$. In the spreadsheet in figure 22.7 a user can vary the initial principal (B1) and the interest rates (B3,C3).

The fields of calculus and numerical analysis are rich sources of iterative and recursive algorithms. The spreadsheet format allows a natural approach to algorithms for numerical integration and differentiation, interpolation, root location, numerical solutions of differential equations, iterative solutions of systems of equations, the evaluation of Taylor's series, and the examination of limits. Example 5 represents such an algorithm.

Example 5—root location: One method for finding the square root of a positive number s is to choose an initial approximation $a(1)$, then divide s

Compound Interest

A	B		C	
1 PRINC	100.00			
2	RATE I		RATE II	
3 YEAR	.08	[.08]	.13	[.13]
4 0	+B1	[100.00]	+B1	[100.00]
5 1	+B1*((1+B3)^A5)	[108.00]	+B1*((1+C3)^A5)	[113.00]
6 2	+B1*((1+B3)^A6)	[116.64]	+B1*((1+C3)^A6)	[127.69]
7 10	+B1*((1+B3)^A7)	[215.89]	+B1*((1+C3)^A7)	[339.46]
8 20	+B1*((1+B3)^A8)	[466.10]	+B1*((1+C3)^A8)	[1152.31]

Fig. 22.7

by $a(1)$. If the quotient is equal to $a(1)$ and the remainder is 0, then $a(1)$ is the square root; otherwise a better approximation is given by $a(2)=.5*[a(1)+(s/a(1))]$. The sequence of approximations generated in this way,

$$a(i+1)=.5[a(i)+(s/a(i))],$$

converges to the desired square root. This algorithm, illustrated in figure 22.8, is a special case of Newton's method for locating roots, using $f(x) = x^2 - s$, and also demonstrates a fixed-point algorithm, using $g(x) = .5*(x+(s/x))$.

Root of $x^2 - n$

	A	B		
1	N =	324	[324]	
2				
3	EST>	15	[15]	
4		.5*(B3+(B1/B3))	[18.3]	
5		.5*(B4+(B1/B4))	[18.002459]	
6		.5*(B5+(B1/B5))	[18]	
7		.5*(B6+(B1/B6))	[18]	

Fig. 22.8

Self and Forward Referencing

The previous examples use separate cells for each computation. It is also possible to design compact spreadsheets in which a few cells are used for all the computations and the display is updated continually through the use of the recalculate command. This is accomplished by incorporating cells that reference either themselves or others that occur later in recalculations. Figure 22.9 illustrates such self and forward referencing combined with recalculation. Note that as the spreadsheet of figure 22.9(a) is constructed, an "extra" calculation is performed: the value of $1 + A1$ is 1 when the expression is entered but immediately becomes 2 as the spreadsheet is updated.

Examples 6, 7, and 8 use self and forward referencing and recalculation. This technique is useful for reducing the number of cells employed, improv-

Spreadsheet		Screen Display				Spreadsheet			Screen Display		
	A				A		A	B			A	B
1	1+A1	original:	1	2		1	+B1	1+A1	original:	1	1	2
		recalculate:	1	3					recalculate:	1	2	3
		recalculate:	1	4					recalcuate:	1	3	4
	(a)						(b)					

Fig. 22.9

ing the screen display, visually emphasizing intermediate results, and designing spreadsheets that require user interaction.

Example 6—factorials: In Figure 22.10, the value of n is computed in A3, the value of $n!$ in B3. Cell B1 is used to initialize the computations. The Boolean @IF expression in A3 is interpreted thus: IF B1=0 THEN 1 ELSE 1+A3. While B1 is 0, 1 is entered into both A3 and B3. Once B1 is set to a nonzero value, the value of A3 is increased by 1 and the value of B3 is multiplied by the value of A3 each time the spreadsheet is recalculated.

Factorials

	Spreadsheet		Screen Display (line 3 only)			
	A	B			A	B
1	START>	0	Initial:	3	1	1
2	N	N!	Change B1 to 1:	3	2	2
3	@IF(B1=0,1,1+A3)	@IF(B1=0,1,A3*B3)	Recalculate:	3	3	6
			Recalculate:	3	4	24

Fig. 22.10

Example 7—bisection algorithm: If a function is continuous on the interval $[a,b]$ and $f(a)$ and $f(b)$ have opposite signs, that is, $f(a)f(b)<0$, then f has a root in $[a,b]$. Using this fact, the bisection algorithm generates a sequence of decreasing intervals $[a(n),b(n)]$, the midpoints of which converge to the root (Burden, Faires, and Reynolds 1981, p. 22). In figure 22.11 an initial interval is entered into A3,B3 and is copied into A4,B4 while the entry in B1 is 0. The midpoint of the interval $[A4,B4]$ is computed in C4. Once B1 is set to a nonzero value, a new interval, either $[A4,C4]$ or $[C4,B4]$, is obtained

Bisection Algorithm

	Spreadsheet			Screen Display (line 4 only)			
	A	B	C		A	B	C
1	START>	0		Initial:	4	1	2	1.5
2	LEFT	RIGHT	MID	Change B1 to 1:	4	1	1.5	1.25
3	1	2		Recalculate:	4	1.25	1.5	1.375
4	<below>	<below>	(A4+B4)/2	Recalculate:	4	1.375	1.5	1.4375

A4: @IF(B1=0,A3,@IF((A4*A4−2)*(C4*C4−2)>0,C4,A4))
B4: @IF(B1=0,B3,@IF(A4=C4,B4,C4))

Fig. 22.11

with each recalculation and entered into A4,B4. The function used in the example is $f(x) = x^2 - 2$.

The technique illustrated in examples 6 and 7 must be modified for algorithms in which expressions refer to cells from more than one line, as in example 8, since during each recalculation the values in the first line are changed before they can be used in subsequent lines.

Example 8—powers of a matrix: In figure 22.12 successive powers of a stochastic matrix (the columns are nonnegative and add to 1) are computed with each recalculation. Cell C1 is used to initialize the spreadsheet, as in the examples above. After C1 is set to a nonzero value, then with each recalculation a copy of the previously computed power is first made (rows 4,5) and then used to compute the next power (rows 7,8). A slight modification will cause only the powers 1,2,4,8,16 . . . to be generated.

Powers of a Matrix

	Spreadsheet				Typical Display		
	A	B	C		A	B	C
1	.3	.2	0	1	.3	.2	1
2	1−A1	1−B1	POWER	2	.7	.8	POWER
3				3			
4	@IF(C1=0,A1,A7)	@IF(C1=0,B1,B7)	@IF(C1=0,1,C7)	4	.23	.22	2
5	@IF(C1=0,A2,A8)	@IF(C1=0,B2,B8)		5	.77	.78	
6				6			
7	(A1*A4)+(B1*A5)	(A1*B4)+(B1*B5)	1+C4	7	.223	.222	3
8	(A2*A4+(B2*A5)	(A2*B4)+(B2*B5)		8	.777	.778	

Fig. 22.12

Conclusion

The examples above indicate some of the many possible mathematical uses of an electronic spreadsheet. In statistics, spreadsheets can be used to compute means, standard deviations, correlation coefficients, and least-squares approximations in a format that allows a user to see the effects of modifications in data (see Arganbright [1984a]). In linear algebra, spreadsheets can be used with inverses, determinants, eigenvalues, and Gaussian elimination. Other topics adaptable to the spreadsheet include synthetic division, continued fractions, modular arithmetic, number-base conversions, game theory, and linear programming (including postoptimal analysis). An extensive collection of mathematical applications of spreadsheets is presented in Arganbright (1984b).

Electronic spreadsheets also have many useful features besides the ones mentioned, including built-in mathematical functions (e.g., exponential, trigonometric, and max/min). Details on these features can be found in user's manuals, books, and magazines (see Beil [1982] and Fylstra and King [1981]).

The electronic spreadsheet has much to recommend it for classroom use. It gives students access to a widely used financial tool; its operation is easy to learn and requires no previous programming knowledge; it provides a natural way to implement algorithms on a computer that allows for interactive experimentation and modeling; and it furnishes an intuitive, concrete means to visualize mathematical algorithms and manipulations. It can be used both by teachers for classroom demonstrations and by students for projects and assignments. Its use by students may be in various modes:

- *Predesigned templates.* A basic spreadsheet illustrating an algorithm or concept is designed in advance and stored on a disk. Students load the disk, change the data and parameters, and observe the results. (Example 4)

- *Parallel adaptations.* Students design spreadsheets that parallel standard pencil-and-paper algorithms. Creating the spreadsheets becomes a productive activity in its own right, reinforcing the concepts being studied. (Examples 1 and 5)

- *Original creations.* Students devise their own techniques to create spreadsheets to model problems.

REFERENCES

Arganbright, Deane E. "The Electronic Spreadsheet and Mathematical Algorithms." *Two-Year College Mathematics Journal* (March 1984*a*).

———. *Mathematical Applications of Electronic Spreadsheets.* New York: McGraw-Hill Book Co., 1984*b*.

Beil, D. *The VisiCalc Book.* Apple ed., IBM ed. Reston, Va.: Reston Publishing Co., 1982.

Burden, R. L., J. D. Faires, and A. C. Reynolds. *Numerical Analysis.* 2d ed. Boston, Mass.: Prindle, Weber & Schmidt, 1981.

Fylstra, D., and B. Kling. *VisiCalc User's Guide for the Apple II Plus.* Sunnyvale, Calif.: Personal Software, 1981.

23

Advanced Placement Computer Science

Stephen J. Garland

T HE Advanced Placement (AP) Program is a cooperative educational endeavor of the College Board. Since many students can complete college-level studies in their secondary schools, AP represents a desire of schools and colleges to foster such experiences. Like other programs of the Board, this program is national, its policies are determined by representatives of member institutions, and its operational services are provided by the Educational Testing Service.

Advanced Placement serves three groups: *students* who wish to pursue college-level studies while they are still in secondary school, *schools* that desire to offer these opportunities, and *colleges* that wish to encourage and recognize such achievement. AP does this by providing practical descriptions of college-level courses to interested schools and the results of examinations based on these descriptions to colleges on the request of individual students. Participating colleges, in turn, grant credit or appropriate placement to students who have done well on the examinations.

The decision to include computer science among the AP offerings was made in 1981. The computer science panel cited two reasons in particular for introducing an AP computer science course: (1) a significant amount of computer-related activity in both elementary and secondary schools already existed and was on the rise; (2) the introduction of such a course would foster further development of both secondary and undergraduate curricula in computer science in much the same way that the introduction of an AP calculus course twenty-five years ago fostered new developments in the mathematics curriculum. At the secondary level, the visibility of an AP course would help guide the development of the computing curriculum at lower grade levels. And at the college level, the presence of students who had completed an AP course would give colleges an incentive to upgrade their introductory courses in keeping with curricular recommendations issued by professional societies in computing (ACM 1979; IEEE 1976).

The College Board accepted the panel's recommendations and appointed a Computer Science Development Committee, composed of representatives from secondary schools and universities, to draft a course description and

194

related materials. The board designated the 1983–84 school year as the date for having the course in place, with the first examination to be given in May 1984. The information that follows is based primarily on the contents of the course description developed by the committee (College Board 1983*a*). There is also a teacher's guide (College Board 1983*b*).

Goals of the Course

The goals of an AP computer science course are comparable to those of a year-long introductory course offered in college and university computer science departments. Thus the course covers topics that normally comprise six or more semester hours of college-level work in computer science and is based on courses that could be credited toward a computer science major. As such, an AP course is more than an introduction to programming in a specific computer language; such courses at the college level rarely occupy a full year and often carry only one or two semester hours of credit.

It is not expected that all students in an AP computer science course will major in computer science at the college level. The course serves both as an introduction for students interested in a computer science major and as a substantial service course for those who will major in other disciplines that require a significant involvement with computing.

The broad goals of the course are for the student to acquire the following skills:

- To design and implement computer-based solutions to problems in several application areas
- To recognize and use well-known algorithms and data structures
- To develop and select appropriate algorithms and data structures to solve problems
- To code fluently in a well-structured fashion using an accepted high-level language (The first offerings of the AP Computer Science Examination will require a knowledge of the Pascal language.)
- To identify the major hardware and software components of a computer system, their relationship to one another, and the roles of these components within the system
- To recognize the ethical and social implications of computer use

This course is not intended to be the sole, or even the primary, course in computing at the secondary level. Just as secondary schools offering AP calculus teach many other courses in mathematics, secondary schools may well teach other courses in computing to larger numbers of students. Though some students may be introduced to computing through an AP course, the course is intended (as are all AP courses) as a first-year college course capable of being taught in those secondary schools that choose to do so.

Prerequisites

Since secondary schools differ widely in the ways they introduce students to computing, there are no mandated computing prerequisites for an AP computer science course. Instead, the course's prerequisites include a familiarity with mathematical notation at the level of a second course in algebra, experience in problem solving, and an appreciation of the need to structure and develop a given topic in a logical manner. A knowledge of any particular mathematical notation is less important than a well-founded confidence that unfamiliar symbolism can be mastered and will eventually serve as an aid to understanding.

Mathematics courses have traditionally offered the best opportunity for secondary school students to acquire such confidence. It is important for secondary school students and their advisors to understand that any significant computer science course builds on a foundation of mathematical reasoning that should be acquired prior to attempting such a course. Therefore, a computer science course is not a substitute for the usual college-preparatory mathematics courses.

Course Content

The major emphases in an AP computer science course are programming methodology, algorithms, and data structures. These subjects are treated in the context of applications of computing. The applications demonstrate the need for particular algorithms and data structures and also provide topics for programming assignments to which students can apply their knowledge. A particular programming language is the vehicle for implementing computer-based solutions to particular problems, but the language is not the focal point of the course. Treatments of computer systems and the social implications of computing are integrated into the course.

Some comments about the major topics of the course follow; more detailed information can be found in the *Course Description* (College Board 1983*a*).

Programming methodology

Programming methodology, or, more broadly, software methodology, concerns itself with the development of high-quality software systems, that is, useful, usable, reliable, maintainable, and extensible software systems. Since most of what students learn in an AP course will be applied to the process of creating computer programs, methodologies that enhance this process are of central concern.

Good programming methodology provides the means for producing quality software in an economical and timely fashion, whether that software is for a student's own use or for use in a commercial application. Modern programming languages have done much to enhance the quality of software by facilitating modular programming, structured programming, and top-down design. Disciplined approaches to the program development process have guided programmers in making use of these facilities.

But there is more to programming methodology than a modern programming language and disciplined techniques. Programming also involves many other skills: recognizing and selecting appropriate data structures; selecting comprehensible, verifiable, and extensible algorithms over algorithms that simply minimize length of code or execution time; analyzing an algorithm for speed, space, and clarity and then making reasonable trade-offs among these factors; and knowing when and how to document a program. In short, programming in its truest sense encompasses the entire subject matter of an AP course.

Programming methodology, then, is not meant to be taught as a self-contained package at the beginning of the course but rather to be integrated throughout. Methodology is taught and assimilated best, not by dictum, but by repeated applications of general principles to the construction and analysis of sample programs.

Features of programming languages

For students to practice principles of programming methodology and to apply their knowledge of algorithms and data structures to actual problems, it is essential that they spend a substantial amount of time writing computer programs. For this activity to be fruitful, students must be able, or must learn, to program well in a language that supports good methodology and facilitates the implementation of specific algorithms and data structures.

The development committee spent much time discussing which programming languages offered adequate support for an AP course not only in terms of their structures for organizing data, the flow of control, and the modular structure of a program but also in terms of their suitability for various applications. It also debated whether or not to constrain the choice of a language, for it recognized that although good programmers can write well in almost any language, certain languages encourage good programming habits more than others. And it considered the support for teaching computer science in conjunction with a particular language that is available through existing textbooks and computer systems commonly used in secondary schools.

As a result of its deliberations, and after surveying secondary schools for their reactions to its options, the committee selected Pascal as the sole language to be used in the AP examination. In making this selection, the committee was fully aware that, in isolated instances, the goals of an AP computer science course might be accomplished in an existing secondary school computing environment with a language other than Pascal. However, the chances seemed too great that a large number of secondary schools would try to teach such a course with a less-than-adequate language, with disastrous consequences for their students taking the examination. Consequently, the committee decided that it could better serve the interests of these students, nationwide, who take the examination by being possibly too restrictive than by being too permissive.

Because BASIC now enjoys such wide use at the secondary school level, some comments are probably in order to explain why the commonly available versions of BASIC are not acceptable vehicles for an AP course. (Schools may still choose, however, to use BASIC in other, more elementary courses.) Most versions of BASIC have many inadequacies, and no attempt will be made to illustrate them all. Two examples should give the flavor of the kind of shortcomings that permeate this language. In Pascal it is easy to distinguish a loop

$$\textbf{while } x < y \textbf{ do } x := 2 * x$$

that doubles a quantity x repeatedly until the resulting quantity either equals or exceeds a quantity $y,$ from a conditional

$$\textbf{if } x < y \textbf{ then } x := 2 * x$$

that simply doubles x once if it is less than y and does nothing otherwise. In standard BASIC, these constructs are expressed indirectly and are harder to distinguish. For example,

```
100 IF X > = Y THEN 130
110 LET X = 2*X
120 GOTO 100
130 . . .
```

performs the same task as the Pascal loop displayed above. But it differs from

```
100 IF X > = Y THEN 130
110 LET X = 2*X
130 . . .
```

only by the omission of one out of four lines, and from

```
100 IF X > = Y THEN 130
110 LET X = 2*X
120 GOTO 130
130 . . .
```

only be what might appear to be a superficial change in one out of four lines. Yet the latter two constructs perform a different task entirely, namely, the same task accomplished by the Pascal **if-then** statement displayed above. The experienced teacher of BASIC can easily imagine further complexities that would be introduced if there were other GOTO statements leading out of the body of the loop. The ease with which one may write a program that is totally incomprehensible, even to its author, quickly becomes obvious in such situations.

As a second and more important example, some versions of BASIC widely available on personal computers have no mechanism for passing parameters to subroutines; this severely limits their usefulness for modular programming. Some dialects of BASIC do possess features akin to those of Pascal, but those dialects having at least the minimum features required for an AP course are not commonly available and are not supported by published texts.

Data types and structures

Data types and structures enable programmers to represent and organize the information manipulated by a program. They range from simple structures (e.g., numbers and characters) included as primitive data types within a programming language to more intricate structures that are either provided by the programming language (e.g., arrays and strings) or constructed by the programmer (e.g., linked lists, stacks, queues, and binary trees) with the aid of more primitive language features.

A treatment of data types and structures cannot be divorced from a study of the algorithms used to manipulate various structures or from a study of applications in which various structures prove useful. Hence material in this section, like the material in the first, is meant to be integrated throughout the course.

Algorithms

Algorithms and algorithmic thinking are at the heart of computer science. To program is to implement algorithms. Searching and sorting algorithms, in particular, yields excellent examples for use in studying the design, development, and analysis of algorithms in general. These algorithms arise naturally in applications concerning information storage and retrieval, and they can be used to illustrate the variety of ways in which one may approach a single problem. Furthermore, this variety of approaches helps illustrate that the efficiency of a particular algorithm is determined more by its approach to a problem than by the ingenuity of the way it is coded. For example, students often take great delight in inventing quite sophisticated "improvements" to intrinsically inefficient algorithms (such as the bubble sort), whereas a different approach altogether (such as repeated merging) is usually required to achieve a true gain in efficiency.

Another feature of an AP course is the emphasis it places on recursive algorithms, that is, algorithms that solve a problem by reducing it to simpler instances of the same problem. Such algorithms constitute a powerful and important means for manipulating data structures and solving problems. All too often they are treated as an advanced or optional topic; instead, students should be well grounded in their use.

Though nonnumerical algorithms play a more central role in computer science today than numerical ones, students should still learn how the latter can be used to approximate solutions to problems that are difficult or impossible to solve analytically (such as finding roots of functions) or that require more advanced mathematical knowledge than they possess. They should also learn how to compute statistical measures such as the mean, variance, mode, and median.

Applications of computing

Though it should not be the intent of an AP computer science course to develop expertise in particular application areas, students should nonetheless become familiar with typical applications in several areas, and they should appreciate how a knowledge of computer science can be brought to bear on problems in these areas. Simple examples of applications related to text processing, simulation and modeling, data analysis and management, system software, graphics, and games are studied in order to acquaint students with the general nature of these applications and to introduce the data structures and algorithms inherent in these applications.

Computer systems

A first course in computer science should give students a working knowledge of the major hardware and software components of computer systems. At this level only a general understanding of the purposes and characteristics of these components is required; a more detailed understanding of how such components operate or how they are constructed should be left to later courses.

Social implications

Given the tremendous impact computers and computing have on almost every aspect of society, it is important that intelligent and responsible attitudes about computers be developed as early as possible. Students in a first course should come to regard computer systems, not as opponents to be bested by whatever wiles they themselves possess, but rather as powerful tools whose nature and use they in part determine.

Attitudes are acquired, not taught. Hence the ethical and social implications of computing should be stressed whenever an opportunity is available. For example, privacy and individual rights can be discussed in the context of the responsible student use of a shared computer system. However, no systematic coverage of these implications is required.

The Examination

A three-hour examination seeks to determine how well a student has mastered the concepts and techniques of the course. The examination consists of (1) a multiple-choice section and (2) a free-response section requiring students to demonstrate their ability to design, write, and document programs and procedures. Such topics as programming methodology may be tested less thoroughly by the multiple-choice questions and more thoroughly by the free-response questions.

The student's knowledge of computer systems and the social implications of computing will usually be tested in questions on other topics, although occasionally single questions in either section will be devoted exclusively to these topics.

For purposes of calculating the grade for the examination, the two sections are given equal weight. Since the examination is designed for full coverage of the subject matter, it is not expected that many students will be able to answer correctly all the questions in either the multiple-choice section or the free-response section.

Conclusion

In summary, an AP computer science course seeks to develop its students' abilities to use computing in powerful, intelligent, and responsible ways. The mastery of programming methodology, algorithms, and data structures raises a student's ability to program considerably above the novice level. An acquaintance with major applications of computing suggests both where and how that programming ability can be put to use. And an awareness of the ramifications of computer use contributes to the ability of society at large to make responsible and intelligent use of computing.

REFERENCES

Association for Computing Machinery. "Curriculum '78: Recommendations for the Undergraduate Program in Computer Science." *Communications of the Association for Computing Machinery* 22 (March 1979): 147–66.

College Board. *Advanced Placement Course Description: Computer Science.* Princeton, N.J.: The Board, 1983*a*. (The College Board, Advanced Placement Program, Box 2899, Princeton, NJ 08541.)

———. *Teacher's Guide to Advanced Placement Courses in Computer Science.* Princeton, N.J.: The Board, 1983*b*. (The College Board, Advanced Placement Program, Box 2899, Princeton, NJ 08541.)

IEEE (Institute of Electrical and Electronics Engineers) Computer Society. *A Curriculum in Computer Science and Engineering* (IEEE Computer Science Education Committee Report, revision 1). New York: The Society, 1976.

24

Microcomputer Arithmetic

John Blattner

$\mathbf{I}$ READ a number of microcomputer magazines, in which it is common to find a reader's letter—or even an article—expressing consternation at the "fact" that this or that small computer has a bug in its arithmetic processing routines. I also own one of the popular makes of home computer, and I can testify that even mathematicians will sometimes get anomalous results if they pay insufficient attention to the realities of computer arithmetic. For example, my computer thinks that the twelfth power of 2 is 4095.998, a value that is perfectly acceptable for most applications. However, in my particular application, I was using this value to extract (by means of the logical AND) a bit from a word, and instead of getting bit 12, I got all the bits 0 through 11. (That's because the AND operator requires integer operands, and so quite naturally truncated the 4095.998 to 4095.)

Here's a problem you can try on your computer: Find the solutions of the quadratic equation

$$x^2 - 10\,000\,000x + 10\,000\,000 = 0.$$

When I do this using the quadratic formula, my computer says that the roots are 10 000 000 and 1.5. The first answer is quite good, but the second is poor, since the actual root is about 0.999 999 9. (I have a second, inexpensive computer that does nine-digit arithmetic; it gives 0.962 89 for the second root, which is still off by nearly 4 percent.) I'll leave it as an exercise for you to make your machine compute this second root with six-digit precision. But here is a hint: Rationalize the numerator of the standard quadratic formula to obtain an alternative form that is sometimes useful.

These examples tell us that if we are to prosper as mathematicians in the brave new world of microcomputers, we need to know how these machines do arithmetic. And, of course, what we will be talking about is not the hardware but the software, for that is where the arithmetic is. In particular, it is the BASIC interpreter that concerns us here. (You may write an occasional program in a highbrow language like Pascal or an exotic one like FORTH, but most of what follows will still apply.)

Integers

Clearly the problems in the examples above stem from the loss of precision that is unavoidable in approximate arithmetic. Since a computer is a digital machine, it is capable of carrying out integer arithmetic exactly. But microcomputer BASIC interpreters put a severe limit on the size of the integers we can use. You know what this limit is: All integer constants and variables must take values between −32768 and +32767, inclusive. This constraint was a sensible compromise when memory was expensive and BASIC was a language for the uninitiated. Today, memory costs next to nothing, and there are small businesses that do all their computing in BASIC; integers, however, are still prisoners in 16-bit cells.

Each microcomputer integer is held in one 16-bit word in two's complement form. Perhaps the easiest way for a mathematician to understand the meaning of "two's complement form" is to think of the system of microcomputer integers as being the ordinary integers taken modulo 65536 (2 to the power of 16), except that as a system of distinct representatives we use the integers from −32768 to 32767 rather than those from 0 to 65535. Thus there are as many negative microcomputer integers as nonnegative ones, and the negative integers all have their most significant bit (bit 15) set to 1. As an example, an integer that to you or me would look like 50000 is considered by the BASIC interpreter to be −15536. (It's modulo 65536, remember.)

All this tells us how integers are represented in a microcomputer's memory; it does not tell us how the BASIC interpreter performs arithmetic operations on these integers. Addition and subtraction are easy, since the microprocessor itself provides at least an 8-bit modular addition and subtraction. The BASIC interpreter may have to cascade two of these operations, with a carry from the low-order to the high-order byte, but that is simple. (A Z-80- or 8088-based microcomputer performs 16-bit modular additions and subtractions directly.) Besides the actual addition or subtraction, the BASIC interpreter also has to test for overflow. For example, if you add 20 000 to 30 000, you want the answer to be 50 000, but 50 000 is not an integer in our system; so, what you end up with is an overflow error.

Multiplication is much harder, since neither the 6502 nor the X-80 microprocessor (two of the most commonly used chips in today's machines) has a hardware multiply instruction. Therefore, multiplication has to be programmed bit by bit in a manner quite similar to the algorithm that is taught in the elementary schools. (The similarity would be greater if, to borrow from Tom Lehrer, our species had developed only one finger on each hand.) Again, the BASIC interpreter must check for overflow, and overflow is much more likely to occur in multiplication than in addition. (If your BASIC interpreter performs floating-point arithmetic, an overflow in an integer operation may cause the result to be converted to floating-point representation, in which case the overflow doesn't show up unless you try to store this result as an integer.)

Division is the hardest of all, and true integer division with a quotient and remainder is not even attempted by the BASIC interpreter. Instead, the operands are converted to floating-point representation (if the interpreter has that capability), the quotient is calculated, and the rounded result is converted back to an integer. Besides overflow, the interpreter must also check for division by zero.

If we could have whatever we wanted in our BASIC interpreters, what would we ask for in the way of integer arithmetic? Bigger integers — at least 24 bits, and preferably 32. (Thirty-two bits would permit integers as large as two billion.) Also, a MOD function (which returns only the remainder of an integer division) is nearly essential for many of the things we would like to do. You have undoubtedly programmed your own MOD function many times; a MOD function built into the interpreter would be much faster and easier to use. As long as we're at it, we might as well wish for a true integer division that returns both quotient and remainder. But until the professional software houses and the computer manufacturers find out how much we need these capabilities, we'll either have to program our own or do without.

Floating-Point Numbers

The microcomputer representation of a floating-point number has two parts: a characteristic (usually called "exponent") and a mantissa. The characteristic occupies one (8-bit) byte, and its actual value is 128 greater than the power of 2 that needs to be multiplied by the mantissa to produce the value of the number represented. As examples, a characteristic of 140 signifies that the mantissa is to be multiplied by 4096 (2 to the power of 12) to give the value of the floating-point number, whereas a characteristic of 120 means that the mantissa is to be multiplied by 2 to the power of -8. (One hundred forty is 12 greater than 128, and 120 is 8 less than 128.) A characteristic of zero is used to represent the number zero, and the value of the mantissa is immaterial in this instance.

The mantissa of a floating-point number occupies several bytes. My microcomputer has two floating-point formats: *single precision*, in which mantissas are three bytes (24 bits) long, and *double precision*, in which mantissas have a length of seven bytes. Thus, my single-precision operations yield about 6½ decimal digits of precision, and my double-precision operations are good to about 16 decimal digits. Your computer may have only one floating-point format, in which case mantissas are probably four bytes long (about 9 decimal digits). Clearly, the precision to which a microcomputer can work is determined by the length of the mantissas of its floating-point numbers. To achieve the maximum precision this length permits, it is necessary to represent every floating-point number in normalized form, which is simply that form in which the most significant bit of the most significant byte of the mantissa is a 1. To normalize a nonnormalized number requires shifting the mantissa left and concomitantly reducing the characteristic. To see this idea more clearly, consider the following example, in which the analogous operation is performed on a decimal number in floating-point notation:

$$0.000025 \times 10^6 = 0.25 \times 10^2.$$

As a standard convention, the binary point of a microcomputer floating-point number is assumed always to be immediately to the left of the most significant bit of the mantissa. Thus the mantissa of any number except zero has a value between ½ and 1.

How are negative numbers distinguished from positive numbers? Where is the sign bit kept? Reread the description of floating-point representation above, and you still won't have the answer to this question. The sign bit is "stolen" from the mantissa. Since the most significant bit of the mantissa must be a 1, it doesn't matter whether the actual value of that bit is 0 or 1. Think about that. Have you ever been frustrated by a compiler or an operating system that could tell you exactly what character you should have typed instead of the one that you did type but couldn't simply accept the input with the mistyped character? It's the same here: if the microcomputer software knows that there must be a 1 bit in the most significant position in the mantissa, then it doesn't really matter whether that bit is there or not. Thus the bit can be used for the sign of the floating-point number—0 for positive, 1 for negative. There is no two's complement form here; a negative number looks exactly like its positive counterpart except for the sign bit.

As with integers, a knowledge of floating-point representation does not tell us how the BASIC interpreter does arithmetic with these numbers. But it's not difficult to surmise how the operations are performed. Addition and subtraction are considerably more difficult for floating-point numbers than they are for integers. One mantissa must be shifted right until the characteristics are equal (the "binary points are lined up") before the two operands can be added or subtracted. Then the result must be normalized and rounded. Clearly, a normalization that requires a left shift of several bits entails a corresponding loss of precision in the answer. This merely reflects the fact that when two approximate numbers of nearly the same value are subtracted, the difference has less precision than either the minuend or the subtrahend. Multiplication is accomplished by a multiplication of the two mantissas and an addition of the two characteristics, followed by normalization and rounding. Division is similar, except that the mantissas are divided and the characteristics are subtracted. (Actually, the handling of the characteristics in multiplication and division is slightly more complicated than just described. In multiplication, after the characteristics are added, 128 must be subtracted from the total, because each characteristic contained an excess

128. Similarly, in division, 128 must be added to the difference of the characteristics.) In all arithmetic operations, there is also the problem of taking into account the signs of the numbers on the one hand while on the other hand pretending that the sign bit is always a 1.

A floating-point operation may be aborted because of an attempted division by zero, or because of an overflow, which is the production of a number whose characteristic is greater than 255—too large to fit into a single byte. It is also possible for a floating-point operation to "underflow," which means that the result is a number whose characteristic is smaller than 1. The computer will not tell you when an operation underflows. It will simply report the result as zero, which is inelegant but not horrible.

Floating-point operations may be employed to perform integer arithmetic with higher precision than is possible with the integer operations. In my microcomputer, for instance, the 24-bit mantissas permit exact addition, subtraction, and multiplication of integers from $-16\,777\,215$ to $+16\,777\,215$, though not all the digits can be easily printed. With the double-precision routines, I can handle integers to sixteen digits. However, I still do not have a true integer division, and the computer gives no warning of inexactness that results from exceeding the limits just mentioned.

Since the arithmetic operations in a microcomputer are software functions, achieving higher precision in calculations can be very costly in time. For example, double-precision division in my machine is ten times as slow as single-precision division. The converse is also true: lower-precision arithmetic could be much faster. I have written a complete floating-point package for my microcomputer that works with numbers with 16 bits of mantissa. I use this package for drawing graphs, for which the precision of about $4\frac{1}{2}$ digits is entirely adequate. My 16-bit floating-point operations (including a larger catalog of functions than that offered by the BASIC interpreter) are five times as fast as the 24-bit operations that are built into BASIC. As a result, my computer can typically calculate and plot a thousand points in under ten seconds.

Functions

If your computer's BASIC interpreter provides floating-point arithmetic, then it also offers a number of standard functions, such as SIN, COS, LOG, and EXP. In the past twenty-five years, the confluence of powerful mathematics and powerful computers has resulted in the development of superb algorithms for approximating these standard functions. Your microcomputer incorporates not just the best methods known but practically the best methods possible for the computation of function values.

The calculation of function values is based on approximations by polynomial or rational functions. A best algorithm is one that requires the least amount of computation to approximate a given function on a given interval with a given precision. If your principal experience with approximation has been with Taylor polynomials, you might be amazed at how efficient a best rational function approximation can be. In more concrete terms, you might be amazed at how little work your microcomputer has to do to calculate the values of the LOG function, for example. No doubt you have been impressed by the speed with which it churns out such numbers.

Any approximation can only work well on a finite interval, and some of the most efficient approximations are designed for very narrow intervals. Yet we require usable values of our functions for widely varying values of the arguments. How can our needs be matched to the severe restrictions of the approximation algorithms? The answer lies in the fact that each elementary function has some special properties that allow all its values to be derived from its values over some rather small interval. As examples, let us consider the SIN, COS, and EXP functions.

The SIN function is periodic with period 2π. It follows that the values of SIN(X) for $-\pi \leq X \leq \pi$ determine all other values of SIN. SIN is also an odd function, which means that $SIN(-X) = -SIN(X)$. Therefore, the values of SIN(X) for $0 \leq X \leq \pi$ determine all other values. There is an addition formula for SIN, and one special case of this formula shows that $SIN(\pi - X) = SIN(X)$. Thus, the values of SIN(X) for $0 \leq X \leq \pi/2$ determine all other values.

Now, COS is the cofunction of SIN, which means that $SIN(\pi/2 - X) = COS(X)$, from which it follows that the values of SIN(X) and COS(X) for $0 \leq X \leq \pi/4$ determine all other values of both functions. It is sufficient, therefore, to have approximation algorithms for SIN and COS that work for $0 \leq X \leq \pi/4$. Of course, some clever conversions of the argument have to be performed, but these take little time. The interval $0 \leq X \leq \pi/4$ is by no means the smallest possible; we've hardly begun to exploit the special properties of SIN and COS in reducing to this interval. (A theorem in the theory of functions of a complex variable guarantees that any interval would suffice, no matter how small.) Very high precision algorithms may use much smaller intervals. Clearly, though, there is a trade-off: Smaller intervals require more conversions of the argument. An efficient algorithm has to balance these conflicting demands along with the precision requirement.

The fundamental property of EXP is that $EXP(X + Y) = EXP(X)*EXP(Y)$. This equation already suggests a method of reducing arguments. However, the key idea in the calculation of EXP is to relate this function to the exponential with base two function. It isn't hard to guess why this is a useful thing to do—2 is the base of the computer's number system. The magic equation, then, is

$$EXP(X) = 2^{X*LOG_2(e)}.$$

$LOG_2(e)$ is thus a constant that is as necessary for the calculation of EXP as the constant π is for the calculation of SIN. I won't give the details of the argument conversions that are required here; suffice it to say that the

208 COMPUTERS IN MATHEMATICS EDUCATION

computation of EXP can easily be reduced to the calculation of its values for $0 \leq X \leq 1/2$. (Again, even smaller intervals are possible at the cost of more elaborate conversions.)

From the tone of this section, you might judge that I am well satisfied with the present state of microcomputer function calculations. That is only partly true. Existing algorithms are excellent, and their software implementations are very good. What is needed, however, is to have these algorithms implemented in hardware for higher precision and far greater speed. At least one auxiliary microprocessor does exist that contains a full implementation of integer and floating-point arithmetic and all elementary functions; this chip is about a thousand times as fast as present microcomputer software and also works to considerably higher precision. With sufficient demand, the cost of such a processor could undoubtedly be brought low enough to justify its inclusion in the standard microcomputer. Real-time computer graphics could then be a reality.

We could also use a few more functions in our standard set, such as SEC and ASN (arcsine). It would be nice if the exponentiation operator were given a bit more flexibility. Here's an experiment to try: Have your computer calculate 10*10 a thousand times and record the time. Now have it calculate 10 to the power of 2 a thousand times. Why did the second calculation take so much longer? Because the microcomputer calculates the square of 10 as EXP(2*LOG(10)), and this is much slower than 10*10. A better exponentiation routine would see that the exponent is an integer and perform the faster calculation. Also, a better exponentiation routine would permit you to calculate -3 to the power of 1/3, for example; your present microcomputer software will not.

Evaluation of Expressions

Having seen how the microcomputer performs its calculations, we can now look at how it parlays these operations into the evaluation of a full-blown arithmetic expression. The key elements of expression evaluation are (1) attention to the priority of operators, (2) the use of a stack for holding operands and operators, and (3) recursion. The BASIC interpreter in your microcomputer has an evaluation subroutine whose performance depends heavily on all these ideas. Let's call this subroutine EVAL and see how it works with this expression:

$$X*(A*SIN(Y)+B*COS(Y))$$

EVAL scans the expression from left to right. In the example, X is the first symbol encountered, and EVAL will fetch the value of X from variable storage and place it in a special location in memory that I shall call the accumulator. Next, the * (multiplication) operator is put into an operator register for later use; it cannot be used yet, because there is only one operand so far. The left parenthesis (next character) causes EVAL to stack the accumulator (which contains the value of X) and the operator register (which contains *). (The stack is a first-in, first-out list of memory cells maintained by the microprocessor.) After the stacking operations, EVAL calls itself (recursion) to evaluate the expression between this left parenthesis and the closing right parenthesis, which is the final character of the expression.

EVAL (having been entered recursively) now transfers the value of A to the accumulator and puts the following * into the operator register. Encountering the SIN (a function), EVAL stacks the accumulator and the operator register and calls the routine that calculates $SIN(Y)$; the result of this computation is placed in the accumulator. (Note that if $SIN(Y)$ had been $SIN(2*Y)$, EVAL would have been called again in the calculation of the argument of the SIN.)

Next, EVAL sees the +, whereupon it pops the * off the stack and compares the priorities of the two operators. Since * has the higher priority, its implied operation (multiplication) is now performed on the operands in the accumulator and at the top of the stack. The result of this multiplication $(A*SIN(Y)$ is left in the accumulator, and the + is still in the operator register. (Observe that the value of A has been removed from the stack.)

Next, the symbol B causes EVAL to stack the accumulator and the operator register and to transfer the value of B from variable storage to the accumulator. The next operator (*) has higher priority than the stacked +, so + is kept pending on the stack. The COS (a function) causes the accumulator and operator register to be stacked while $COS(Y)$ is evaluated and placed in the accumulator. The right parenthesis following $COS(Y)$ signals EVAL to complete all calculations back to the preceding left parenthesis (that is, all the calculations that are pending in this recursive call to EVAL). Thus the stack is popped to produce the *, multiplication is performed on $COS(Y)$ (in the accumulator) and B (on the stack), with the result going into the accumulator. The stack is popped again, producing the +, and addition is then performed on $B*COS(Y)$ (in the accumulator) and $A*SIN(Y)$ (on the stack), with the result going into the accumulator. This terminates EVAL's actions in the recursive call, and the return is to EVAL at the next level (where it was first entered). EVAL at this level completes its job by popping the stack (to produce *) and then multiplying $A*SIN(Y)+B*COS(Y)$ (in the accumulator) by X (on the stack), leaving the final result in the accumulator.

If this description seems hard to follow, try it with pencil in hand, writing down at each step what goes into, or comes out of, the stack, the accumulator, and the operator register. The entire operation is so efficient that it is well worth the effort required to understand its workings. If it still seems like legerdemain, be assured that it does to me too. It is truly computer magic.

Conclusions

By obtaining a working knowledge of microcomputer arithmetic, we can free ourselves from a total dependence on the software houses that write our BASIC interpreters. Then, if we have a special requirement for greater speed, higher precision, or a greater range of representation of numbers, we have a fighting chance of producing the specialized programs needed to achieve these ends. If enough of us can identify common needs beyond the reach of present hardware or software and if we can make these needs known to manufacturers, designers, and professional programmers, then we have a good chance of getting the equipment and programs that we deserve.

25

Computer Diagnosis of Algorithmic Errors

Betty Travis

ADULTS who are unable to perform basic arithmetic operations appear in every developmental mathematics course that community colleges offer. Many schools have established remedial programs to meet the needs of the large number of learning disabled students. These programs often suffer, however, because few teachers know how to carry them out effectively. Teachers are often unfamiliar with basic diagnostic techniques and cannot construct specific, individualized remediation plans. The community college teacher needs an instructional tool that can diagnose learning difficulties, prescribe appropriate remediation, provide successful experiences, and handle the tremendous amount of data involved in such an undertaking. This essay describes a research study in which the problems of diagnosis and remediation were addressed through computer technology.

The purpose of the study was to describe and apply a theoretical scheme whereby computers could be used to diagnose and prescribe remediation for whole-number multiplication difficulties of students in community college developmental mathematics courses. A computer program in BASIC was developed to analyze students' answers to ten specially constructed whole-number multiplication exercises. On the basis of that analysis, the program identified errors and partitioned them into a classification system. This yielded diagnostic information from which a remediation plan was developed that proposed to correct the particular deficiency.

Related Research

Since the early 1960s, investigators have been developing computer applications for educational purposes. One of the most important applications has been in the area of computer-assisted instruction (CAI), in which material can be sequenced according to individual progress. Intelligent CAI (ICAI) programs use the strengths and weaknesses of each student to provide diagnostic information so that incorrect answers produce a branching to remedial material (Barr and Atkinson 1975; Brown 1977; Koffman and Blount 1975).

211

BUGGY (Brown and Burton 1978) is one example of an ICAI program for diagnosing basic arithmetic skills. BUGGY has procedures for explaining the reason underlying an arithmetic error instead of simply identifying a mistake in the calculation. The natural expansion and continuation of the BUGGY research is the development of an ICAI tutor, which after recognizing student inaccuracies can diagnose particular errors and provide appropriate remediation.

The Study

This study on the multiplication of whole numbers had two components, the development and evaluation of a computer-based diagnostic program and the development and use of a CAI remediation package.

For the remediation component of the ICAI instructional packets, the design was based on the student's errors identified by the diagnostic routine. The design of the diagnostic program was derived from a logical analysis of the choice and execution of the mathematical operations implicit in the task. Based on a review of the literature as well as previous experience in working with several hundred remedial adult students, the program was written to identify and classify specific errors in whole-number multiplication:

- Errors with an internal zero in one of the multipliers
- Errors with a unit zero
- Incorrect addition of partial products
- Errors in basic multiplication facts

Certain assumptions were made concerning the possibilities of errors. One assumption was that errors in basic multiplication facts would occur with a higher probability when both factors fell in the range of 6 through 9. Another assumption was that a correct answer would not result from two or more combined errors, that is, that no two errors would cancel each other.

Ten problems were constructed for which the probability of certain types of errors or combinations of errors would be high. Table 25.1 illustrates the correspondence between the problems and the errors.

The sample problem in figure 25.1 illustrates the error analysis proce-

$$
\begin{array}{r}
409 \\
\times\ 285 \\
\hline
2045 \\
3272 \\
818\ \ \\
\hline
116565
\end{array}
$$

Fig. 25.1

TABLE 25.1
Classification System

Problem	Carry	Internal zero	Unit zero	Place value	Addition of partial products	Basic Facts			
						6	7	8	9
62 × 13				x	x				
53 × 18	x			x	x				
38 × 27	x			x	x		x	x	
307 × 49	x	x		x	x		x		x
519 × 40	x		x	x					
112 × 234				x	x				
319 × 124	x			x	x				
795 × 463	x			x	x	x	x		x
409 × 285	x	x		x	x			x	x
843 × 560	x		x	x	x	x		x	

dure. An analysis of this problem for possible error sources revealed the following:

- *Carrying.* It was necessary to carry to an internal zero in finding all three partial products.
- *Basic multiplication facts.* In finding the second partial product, the most probable error was in the basic fact 8×9.
- *Addition of partial products.*
- *Position of partial products.*

These sources of possible errors were monitored by inspecting the partial products. An incorrect answer to the multiplication problem caused the program to ask for the first partial product. An error in the first partial product was considered to result from carrying to an internal zero, since no addition or positioning errors were likely at this stage and no basic fact errors (as previously defined) were likely. The program then branched to the second partial product. If this was incorrect, an analysis was made of the student's response to the question "$8 \times 9 = ?$" If the response was incorrect, then a basic fact error was catalogued along with a notation of $\times 8$ and $\times 9$, accumulating a total count for each of the factors. An examination was then made of the third partial product. If this value was incorrect, then carrying to an internal zero was catalogued as the cause of the error; if it was correct, the program considered further possible causes: (1) incorrect addition of the partial products and (2) incorrect position of the partial products. This analysis was accomplished by examining the student's answer with a predetermined value, which for this problem was 116 000. Since the greatest difference between 116 565 (the correct answer) and 116 000 (the value in computer memory) is 565, it was determined that if the difference between a student's answer and the correct answer was greater than 565, the incorrect position of partial products was the most probable cause of the error. If the difference between the student's answer and the prescribed value of 116 000 was less than 565, then the addition of partial products was catalogued as the cause of the error. The computer was programmed to handle eighteen different error combinations for this one problem.

The study was a developmental effort aimed at demonstrating the feasibility of the computer as a tool useful in the diagnosis and remediation of learning difficulties in mathematics. Although the major components of the work included clarifying the theoretical position, developing the software, and assessing the effectiveness of the procedure, this essay focuses on the analysis and interpretation of data that investigates the efficacy of the computer as a diagnostic tool.

Procedures

In the selected setting for the study, the normal treatment of the addition and subtraction of whole numbers preceded the treatment of multiplication. The study began with the multiplication of whole numbers using the diagnostic and prescriptive approach and made use of computer facilities in the mathematics laboratory at the college. Each student in the study group made an appointment with the instructor for thirty minutes with an IBM 370 computer terminal. The students were first given a worksheet of ten multiplication problems, randomly sequenced for each student. After completing the problems using paper and pencil, the students, under the supervision of the instructor, activated the computer program. The BASIC program driving the terminal displayed initial greetings and introductory statements. Each problem was then presented, with time allowed for the student to respond. The program recorded all responses; students with no errors, or one, were not given remediation. In such cases, the computer automatically ended the program with concluding remarks. Two mistakes resulted in the program requesting partial products for the incorrect answers. By examining these partial products and answers, the computer classified the various types of errors. This made possible an error profile, such as a specific difficulty with basic multiplication facts. For errors that occurred more than once, remediation was given on the computer. Remediation time varied from one to thirty minutes. After the remediation effort students were asked to solve additional problems. If they were still unable to multiply correctly, they were instructed individually by the teacher. All the needed information concerning the diagnosis of errors was available from a computer printout.

Analysis of data

The effectiveness of the computer as a diagnostic tool was investigated through a program verification design. A comparison was made between the errors as diagnosed by the computer program and the errors as diagnosed by the investigator. An examination of each student's worksheet was made and an error list was compiled. A *hit* was scored for the computer for each particular error on the investigator list that was also computer diagnosed; otherwise a *miss* was catalogued. If the computer identified an "error" that wasn't really an error, students received remediation anyway. It was felt that they would benefit from remediation even if they did not have a deficiency; thus an overdiagnosis of errors by the program was not considered a miss.

Several students had a total error count of 1. In such an instance the computer did not attempt any diagnostic procedures but automatically ended the program under the assumption that the student had demonstrated adequate competency in working through the algorithm but had made a careless mistake. When errors of this type were omitted in the analysis, the percentage of accurate diagnostic successes by the computer was 72 percent. However, further investigation suggested that the true adequacy of the computer's diagnostic features was not totally revealed by the preceding analysis.

In some instances the investigator diagnosed a basic fact error when the computer did not. This occurred because students could correct such an error during their interaction with the computer. At the point when a basic fact error was suspected, the computer asked the student for the answer to the fact in question (such as 8×9). If the student answered correctly, the computer did not record an error, even though the paper-and-pencil work was incorrect.

In the reanalysis of the data, a miss was not recorded if the student was able to correct basic fact errors in the evaluation process with the computer. Using this restriction, an accuracy index of 100 percent was achieved.

Furthermore, on a multiplication retention test administered approximately a month later, the group of students who received computer diagnosis and remediation exhibited a mean score of 90.42 percent correct, reflecting a gain of 23 percent from a pretest. A control group taught in a regular classroom over the same time period achieved a mean of 84.09 percent, reflecting a corresponding gain of 11 percent (Travis 1978, p. 91).

Conclusions

The study investigated the use of computer technology in the diagnosis and remediation of learning difficulties of community college developmental students. Data analysis indicated that the diagnostic and remedial plan was an effective procedure for identifying and rectifying student errors in the multiplication process. In this study the computer was shown to be an effective classroom diagnostic instrument, capable of not only identifying error origins with adequate and acceptable precision but also remedying the errors. The efficacy of the computer as a tool for diagnosis and remedial instruction was demonstrated.

216 · COMPUTERS IN MATHEMATICS EDUCATION

REFERENCES

Barr, Avron, and Richard C. Atkinson. "Adaptive Instructional Strategies." In *Structural Models of Thinking and Learning,* edited by Hans Spada and W. F. Kempf. Bern: Hans Huber, 1977.

Brown, John Seely. "Uses of Artificial Intelligence and Advanced Computer Technology in Education." In *Computers and Communications: Implications for Education,* edited by Robert J. Seidel and Martin Rubin, pp. 253–70. New York: Academic Press, 1977.

Brown, John Seely, and Richard R. Burton. "Diagnostic Models for Procedural Bugs in Basic Mathematical Skills." *Cognitive Science* 2 (1978): 155–92.

Koffman, Elliot B., and Sumner E. Blount. "Artificial Intelligence and Automatic Programming in CAI." *Artificial Intelligence* 6 (1975): 215–34.

Reisman, Fredericka K. *A Guide to the Diagnostic Teaching of Arithmetic.* Columbus, Ohio: Charles E. Merrill Publishing Co., 1972.

Travis, Betty P. "The Diagnosis and Remediation of Learning Difficulties of Community College Developmental Mathematics Students Using Computer Technology." Unpublished doctoral dissertation, University of Texas, 1978.

26

Diagnostic Uses of Computers in Precalculus Mathematics

Ronald H. Wenger
Morris W. Brooks

Success in using technology to improve the learning of mathematics has been seriously limited by the lack of suitable research and diagnostic tools for modeling the student's behavior or relevant mathematical knowledge. Significantly more attention is now being paid to such topics.

One of the most intriguing efforts to combine cognitive science and the use of technology in the mathematics context is provided by the Buggy and DEBUGGY research and computer programs of Brown and Burton (1978). Although this work dealt with addition and subtraction of integers, several of the objectives and byproducts of their work, and certainly its general philosophy, provide useful metaphors for work on higher-level mathematics topics such as algebra and elementary functions.

There is a risk, however, that the "trees and the forest" will be confused if attention is paid solely to the many observed "bugs" or errors in algebraic technique. Such potential confusion has two important consequences. First, it has serious implications for what mathematics is taught and how it is taught (e.g., excessive emphasis on low-level algorithmic techniques). Second, even with the speed and power of computers, there is no way to effectively develop intelligent tutors that identify and treat nearly all combinations of the errors that, theoretically, could occur—even if this were pedagogically wise.

Examples of hypotheses that have such unifying potential, that are testable, and that have important pedagogical implications are provided by the work of Matz (1980, 1982). One example of a higher-level means of organizing observations of patterns is familiar to anyone who has taught algebra. She examines the ubiquitous "linearity errors," $f(a + b) \rightarrow f(a) + f(b)$, which occur in settings involving many types of operators and functions; for example,

This work is supported, in part, by National Science Foundation CAUSE Grant Number SER 8103901.

217

$$(a + b)^n \rightarrow a^n + b^n$$

or

$$\log (a + b) \rightarrow \log (a) + \log (b).$$

Matz hypothesizes that many errors are the result of reasonable, although unsuccessful, attempts to adapt previously acquired knowledge to a new situation. She indicates that many common errors are the result of one of two processes: the inappropriate use of a known rule *as is* in a new situation; and the incorrect adaptation of a known rule to solve a new problem.

Activities under way in the Mathematical Sciences Teaching and Learning Center at the University of Delaware demonstrate the ways the DEBUGGY metaphor and work such as that of Matz (1980, 1982) are being used to analyze and enhance mathematics learning. The computer is playing a critical role in virtually all aspects of the project: developing and testing hypotheses, analyzing protocols, and developing and delivering diagnostic and instructional materials.

Our work is similar to several mathematics projects discussed in *Intelligent Tutoring Systems* (ITSs) (Sleeman and Brown 1982) in that we are "performing detailed (protocol) analyses of the learning, mislearning and teaching processes" and "developing theoretical constructs for use within ITSs that may also be psychologically insightful" (p. 3). However, we are not currently developing artificial intelligence techniques that employ such theoretical constructs to improve ITSs. Thus, unlike the necessarily more narrowly focused ITS projects discussed by Sleeman and Brown, we are examining student performance and developing computer-based materials for a full course.

The Problem Data Base and MIPP

For more than five years we have been examining the performance of approximately 1200 students each year (primarily college freshmen) on paper-based, multiple-choice tests in a one-semester precalculus course. This course rapidly reviews intermediate algebra and then emphasizes the concept of function. Functions are illustrated by introducing the usual classes: polynomial, rational, exponential, trigonometric, and their inverses (e.g., radicals, logarithms, and inverse trigonometric functions).

Nearly all the problems from these tests and their solutions (presented in mathematically relevant "chunks") are currently available to students on the university's instructional computing system. The problems can be accessed by the student from menus structured in any way we choose. Currently, for example, the student may see any of the following groups of problems:

- Those associated with each section of the current textbook

- Mixed lists that indicate the variety of sections covered to date in the course
- Those that more than 50 percent of the students got wrong on a test
- Those that are essentially conceptual
- Those that are essentially algorithmic
- Those that require conversion from narrative descriptions of settings or phenomena into a formal mathematical form

This software, called the Mathematics Interactive Problem Package (MIPP), supports several forms of instruction and research. The MIPP permits seven modes of questioning (including judging a wide variety of student-entered algebraic expressions), several contingency levels of questioning, and branching to appropriate instructional resources. It makes full use of high resolution graphics and sophisticated routines for entering and judging mathematical responses. MIPP is used by several hundred individuals each semester. (Further information on MIPP can be obtained from the Mathematical Sciences Teaching and Learning Center at the University of Delaware, Newark, DE 19711.)

In addition to this flexible, menu-driven selection of problems, MIPP is used extensively in an interactive computer-based testing mode. However, the diagnostic process is of greatest interest. It is described below.

The Diagnostic Process

One of the center's main development goals is a collection of computer-based materials to serve as an "intelligent" diagnostic system to provide instructional support for students studying algebra and precalculus topics. In a highly simplified form, the main ingredients of our system consist of an appropriate computer-based environment for student interaction, an individual student model that changes dynamically as a result of the interaction between student and computer, and a diagnostic mechanism that examines the current state of the student model and makes decisions to offer helpful feedback, additional instruction, or advice on seeking help from an instructor.

In its current implementation, the environment consists of a series of interactive computer-based "diagnostic tests" administered at regular intervals throughout a course. Eventually, a less formal environment may be possible. Response data collected in these tests form the raw material for the student model. Initial data are supplied by the results of placement tests, currently administered to all entering freshmen. The students' behavior on all diagnostic problems is stored and their profile is updated. After students complete a diagnostic test, they are presented with a collection of diagnostic messages based on the current state of their model. The messages vary in complexity. Some may be simple statements describing the probable cause of an error with a solution to the problem; others are fairly elaborate, interactive, short tutorial segments. When appropriate, a student may be branched to more extended computer-based tutorials, drills, or other forms of instructional materials.

The screen displays in figures 26.1–9 illustrate, for example, one step in our effort to improve students' ability to solve complex, multistep problems. We believe such ability will be enhanced if their attention is drawn to the importance of learning to distinguish the roles of heuristics, strategies, and relevant procedures for solving such problems. These static screen copies inadequately represent many different displays—each of which dynamically draws the student's attention to an important feature of the message.

```
Using interval notation, describe the complete
solution set for  x - 1  ≤ 2.
                  ──────
                  2x + 1

Your answer, [-1, ∞] was incorrect.
For example, what is the value of  x - 1
                                   ──────
                                   2x + 1
when x = -3/4?    1 no

                No, the answer is 7/2.  Note that
                7/2 is not less than 2.


        Press NEXT to continue.
```

Fig. 26.1

```
Using interval notation, describe the complete
solution set for  x - 1  ≤ 2.
                  ──────
                  2x + 1

You appear to have made a common but serious error.
Namely,

 x - 1
 ────── ≤ 2  ===> x - 1 ≤ 2(2x + 1).
 2x + 1

Before multiplying both sides of an inequality
(unlike equations) by an expression, you must determine
when the expression is positive and when negative.

You could use this technique if you treated separate
cases:
        Press NEXT to continue.
```

Fig. 26.2

Using interval notation, describe the complete
solution set for $\dfrac{x-1}{2x+1} \le 2$.

Case 1. $2x + 1 > \emptyset$: Find all numbers x so that
$2x+1>\emptyset$ and $x-1 \le 2(2x+1)$.

Case 2. $2x + 1 < \emptyset$: Find all numbers x so that
$2x+1<\emptyset$ and $x-1 \ge 2(2x+1)$.

Then the solution set for $\dfrac{x-1}{2x+1} \le 2$ consists of
the solution set for Case 1 together with the
solution set for Case 2.

Another approach to this problem is described
below:

Press NEXT to continue.

Fig. 26.3

Now consider the following problem: $\dfrac{2x - \frac{1}{x}}{1 - x} > -1$.

A reliable strategy often useful for solving inequality
problems involving quotients or products of expressions
containing the variable but with a zero on neither side
is to:

Chunk 1 - Transform the problem into an equivalent one with
a zero on one side;
Chunk 2 - Transform the non-zero side into a product or
quotient (if possible) to obtain an equivalent
form such as $\square/\triangle \le \emptyset$ (or $\ge \emptyset$) or $\square\triangle \le \emptyset$
(or $\ge \emptyset$);
Chunk 3 - Solve the form $\square/\triangle \le \emptyset$ or $\square\triangle \le \emptyset$ by:
Step 1. Understanding the "Critical Idea";
(e.g., that a number is a solution
to $\square/\triangle > \emptyset$ if and only if it causes
the expressions in $\square$ and $\triangle$ to have the
same sign.)
Step 2. Understanding the purpose of and master-
ing the use of "Procedure for Analyzing
Signs.";
Step 3. "Checking endpoints."
Press NEXT to return to the problem.

Fig. 26.4

Using interval notation, describe the complete
solution set for $\dfrac{x-1}{2x+1} \le 2$.

CHUNK 1:
Convert to
inequality
with a zero
on one side.

$\dfrac{x-1}{2x+1} \le 2$ is equivalent to

$\dfrac{x-1}{2x+1} - 2 \le \emptyset$ (since a ≤ b is true iff
                     and only if a+c ≤ b+c).

CHUNK 2:
Convert the
inequality to
one of the
standard forms:
□∆ ≥ ∅   or
□／∆ ≤ ∅ (or
> ∅ or < ∅).

This is equivalent to $\dfrac{x-1-2(2x+1)}{2x+1} \le \emptyset$

or $\dfrac{-3x-3}{2x+1} \le \emptyset$ or, if you wish to

eliminate some minus signs, multiply both
sides by -1/3.

$\dfrac{x+1}{2x+1} \ge \emptyset$ which is of the form □／∆ ≥ ∅

which can be solved as follows.

Press NEXT to continue.

Fig. 26.5

Using interval notation, describe the complete
solution set for $\dfrac{x-1}{2x+1} \le 2$.

Critical
Idea

A value of x is a solution to □／∆ ≥ ∅,

(here $\dfrac{x+1}{2x+1} \ge \emptyset$), if and only if this
value of x causes the values of the
expressions in □ and ∆ (here x+1 and 2x+1)
to have the same signs.

How can all such values of x be determined?
Try a few values, then press NEXT.

Fig. 26.6

Using interval notation, describe the complete
solution set for $\dfrac{x-1}{2x+1} \le 2$.

Solve the
inequality in
standard form.

x + 1 changes sign at x = -1 and 2x + 1
changes sign at x = -1/2. A chart helps
show for what values of x these expressions
have the same signs.

IMPORTANT PROCEDURE

```
x + 1      - - - - + + + + + +
2x + 1     - - - - - - + + + +
          ---------+----+-------->
                  -1  -1/2   Ø
```

Thus, for $x < -1$ or for $x > -1/2$ the signs of the two expressions $x + 1$ and $2x + 1$ are the same so their quotient is positive, as desired.

Press NEXT to continue.

Fig. 26.7

Using interval notation, describe the complete solution set for $\frac{x - 1}{2x + 1} \leq 2$.

Always check to see if endpoints of intervals are contained in the solution set.

Are the endpoints, $x = -1$ and $x = -1/2$, solutions to $\frac{x + 1}{2x + 1} \geq 0$? Simply substitute each of these values to check.

$x = -1$ is a solution but $x = -1/2$ is not since there the denominator is zero.

The solution set in interval notation is:
$(-\infty, -1] \cup (-1/2, \infty)$.

Press NEXT to continue.

Fig. 26.8

Now consider the following problem: $\frac{2x - 1}{1 - x} > -1$.

On paper develop your work for each "chunk" in the strategy.

Press HELP to review the basic strategy for identifying and solving problems of this type, or

press NEXT when you wish to compare your work with ours.

Fig. 26.9

To construct an effective diagnostic system, we must first determine the most important forms of difficulty—strategic, conceptual, and algorithmic—that students exhibit with precalculus topics, especially those that persist after additional instruction. It is essential that this be done in such a way that we constantly search for patterns or phenomena, such as Matz's conjectures, that help explain large numbers of specific "bugs." Such phenomena not only suggest how the technology might be used to improve instruction but also have implications for the curriculum as well as the content and objectives of textbooks. Several examples of these phenomena and their implications are discussed later.

The analysis and treatment of conceptual and algorithmic errors is even more complex than it might at first appear. Their *stability* for a given student and how they are *linked* with other errors are critical both to their diagnosis and to the objectives and design of instructional materials. Some examples of the linearity type will clarify these terms and help to illustrate this point.

By the "stability" of a form of mathematical behavior we mean the tendency of the individual to behave the same way not only whenever a problem of essentially the same type is encountered but also whenever the same technique is needed in a somewhat different context. Consider, for example,

$$(2x + 1)^2 \text{ and } (x^{1/2} + x^{-1/2})^2.$$

While dealing with the multiplication of polynomials, it is possible to convince students to avoid the linearity error

$$(2x + 1)^2 \rightarrow 4x^2 + 1.$$

But two weeks later, after fractional exponents are introduced, the students' attention is focused on these new procedures and often they decide that

$$(x^{1/2} + x^{-1/2})^2 \rightarrow x + x^{-1}$$

is a valid transformation. Our diagnostic process anticipates such behavior and provides appropriate feedback to students who exhibit it.

The problems below (and many others in which such techniques are required) are seeded through several diagnostic tests. These problems are designed to trap linearity errors like those in figure 26.10. The pervasiveness of these errors is indicated by the percentages of students making them in one sample.

    a. $(x^3 - x^{-3})^2 \rightarrow x^6 - x^{-6}$ (57% of 474 students)

    b. $(2^{-1} + 3^{-1})^{-1} \rightarrow 5$ (66% of 546)

    c. $(4a^2 + 4b^2)^{1/2} \rightarrow 2a + 2b$ (69% of 586)

Fig. 26.10

We use "linkage" to describe the tendency of students who make one kind of algebraic error to also make another. To what extent, for example, is a student who makes the error

$$\text{A.} \quad 8^{1/3}9^{-1/2} \rightarrow (72)^{-1/6}$$

(done by 474 students, 34 percent of approximately 2400 entering freshman on our placement examination) likely to also make one of the linearity errors above. Table 26.1 displays the percentages of students making the linearity errors (a), (b), and (c) and all combinations of them. It also shows the corresponding percentages for the subpopulations of students who made error A and who answered the question involving error A correctly. These data, taken from a total sample of 2444 students, suggest that linkage is a relatively common phenomenon.

TABLE 26.1
Relationship of Linearity Errors a, b, and c
to Type A Errors

Student population	No a, b, or c errors	a only	b only	c only	a & b only	a & c only	b & c only	a, b, & c
Percentage of full group	20.4	7.9	8.4	11.7	9.8	8.3	12.1	21.4
Percentage making TypeA error	9.8	5.3	7.7	12.0	9.2	9.5	15.6	31.0
Percentage not making Type A error	33.6	10.5	9.1	10.6	10.5	6.2	8.0	11.6

How are the phenomena referred to loosely here as stability and linkage related to mathematics learning in general and to the use of information technology in particular? We believe that a number of fundamental forms of algebraic behavior may underlie large percentages of the myriad specific and chaotic difficulties or symptoms that students exhibit. The challenge is to attempt to unbundle these complex relationships. This requires methodologies and additional hypotheses, such as those of Matz, which can be used to categorize and clarify the relationships among apparently disparate patterns of behavior. The task also requires access to large numbers of observations over a suitably large domain of mathematical topics.

To assist us in these difficult tasks we have developed software that allows us to scan the entire file of response data for all students and all the diagnostic tests. Within seconds, all students whose responses satisfy an arbitrary pattern of interest are identified, and a list of their names and sections is written on the screen. This capability greatly simplifies the collection of the additional information or written work from relevant subpopulations of students needed to test and refine hypotheses and instructional materials. This software not only supports our research interests but provides a valuable tool for developing individualized instructional units. It also allows instructors instantly to identify groups of students who need special attention.

Selecting and Refining Diagnostic Items

A description of the "genealogy" of a relatively simple diagnostic problem will help illustrate the role of the computer and the close relationship between instructional development and research required of this undertaking. Space permits only one example, but the center has developed approximately two hundred similar ones covering most of the mathematical topics treated in the full precalculus course. The specific diagnostic problems used in the process are probes to help discover deeper, more important, and more powerful information about how individuals process information of the kinds treated in algebra. This point should be kept in mind as examples of the concrete stages in their development are sketched below.

Stage 1

The distribution of responses to multiple-choice questions administered on paper-based examinations in previous semesters is analyzed. The purpose of this analysis is to identify patterns of behavior on a topic that appear to be common to large numbers of students and somewhat independent of the instructor.

For example, consider the following problem. As we shall see, the initial multiple-choice answer options presented to the students were not very consistent with the actual errors students tended to make when they worked out their own answers.

$$ - [x - 2(x - 1)] = \underline{\quad ? \quad} $$

$a)$ $x - 2(x - 1)$ $\quad b)$ $x + 2(x - 1)$ $\quad c)$ $x - 2$ $\quad d)$ $2 - x$
(17%)   (33%)   (41%)   (9%)

The percentage of students choosing each answer option is shown in parentheses. That only 41 percent of these freshman students chose the correct answer (c) was of interest to us, especially since approximately 92 percent of those taking the course had had two years of high school algebra and had averaged more than three years of high school mathematics. Clearly, large numbers of students continue to have difficulty with negative signs and grouping when *nested* brackets are present. Why?

The students' written work during these examinations is collected. However, written work associated with multiple-choice tests often gives relatively little, or misleading, information about students' approaches to the problem. Such a record does not, for example, give clear information about the other answers students arrived at or what steps were used.

Stage 2

Prototype questions selected in the first stage are presented to students in free-response format on the computer as part of the diagnostic process. Students enter their responses using the keyset, and all responses are collected and stored in computer files. Software we have developed analyzes these files and creates frequency tallies of all mathematically equivalent responses. These tallies are then used to revise the variety of responses that are anticipated and for which the computer will provide tutorial feedback. Figure 26.11 shows the major portion of the tally of responses collected (on line) for the free-response version of our sample problem during the spring semester of 1983.

Partial List of Answers Entered

Problem: $-[x - 2(1 - x)] = $ _____?_____ $\qquad N = 171$

Number	Answer	Hypotheses	Formulation to be monitored
$N=91$	$2-3x$	Correct	
$N=13$	$x+2$	$\rightarrow -x+2(1-x)$	"Change nearly all signs inside"
$N=3$	$x-2$	$\rightarrow -x+2(-1+x)$	"Change all signs inside"
$N=3$	1	$\rightarrow -x+2(-1+x)=$ $\rightarrow -x+2-1+x$	"Change all signs inside" and additional error.
$N=2$	x^2+3x+2	$\rightarrow [x+2(x+1)]$ $\rightarrow (x+2)(x+1)$	"Change all negative signs to positive." and parsing error.
$N=1$	$3x+2$	$\rightarrow x+2(1+x)$	"Change all negative signs to positive."
$N=7$	x^2-3x+2	$\rightarrow -[(x-2)(1-x)]$	Parsing error
$N=2$	x^2+3x+2	as above	Parsing error
$N=7$	There were seven other quadratic responses in various forms		Parsing error
$N=17$	$2-2x$	$\rightarrow -[x-2+x]$	$-A(B-C)\rightarrow -AB+C$
$N=2$	$2x-2$	$\rightarrow -[x-2+x]$ $\rightarrow [2x-2]$	$-A(B-C)\rightarrow -AB+C$ and forgot last step.
$N=5$	2	$\rightarrow -[x-2-x]$	$-A(B-C)\rightarrow -AB-C$
$N=5$	$3x-2$	$\rightarrow -[3x-2]=$ $\rightarrow 3x-2$	Did subtasks in brackets but forgot last step.
$N=3$	$2-x$	$\rightarrow x+2(1-x)$	$-[A-B]\rightarrow A+B$

Fig. 26.11

In addition to this gross statistical analysis, off-line protocols of solutions are developed. Students are asked to work the problem on formatted paper. A carbon copy of their work is collected before they see or enter answers on the computer. This written work is then carefully analyzed to determine—

- all strategies (correct and incorrect) that students used in attempting to solve the problem;
- all answers they arrived at and their logic for each;
- what follow-up questions or problems might be used to effectively and efficiently reduce or eliminate inaccurate diagnoses of a strategy (this will be useful for the on-line diagnostics, since the software supports

highly interactive contingency-driven questioning and tutorial activity within the "message" assigned to a specific student);

- the *levels* and kinds of mathematical behavior for which additional forms of instruction are needed (both on and off computers).

Stage 3

A final version of the problem is incorporated into the diagnostic process. Based on the analysis of written work, corresponding diagnostic feedback messages are implemented. The messages often take the form of short tutorials and may be highly interactive. Often, the messages begin by seeking to confirm the accuracy of the diagnosis and may use additional questioning to determine more accurately the cause of the error. For each such message the students are asked (by computer) whether the analysis of their difficulty seemed accurate. These data are also used to determine when important elements in the table of possible difficulties seem to be missing.

What were the results when the problem $- [x - 2(1 - x)]$ was processed in this way? This one problem is used to identify several forms of troublesome mathematical behavior. These are summarized in figure 26.11. In addition to the difficulty with the distributive property, the following patterns illustrate several themes of importance to the curriculum and to pedagogy.

  a. "Change all (or nearly all) the signs inside" (and variations); for example:
  $$-[x - 2(1 - x)] \rightarrow -x + 2(1 + x)$$

  b. "Parsing errors" (and variations); for example:
  $$-[x - 2(1 - x)] \rightarrow -[(x - 2)(1 - x)]$$

The form in *a* is an excellent illustration of Matz's hypotheses. These errors are efforts by students to generalize a procedure that works fine for expressions involving only one set of brackets but fails when students attempt to apply it in settings involving nested sets of brackets. Very few of these forms of the answer were anticipated in the initial design of this as a multiple-choice test problem. None of the parsing errors were anticipated.

Thus, to use the computer effectively one need not (and perhaps should not) attempt to anticipate *all* incorrect answers for a diagnostic problem— but rather should use the problem to develop initial hypotheses about each student's understanding of its *important* algebraic features (e.g., those in the column labeled hypotheses of fig. 26.11). Then the diagnostic messages to which an individual is branched uses the student's particular error as an opportunity to discuss the more general features or concepts. Examining the student's performance history and the information we are acquiring concerning stability and linkages can increase the efficiency and accuracy of the diagnosis.

Another important distinction made by Matz (1982) concerns two ways of interpreting rules: pattern replacement and schemata. Students using the former tend to see an algebraic expression as a "character string" without noticing important patterns or relevant substrings within it. Matz states that "more sophisticated problem solvers view patterns as descriptions of 'expression trees' and match pattern literals to subexpressions, e.g., substituting '3 + x' for 'x' in some pattern" (1982, p. 28). The student's ability to discern relevant patterns or "chunks" in an algebraic expression is very important to success with algebraic technique.

Consider the role of pattern recognition in the solution of our example problem.

$$- [x - 2(1 - x)] = - [x - A] \text{ with } A = 2(1 - x)$$
$$= - x + A \text{ (using the procedure they already know)}$$
$$= - x + 2(1 - x)$$

It may well be that students making the "change all the signs inside" errors have not yet developed the algebraic maturity required to "chunk" or make the substitutions that permit one to perceive a given algebraic expression in a variety of ways. This conjecture is important to the diagnostic process. If it is correct, this problem can also help identify students who require help on this fundamental skill.

The task of helping students acquire the extremely important ability to perceive an algebraic expression in a variety of ways may well be easier to teach dynamically with the help of computers than by using a more static text-based mode.

Implications for Teaching and the Design of Text-based Materials

Several important questions concerning the curriculum are illustrated by our example problem. How many problems of the form $-(a + b)$ should students do, using their procedure that works only for a single set of brackets, before realizing that their procedure breaks down when working problems having expressions with nested brackets such as those of the form $- [a - (b + c)]$? It appears that it may actually be quite detrimental to delay this important step.

Observations of the mathematics performance of our matriculating freshmen motivated our inspection of the lists of exercises in one of the popular algebra texts (Dolciani et al. 1980). To what extent did the lists of exercises help the student or teacher identify this particular bug! That examination illustrates how easy it is for a student to complete at least a year's study of algebra with such a faulty procedure still intact. Problems on negating bracketed numerical expressions first occur on page 40. Not until page 103 do students encounter nested brackets. Only five problems in the text, scattered across three sections, might cause a student to realize that the "change all the signs" procedure no longer applies. The point is not to be critical of that particular text nor to emphasize the importance of this particular mathematical skill. We simply wish to illustrate the value of the longitudinal information we are obtaining on students' preparation in algebra and elementary functions to the study of mathematics learning and instruction.

The information obtained from the kind of analysis described here can be used to make the computer-based diagnostic materials significantly more robust in terms of the varieties of patterns of errant behavior they identify and treat. Large percentages of the students who do these problems incorrectly have the particular reasons for their difficulty explained *and* have their attention drawn to related conceptual or algorithmic errors they may be making.

Dissemination

The mathematics topics in precalculus are common to courses in universities and in high schools. One of the center's highest priorities is to see that the results of our research and the materials we develop are made available to schools. The development of Pascal programs to deliver on microcomputers portions of the software that is found to work especially well on the university's mainframe system is already under way.

BIBLIOGRAPHY

Brown, John S., and Richard Burton. "Diagnostic Models for Procedural Bugs in Basic Mathematical Skills." *Cognitive Science* 2 (1978): 155–92.

Carry, L. R., Clayton Lewis, and J. E. Bernard. *Psychology of Equation Solving: An Information Processing Study.* Austin, Tex.: Department of Curriculum and Instruction, University of Texas at Austin, 1978.

Davis, Robert B. "Some New Directions for Research in Mathematics Education: Cognitive Science Conceptualizations." Paper presented in the Begle Symposium at the Fourth International Congress on Mathematics Education, Berkeley, Calif., 1980.

Davis, Robert, E. Jockusch, and C. McKnight. "Cognitive Processes in Learning Algebra." *Journal of Children's Mathematical Behaviour* 2 (1978): 1.

Davis, Randall, and D. B. Lenat. *Knowledge-based Systems in Artificial Intelligence.* New York: McGraw-Hill, 1982.

Dolciani, Mary, W. Wooten, R. Sorgenfrey, and R. Brown. *Algebra: Structure and Method, Book 1.* Boston: Houghton Mifflin Co., 1980.

Greeno, J. G. "Cognitive Objectives of Instruction: Theory of Knowledge for Solving Problems and Answering Questions." In *Cognition and Instruction,* edited by D. Klahr. Hillsdale, N.J.: Lawrence Erlbaum Associates, 1976.

———. "Understanding and Procedural Knowledge in Mathematics Education." *Educational Psychologist* 12 (1978): 262–83.

Kimball, R. "A Self-improving Tutor for Symbolic Integration." In *Intelligent Tutoring Systems,* edited by D. Sleeman and J. S. Brown. London: Academic Press, 1982.

Lachman, R., J. Lachman, and E. Butterfield. *Cognitive Psychology and Information Processing: An Introduction.* Hillsdale, N.J.: Lawrence Erlbaum Associates, 1979.

Matz, Marilyn. "Towards a Process Model for High School Algebra Errors." In *Intelligent Tutoring Systems,* edited by D. Sleeman and J. S. Brown. London: Academic Press, 1982.

————. "Towards a Computational Model of Algebraic Competence." Master's thesis, M.I.T., 1980.

Newell, A., and H. A. Simon. *Human Problem Solving.* Englewood Cliffs, N.J.: Prentice-Hall, 1972.

Resnick, L., and Wendy W. Ford. *Psychology of Mathematics for Instruction.* Hillsdale, N.J.: Lawrence Erlbaum Associates, 1981.

Sleeman, D. H., and J. S. Brown, eds. *Intelligent Tutoring Systems.* London: Academic Press, 1982.

Sleeman, Derek H. "A Rule-directed Modeling System." *Learning,* in press.

VanLehn, Kurt. "Bugs Are Not Enough: Empirical Studies of Bugs, Impasses, and Repairs in Procedural Skills." Cognitive and Instructional Sciences Series Report CIS-11. Palo Alto, Calif.: Xerox Research Center, 1981.

27

Computers in the Classroom:
A Selected Bibliography

Louise S. Grinstein
Brenda Michaels

Within the past decade materials have proliferated dealing with the impact of computers on education in general as well as on mathematics education in particular. Teachers who were trained before the technological revolution are often unprepared to evaluate the choices; they can be overwhelmed by the quantity and quality of hardware and software that is available. This bibliography was compiled to help the classroom teacher make order out of this seemingly chaotic situation.

The material is presented alphabetically by author and is divided into two sections: journal articles and books. No reference materials predating 1975 are included. A coding system will help the teacher locate materials relative to a particular hardware, software, or mathematical content. In general, the code consists of three entries separated by slashes: the first designates mathematical content, the second, programming language, and the third, teaching level. For instance, an entry of **(Algebra/B/S)** indicates a reference that pertains to the teaching of algebra, involves the use of microcomputers coded in BASIC, and is geared to the secondary level.

The following table summarizes the coding.

Code

2d Entry	3d Entry
Computer Language	**Teaching Level**
A - APL	**E** - K–6
B - BASIC	**J** - 7–9
F - FORTRAN	**S** - 10–12
L - Logo	**T** - 13–14

NA - Category Not Applicable

V - Various (more than two descriptors fit)

The authors would like to express their appreciation to Marilyn N. Suydam for her extensive contributions to an earlier version of this article.

Since technological development is in a state of flux, teachers should also investigate the following additional sources:

- Bibliographies and reviews of books and other media appearing as regular features in such journals as the *Arithmetic Teacher, Mathematics Teacher, Mathematics and Computer Education, Mathematics Magazine, American Mathematical Monthly, Sigcue Bulletin,* and *Journal of Computers in Mathematics and Science Teaching.*

- General indexes of books and journal articles such as ERIC, *Microcomputer Index,* and *Reader's Guide to Periodical Literature.* However, coverage in these sources is not limited to mathematics or mathematics education.

- On-line information retrieval systems such as Lockheed's DIALOG, which use data bases or computerized information banks. These can be accessed by computer terminal and telephone link. Many indexes, such as ERIC and *Microcomputer Index,* are now available on line.

- Organizations that publish ongoing updates on technological advances in mathematics education. A selected list of these appears in Appendix 1. NCTM publishes the *Guide to Resources in Instructional Computing* (first edition prepared by Mary Kay Corbitt), with up-to-date references and sources of use to the mathematics educator.

Journal Articles

(Journal information is given in Appendix 2.)

(Analytic geometry/B/S,T) Aieta, Joseph F. "Getting to the Roots of the Problem." *Mathematics Teacher* 71 (May 1978): 414–17.
Demonstrates how a computer can be used to investigate analytic geometry problems. A BASIC program is given for finding the equations for a pair of parabolas that intersect in exactly three points.

(NA/NA/NA) Anderson, Ronald E., Daniel L. Klassen, and David C. Johnson. "In Defense of a Comprehensive View of Computer Literacy—a Reply to Luehrmann." *Mathematics Teacher* 74 (Dec. 1981): 687–90.
A rebuttal to the Luehrmann paper (see below).

(Number theory/NA/T) Anderson, Sabra S. "Computer-assisted Creativity in Number Theory." *Mathematics and Computer Education* 16 (Spring 1982): 91–94.
Describes a proposed number theory course to be taught using the "discovery" approach. Computer projects are introduced to gather information about concepts to be studied. Conjectures are made on the basis of the data collected. These are then followed by theorem formulations and proofs. Several computer projects are detailed.

(Analytic geometry/B/S,T) Baker, Thomas B. "Sketching the Curve $y = x \sin (1/x)$." *Mathematics Teacher* 72 (Feb. 1979): 129–31.
A study of the function $y = x \sin (1/x)$. Gives a BASIC program that can determine the maxima and minima on the curve.

(Finance/B/T) Barron, Jonathan C. "Successive Approximation by Computer—a Modular Approach." *Creative Computing* 7 (Dec. 1981): 230–34.
Presents a BASIC program for solving a mathematics-of-finance problem.

(Algebra/B/S,T) Carlson, Ronald. "Inequality Tutorial." *Creative Computing* 7 (Oct. 1981): 186–90.
A description and listing of a BASIC program that can tutor algebra students in inequalities. It can also generate the graph of any input linear inequality.

(Probability/B/J,S) Collis, Betty. "Simulation and the Microcomputer: An Approach to Teaching Probability." *Mathematics Teacher* 75 (Oct. 1982): 534–87.
A proposed eighteen-lesson unit of instruction using microcomputers in dealing with probability situations and Monte Carlo simulation techniques.

(Algebra/B/V) Cornelius, Richard. "Instant Hex—a Program for Teaching Hexadecimal Notation." *Computing Teacher* 10 (May 1983): 43–45.
Describes and gives a BASIC program for presenting, comparing, and contrasting three notational systems for number representation (i.e., decimal, binary, and hexadecimal).

(Precalculus/B/S,T) Crothamel, David A. "Graphing Functions on the Microcomputer Video Display." *Computing Teacher* 7 (Dec. 1979–Jan. 1980): 17–20.
Gives a BASIC program for graphing rational functions over a specified interval.

(Linear algebra/B/T) Davis, Elwyn H. "A Use of Computers in Elementary Linear Algebra." *MATYC Journal* 15 (Fall 1981): 171–77.
Gives two BASIC programs for handling the computational problems involved in the simplex method of linear programming. Their use enables the student to focus on the conceptual material rather than get bogged down in arithmetic processes.

(Trigonometry, analytic geometry/B/S,T) De Jong, Marvin L. "Plotting Polar Graphs with the Apple II." *Compute* 4 (Feb. 1982): 62–66.
Gives a program in BASIC to generate various polar coordinate graphs such as rose curves, cardioids, and spirals. With the program, students can experiment with a wide variety of such graphs.

(Geometry/NA/S) Dennis, J. Richard. "Computer Classification of Triangles and Quadrilaterials—a Challenging Application." *Mathematics Teacher* 71 (May 1978): 452–58.
Explores the computer solution of two geometric questions: (1) Given the two-dimensional coordinates of three points, what type of triangle, if any, is formed? (2) Given the two-dimensional coordinates of four points, what type of quadrilateral, if any, is formed?

(Algebra, precalculus/NA/S,T) Dugdale, Sharon. "Green Globs: A Microcomputer Application for Graphing Equations." *Mathematics Teacher* 75 (Mar. 1982): 208–14.
Describes a computer activity developed to initiate graphing equations. Thirteen green objects, or "globs," are scattered on a coordinate grid. The goal is to explode all the objects by hitting them with graphs specified by typing in equations.

(Linear algebra/B/T) Duncan, Richard B. "The Golf Tee Problem." *Mathematics Teacher* 72 (Jan. 1979): 53–57.
Gives a BASIC program for solving a board puzzle with the object being to remove all but one tee by successively "jumping" tees over one another. Involves the use of matrices.

(Analytic geometry/B/S,T) Enns, Don K., and Walter Dodge. "Use of Apple Graphics to Study Conics." *Computing Teacher* 8, No. 3 (1980-81): 47–50.
A BASIC program that graphically illustrates the eccentricity definition of a conic.

(Statistics/B/T) Flynn, Brian J. "How Random Are Sequences of Random Numbers?" *Compute* 4 (Jan. 1982): 59–69.
Presents a BASIC program for testing the randomness of a random-number generator.

(Statistics/B/T) Forsythe, Alan B. "Elements of Statistical Computation." *Byte* 4 (Jan. 1979): 182–84.
Describes BASIC programs for calculating such statistical measures as mean and standard deviation. Stresses that good programming requires the balancing of computational speed, accuracy, and memory capabilities.

(Probability/B/J,S) Ginther, John L., and William A. Ewbank. "Using a Microcomputer to Simulate the Birthday Coincidence Problem." *Mathematics Teacher* 75 (Dec. 1982): 769–70.
Presents a BASIC program for computing the probability of two or more people in a group having the same birthday.

(Calculus/NA/T) Gordon, Sheldon P. "Generalized Cycloids: Discovery via Computer Graphics." *Two-Year College Mathematics Journal* 13 (Jan. 1982): 22–27.
The computer is used to generate pairs of parametric equations. Effects of modifications can readily be seen, and patterns of change can be deduced.

(Statistics/B/V) Harder, Monty J. "Bar Graph: A Program for the PET Microcomputer." *Computing Teacher* 6 (May 1979): 45–46.
Lists a BASIC program for generating a bar graph.

(Algebra/B/S) Hastings, Ellen H., and Daniel S. Yates. "Microcomputer Unit: Graphing Straight Lines." *Mathematics Teacher* 76 (Mar. 1983): 181–86.
Detailed worksheets for use in the study of the straight line on a microcomputer.

(Probability, statistics/B,F/E,J) Hatfield, Larry L. "A Case and Techniques for Computers: Using Computers in Middle School Mathematics." *Arithmetic Teacher* 26 (Feb. 1979): 53–55.
A general discussion of the possible uses of the computer in mathematical instruction. Suggests that in addition to drill and testing, the computer can be used for simulating situations to test hypotheses.

(Statistics/B/T) Hutcheson, James W. "Computer-assisted Instruction Is Not Always a Drill." *Mathematics Teacher* 73 (Dec. 1980): 689–91, 715. Reprinted in *Creative Computing* 7 (Mar. 1981): 96–99.
Shows how the computer can be used to emphasize statistical thinking rather than the arithmetic of statistics. BASIC programs are given to generate random numbers, compute mean and standard deviation, and do multiple linear regression.

(NA/NA/NA) Johnson, David C., Ronald E. Anderson, Thomas P. Hansen, and Daniel L. Klassen. "Computer Literacy—What Is It?" *Mathematics Teacher* 73 (Feb. 1980): 91–96.
Tries to put the whole question of computer literacy in historical perspective. Both cognitive and affective objectives are defined.

(Algebra/B/S,T) Kennedy, Jane B. "Graphing Polynomials with Computer Assistance." *Mathematics Teacher* 74 (Oct. 1981): 516–19.
Describes BASIC programs for graphing a polynomial function over a given interval. These programs are recommended for beginning the study of polynomial theory.

(Number theory/B/S,T) Kimberling, Clark. "Primes." *Mathematics Teacher* 76 (Sept. 1983): 434–37.
Gives several BASIC programs for discovering divisibility properties of the positive integers. Other possible directions of exploration include finding primes representable as prescribed sums or differences of squares, cubes, Fibonacci numbers, or other primes.

(V/B/V) Koetke, Walter. "Computers and the Mathematically Gifted." *Mathematics Teacher* 76 (Apr. 1983): 270–72.
Eight problems involving number theory, recreational mathematics, and probability.

(Algebra/B/S) Landry, Michael. "Algebra and the Computer." *Mathematics Teacher* 73 (Dec. 1980): 663–67.
A BASIC program for solving a linear equation with decimal coefficients.

(Precalculus/B/S,T) Lappan, Glenda, and M. J. Winter. "A Unit on Slope Functions: Using a Computer in Mathematics Class." *Mathematics Teacher* 75 (Feb. 1982): 118–22.
The computer is used to generate examples that serve as a basis for conjectures about functions and their slope functions.

(NA/NA/S,T) Lawson, Harold W., Jr. "Explaining Computer-related Concepts and Terminology." *Creative Computing* 7 (Oct. 1981): 92–102.
Shows how students can be introduced to computer systems concepts and terminology in an integrated manner.

(Number theory/NA/V) Leonard, William A., and David L. Pagni. "A Computer Meets a Classical Problem." *Mathematics Teacher* 73 (Mar. 1980): 207–12.
An application of computers to a problem in number theory provides insight into the limitations of the computer. The discussion also emphasizes the need for analyzing a problem carefully before attempting computer runs.

(NA/NA/NA) Luehrmann, Arthur. "Computer Literacy: What Should It Be?" *Mathematics Teacher* 74 (Dec. 1981): 682–86.
A critique of the computer literacy objectives postulated in the Johnson-Anderson-Hansen-Klassen paper (see above).

(Algebra/B/V) Lund, Charles. "Pascal's Triangle and Computer Art." *Mathematics Teacher* 72 (Mar. 1979): 170–84.
BASIC programs create artistic patterns using Pascal's triangle.

(V/B/S,T) McCall, Michael B., and Jean L. Holton. "Integration of CAI into a Freshman Liberal Arts Math II Course in the Community College." *Journal of Computers in Mathematics and Science Teaching* 2 (Winter 1982): 35–37.
CAI packages dealing with polynomial equation theory, differential calculus, trigonometry, and matrix algebra.

(Probability, statistics/B/S,T) McGrath, Gary, and Forrest Coltharp. " '97 Coins': An Example of Computing Power." *Computing Teacher* 10 (Sept. 1982): 66–69.
An analysis of a contest in which people were required to guess the value of ninety-seven coins. Shows that the computer is an indispensable aid in processing large amounts of data.

(Linear algebra/B/T) McGuire, Patrick E. "A Gauss-Jordan Elimination Method Program." *Byte* 8 (Aug. 1983): 394–400.
Gives a BASIC program for the computer solution of n linear equations in n unknowns by Gauss-Jordan elimination.

(Geometry, algebra/B/S) Mazen, Henrietta, Abraham M. Glicksman, and Sherrill Mersky. "A Symbiosis between the Computer and the Curriculum." *Mathematics Teacher* 71 (May 1978): 435–38.
BASIC programs are discussed and listed for such geometric and algebraic problems as determining whether three numbers can form a triangle, evaluating a polynomial by synthetic division, and solving polynomial equations of degree no greater than three by successive approximation.

(Precalculus, calculus/V/S,T) Mechner, Jordan. "In Search of Pi." *Creative Computing* 6 (May 1980): 124–27.
Gives a brief history of the calculation of pi and several formulas useful in computing its value. Programs for approximating pi are provided in several languages.

(Precalculus/B/S,T) Millikan, Roger C. "Curious Coordinates for Computer Graphics." *Byte* 8 (Aug. 1983): 386–91.
Shows how different types of coordinate systems can be used to produce computer graphics. As an example, polar coordinates are generalized to so-called elliptical polar coordinates of a specified scale.

(Probability/B/T) Millikan, Roger C. "The Magic of the Monte Carlo Method." *Byte* 8 (Feb. 1983): 371–73.
Gives descriptions and BASIC programs for applying Monte Carlo simulation techniques to such diverse problems as neutron motion and area calculation.

(NA/NA/NA) Milner, Stuart D. "How to Make the Right Decisions about Microcomputers." *Instructional Innovator* 25 (Sept. 1980): 12–19.
Background information on microcomputer hardware and software. Discusses such questions as, Will computer-based instruction improve learning? Is it cost-effective? What system is best for specific needs?

(Geometry, trigonometry/B/J,S) Muller, Richard C. "An Investigation of Integral 60° and 120° Triangles." *Mathematics Teacher* 70 (Apr. 1977): 315–18.
Examples for using the computer in the inductive process bridging the gap between algebra and geometry. Gives a BASIC program for searching for triangles of the desired format.

(Differential equations/B/T) Musgrove, Charles P. "Differential Equations and the Computer in the Freshman-Sophomore Calculus Curriculum." *Mathematics and Computer Education* 16 (Winter 1982): 11–21.
Describes several examples involving differential equations in which the computer can play an illuminating role. These include examining residual electrical inductance, studying population growth, and modeling drug concentration.

(Calculus/B/T) Norris, Donald O. "Some Thoughts on Using Microcomputers to Teach Calculus." *Journal of Computers in Mathematics and Science Teaching* 2 (Spring 1983): 28–30.
Gives illustrative programs for such topics as differentiation, numerical integration, functional graphing, and iterative equation solution. Also points out that what is really needed are interactive programs enabling students to experiment with and experience the calculus.

(V/A/S,T) Peelle, Howard A. "Learning Mathematics with Recursive Computer Programs." *Journal of Computer Based Instruction* 3 (Feb. 1977): 97–102.
Shows the effectiveness of recursive computer programs in solving some number theory problems.

(V/A/S,T) Peelle, Howard A. "Teaching Mathematics via APL (A Programming Language)." *Mathematics Teacher* 72 (Feb. 1979): 97–116.
A brief introduction to APL is followed by illustrative examples from logic, set theory, algebra, number theory, and calculus.

(Algebra/L/S) Piele, Donald T. "Beyond Turtle Graphics." *Creative Computing* 9 (Mar. 1983): 180–85.
Describes in detail the application of Logo to the nongraphic problem of factorial generation.

(Algebra, number theory/B/V) Piele, Donald T. "How to Solve It—with the Computer." *Creative Computing* 6 (Sept. 1980): 126–31; (Oct. 1980): 98–104; (Nov. 1980): 66–71; 7 (Jan. 1981): 142–51; (Feb. 1981): 82–92; (Mar. 1981): 158–64.
An article in six parts in which BASIC programs demonstrate some advantages of computer solution for problems from both algebra and number theory. The suggested problems are graded according to student level.

(Number theory/B/S,T) Piele, Donald T. "Prime Time." *Creative Computing* 8 (June 1982): 107–12.
Gives BASIC programs for factoring a given number into prime factors as well as for generating prime numbers between two given limits. Possible modifications are noted which can increase the speed of solution.

(Precalculus/B/S,T) Priest, Douglas. "Circles and Ellipses on the Apple II." *Byte* 8 (Mar. 1983): 380–84.
Gives two BASIC programs for generating the graphs of circles and ellipses. The first program plots a circle from three given points on the circumference. The second constructs an ellipse after the two foci and a point on the circumference are entered.

(Statistics/NA/T) Rappaport, K., and T. Stafford. "A Statistics Course with Computer Applications." *Sigcue Bulletin* 11 (Oct. 1977): 8–19.
A syllabus for a course in which the computer is integrated into the statistics curriculum.

(Trigonometry/B/S,T) Rheinstein, John. "Simple Algorithms for Calculating Elementary Functions." *Byte* 2 (Aug. 1977): 142–45.
Flowcharts and BASIC programs for the computation of the tangent and hyperbolic tangent functions as well as their inverses.

(Statistics/B/T) Ruckdeschel, Fred. "Curve Fitting with Your Computer." *Byte* 4 (Oct. 1979): 150–60.
A general technique for generating one-dimensional least-squares fitting algorithms. Also shows how such algorithms can be used to regress multidimensional data. Gives a BASIC program for calculating a least-squares parabolic fit to any data set having more than three points.

(Calculus/B/T) Scheidler, Alan. "Numerical Integration on a TRS-80." *Creative Computing* 7 (Oct. 1981): 192–96.
A BASIC program for numerical integration using the trapezoidal rule. The application of this program to practical problems is also discussed.

(Analytic geometry/B/T) Scheuer, Don W., Jr., and James M. Rubillo. "Conic Sections and lima$_5$cons—an Interesting Connection." *Mathematics Teacher* 75 (May 1982): 382–85.
A BASIC program for illustrating the reciprocal relationship between lima$_5$cons and conics.

(Algebra/B/J) Seber, Robert E. "Systems of Linear Equations with Minicalculators or Computers." *School Science and Mathematics* 81 (Oct. 1981): 512–16.
A successive approximation method (i.e., the Gauss-Seidel method) for solving a system of linear equations appropriate for use with calculators or computers. Included are curricular implications.

(Precalculus/B/S,T) Shilgalis, Thomas W. "Geometric Transformations on a Microcomputer." *Mathematics Teacher* 75 (Jan. 1982): 16–19.
Deals with the application of microcomputers to the study of such geometric transformations as translations, rotations, reflections, and glide reflections as well as expansions and contractions.

(Group theory/B/T) Simmonds, Gail. "Computer Discovery of a Theorem of Modern Algebra." *Mathematics and Computer Education* 16 (Winter 1982): 58–61.
Describes how microcomputers can be used as a discovery tool in learning group theory.

(Geometry/B/S,T) Sipser, Kenneth. "A Computer Search for Almost-Regular Polygons." *Mathematics and Computer Education* 17 (Winter 1983): 15–23.
Shows how to use the computer in constructing almost-regular polygons.

(Algebra/B/E) Spaans, Z. T. "Algebra." *Creative Computing* 7 (Oct. 1981): 210–14.
Presents a BASIC program for training students to work with positive and negative numbers using a game approach.

(Number theory/B/T) Stevens, Gary E. "Forward and Backward with Euclid." *Two-Year College Mathematics Journal* 12 (Nov. 1981): 302–6.
Describes a BASIC program for calculating the greatest common divisor of two given numbers and also for expressing the greatest common divisor as a linear combination of the two given numbers.

(V/V/S,T) Stoutemyer, David R. "Nonnumeric Computer Applications to Algebra, Trigonometry and Calculus." *Two-Year College Mathematics Journal* 14 (June 1983): 233–39.
Describes the capabilities of software packages that allow the user to simplify algebraic, logarithmic, exponential, and trigonometric expressions; factor polynomials; perform matrix operations on matrices with nonnumeric entries; solve equations and sets of simultaneous equations; and perform differentiation and indefinite integration.

(Applied mathematics/B/S,T) Vest, Floyd. "Bodies Falling with Air Resistance: Computer Simulation." *School Science and Mathematics* 82 (Oct. 1982): 506–10.
The computer is used to generate simulations of realistic rather than idealized situations.

(Precalculus, calculus/B/V) Wagner, William J. "Circles, Polar Graphs, and a Computer—Some Unexpected Results." *Mathematics Teacher* 75 (Apr. 1982): 323–28.
A creative computer project in which students experiment with BASIC programs generating various graphic displays.

(Number theory/B/J,S) Walling, Matthew, and David Meger. "Modular Arithmetic and Computer Art." *Creative Computing* 9 (Oct. 1983): 210–20.
Describes a method for teaching modular arithmetic using the graphics capability of the computer.

(Number theory/L/V) Watt, Dan. "Logo: What Makes It Exciting?" *Popular Computing* 2 (Aug. 1983): 106–13, 148–66.

Presents an overview of Logo. Describes features of the language and gives some applications. Reviews some currently available implementations of Logo.

(V/B/E,J) Wiebe, James H. "Needed: Good Mathematics Tutorial Software for Microcomputers." *School Science and Mathematics* 83 (Apr. 1983): 281–92.
A plea for good software to teach mathematical concepts and procedures at an elementary level. Gives examples of how greater use of computer graphics capability and user-computer interaction can produce more effective software.

(Topology, statistics/B/E,J) Winner, Alice-Ann. "Elementary Problem-Solving with the Microcomputer." *Computer Teacher* 9 (Feb. 1982): 11–14.
Shows how the microcomputer can serve as an instructional aid for teaching topological and statistical problems in elementary schools.

(Number theory/B/T) Woods, Dale, and Joe D. Flowers. "A Computer Program to Determine the Digits of Perfect Numbers." *School Science and Mathematics* 76 (Dec. 1976): 635–38.
A BASIC program produces the base-ten digits of the known Mersenne primes and their associated perfect numbers.

(NA/NA/E,J) Worth, Joan. "Action for Middle Schoolers." *Arithmetic Teacher* 28 (Jan. 1981): 2.
NCTM's *An Agenda for Action* (1980) recommends that the mathematics curriculum take full advantage of the power of calculators and computers. The significance of this recommendation for middle schoolers is discussed.

(Algebra/B/S) Zabinski, Michael P., and Benjamin Fine. "A Computer Discovery Approach for Quadratic Equations." *Mathematics Teacher* 72 (Dec. 1979): 690–94.
Describes a unit on quadratic equations using the "discovery" method to deal with the subject matter. The computer serves as a much-needed computational tool.

(NA/B/E) Zukas, Walter X., L. H. Berka, and Judith T. Martin. "Teaching Fourth and Fifth Graders about Computers." *Arithmetic Teacher* 28 (Oct. 1980): 24–27.
A description of a minicourse about computers that capitalizes on the interest of fourth and fifth graders in games and secret codes.

Books/Special Journal Issues

(V/V/V) Ahl, David H. *Computers in Mathematics: A Sourcebook of Ideas.* Morristown, N.J.: Creative Computing Press, 1979.
A collection of articles and activities published in *Creative Computing* from 1974 to 1979. Some representative titles include "Problems in Probability and Compounding," "Trigonometric Functions," and "Pascal's Triangle." Suggests many exercises and projects.

(V/B/E) *Arithmetic Teacher* 30 (Feb. 1983). "Teaching with Microcomputers."
A special issue containing articles on a hardware and software selection, computer literacy, instructional usage, and computer games.

(Arithmetic/B/V) Bezuszka, Stanley J., and Margaret Kenney. *Number Treasury: A Sourcebook of Problems for Calculators and Computers.* Palo Alto, Calif.: Dale Seymour Publications, 1982.
The problems in this collection can stimulate thinking about numbers and practice on arithmetic skills while involving the use of calculators or computers.

(V/L/V) *Byte* 7 (Aug. 1982). "Logo."
A special issue that gives an introduction to Logo and examines its use in the mathematics classroom.

(V/B/S,T) Coan, James. *Basic BASIC: An Introduction to Computer Programming in BASIC Language.* 2d ed. Rochelle Park, N.J.: Hayden Book Co., 1978.
Not only presents the elements of BASIC but also deals with many programming applications selected from such areas as quadratic equations, trignometry, complex numbers, polynomials, matrices, and probability.

(V/B/V) Doerr, Christine. *Microcomputers and the 3 R's: A Guide for Teachers.* Rochelle Park, N.J.: Hayden Book Co., 1979.
Contains background information on microcomputers, an overview of educational computing, and information on computer products. The mathematical applications include quadratic equations, number theory, trigonometry, and mathematics of finance.

(V/B/S,T) Dwyer, Thomas, and Margot Critchfield. *A Bit of BASIC.* Reading, Mass.: Addison-Wesley Publishing Co., 1980.
This revision of an earlier book entitled *BASIC and the Personal Computer* covers fundamental programming in BASIC as well as extensions for such operations as word processing and computer graphics.

(Calculus, differential equations/B/T) Fossum, Timothy V., and Ronald W. Gatterdam. *Calculus and the Computer: An Approach to Problem Solving.* Glenview, Ill.: Scott, Foresman & Co., 1980.
Presents many BASIC programs dealing with such topics as limits, differentiability, approximate antidifferentiation, numerical integration, and exponential and logarithmic functions. In each instance, a flowchart of the algorithm is followed by a discussion of the necessary theory. Sample runs are listed.

(NA/B/V) Heck, William P., Jerry Johnson, and Robert J. Kansky. *Guidelines for Evaluating Computerized Instructional Materials.* Reston, Va.: NCTM, 1981.
Discusses issues pertinent to software evaluation and presents sample evaluation instruments.

(V/NA/V) Higgins, Jon L., and Vicky Kirschner, eds. *Calculators, Computers, and Classrooms.* Columbus, Ohio: ERIC/SMEAC, 1981.
Computer articles in this compilation focus on the use of computers in schools, their role in the curriculum, and computer literacy.

(Probability/B/T) Inhelder, William. "Solving Probability Problems through Computer Simulation." In *Teaching Statistics and Probability,* 1981 Yearbook of the National Council of Teachers of Mathematics, edited by Albert P. Shulte, pp. 220–24. Reston, Va.: The Council, 1981.
Shows how computer simulation can serve as a teaching aid in the study of probability; presents a BASIC program for investigating extrasensory perception.

(Probability, statistics/B/S,T) Kellogg, Howard M. "In All Probability, a Microcomputer." In *Teaching Statistics and Probability,* 1981 Yearbook of the National Council of Teachers of Mathematics, edited by Albert P. Shulte, pp. 225–32. Reston, Va.: The Council, 1981.
The computer in probability instruction. Gives BASIC programs for studying a tontine, estimating areas, and simulating Buffon's needle problem.

(Probability, statistics/B/T) Lilly, Catherine. "Simulating Sampling from Normal Populations." In *Two-Year College Mathematics Readings,* edited by Warren

Page, pp. 194–97. Washington, D.C.: Mathematical Association of America, 1981.
A BASIC program simulates the process of sampling from a normal population.

(V/B/S,T) *Mathematics Teacher* 74 (Nov. 1981). "Microcomputers."
A special issue containing articles on hardware and software selection, computer literacy, instructional usage, and computer games.

(V/B/S,T) Oldknow, Adrian, and Derek Smith. *Learning Mathematics with Micros.*
Chichester, West Sussex, England: Ellis Horwood; and New York: Halsted Press (a division of John Wiley & Sons), 1983.
Describes the use of the computer in developing mathematical ideas. Shows how numerical experiences can be used to emphasize understanding. Provides BASIC programs covering a wide range of concepts from such areas as calculus, linear algebra, and statistics.

(Geometry/L/E,J) Papert, Seymour. *Mindstorms: Children, Computers, and Powerful Ideas.* New York: Basic Books, 1980.
This book, written by the developer of Logo, contains the author's personal reflections on the Logo project.

(NA/V/T) Sloan, Martha E. *Introduction to Minicomputers and Microcomputers.*
Reading, Mass.: Addison-Wesley Publishing Co., 1980.
An introduction to small computers. Its purpose is to help students develop the skills and understanding necessary to enable them to use small computers to solve problems.

(Problem solving/B/V) Snover, Stephen L., and Mark A. Spikell. *Brain Ticklers: Puzzlers and Pastimes for Programmable Calculators and Personal Computers.* Englewood Cliffs, N.J.: Prentice-Hall, 1981.
Supplementary problem-solving activities.

(V/B/S,T) Spencer, Donald D. *Fun with Microcomputers and BASIC.* Reston, Va.: Reston Publishing Co., 1981.
Games, puzzles, and problems to introduce programming with BASIC. Problems are selected from such areas as algebra, geometry, number theory, probability, and mathematics-of-finance.

(V/NA/J,S) Spencer, Donald D. *Problems for Computer Solution.* Rochelle Park, N.J.: Hayden Book Co., 1979.
Problems for computer solution taken from such areas as algebra, geometry, trigonometry, probability, statistics, and number theory.

(NA/NA/S,T) Spencer, Donald D. *The Illustrated Computer Dictionary.* Columbus, Ohio: Charles E. Merrill Publishing Co., 1980.
An easy-to-read glossary of computer-related words, phrases, and acronyms.

(NA/NA/E,J) Spencer, Donald D. *The Story of Computers.* Ormond Beach, Fla.: Camelot, 1977.
An illustrated children's introduction to computers, input/output, and simple programming.

(NA/NA/NA) Willis, Jerry. *Peanut Butter and Jelly Guide to Computers.* Forest Grove, Oreg.: Dilithium Press, 1979.
An introduction to the basics of computers. The discussion explains what computers can do and how they do it.

(V/V/V) Zalewski, Donald L., ed. *Microcomputers for Teachers—with Application to Mathematics and Science.* Bowling Green, Ohio: School Science and Mathematics Assoc., 1982.
Background information on computers in general and their use in education. Microcomputer hardware and software are discussed. Examples of computer languages are given as well as ready-to-use programs in science and mathematics.

Appendix 1: Organizations

Association for Computing Machinery
(ACM)
11 West 42d Street
New York, NY 10036

Association for Educational Data
Systems (AEDS)
1201 16th Street, NW
Washington, DC 20036

Association for Supervision and
Curriculum Development
225 N. Washington Street
Alexandria, VA 22314

Compendium CCN
P.O. Box 266
Cambridge, MA 02138

CONDUIT
P.O. Box 388
Iowa City, IA 52244

Mathematical Association of America
1529 18th Street, NW
Washington, DC 20036

Microcomputer Education Applications
Network
Suite 800
1030 15th Street, NW
Washington, DC 20005

Microcomputer Software Information
for Teachers (MicroSIFT)
Computer Technology Program
Northwest Regional Educational
Laboratory
300 SW Sixth Avenue
Portland, OR 97204

Minnesota Educational Computing
Consortium (MECC)
2520 Broadway Drive
Saint Paul, MN 55113

National Council of Teachers of
Mathematics (NCTM)
1906 Association Drive
Reston, VA 22091

Appendix 2: Journals

AEDS Journal
Association for Educational Data
Systems

American Mathematical Monthly
Mathematical Association of America

Arithmetic Teacher
National Council of Teachers of
Mathematics

Byte
Byte Publications
70 Main Street
Peterborough, NH 03458

Classroom Computer News
341 Mt. Auburn Street
Watertown, MA 01272

Compute!
Small System Services
P.O. Box 5406
Greensboro, NC 27403

Computing Teacher (formerly *Oregon
Computing Teacher*)
135 Education
University of Oregon
Eugene, OR 97403

Creative Computing
P.O. Box 789-M
Morristown, NJ 07960

Educational Technology
140 Sylvan Avenue
Englewood Cliffs, NJ 07632

80 Microcomputing
P.O. Box 981
Farmingdale, NH 11737

Instructional Innovator
1126 16th Street, NW
Washington, DC 20036

Instructor (see *Instructor and Teacher*)

Instructor and Teacher (formerly two
separate journals: *Instructor* and
Teacher)
Instructor Publications
757 Third Avenue
New York, NY 10017

*Journal for Research in Mathematics
Education*
National Council of Teachers of
Mathematics

Journal of Computer Based Instruction
Association for the Development of
Computer Based Instructional
Systems
Computer Center
Western Washington University
Bellingham, WA 98225

*Journal of Computers in Mathematics
and Science Teaching*
Association for Computers in
Mathematics and Science Teaching
P.O. Box 4455-C
Austin, TX 78765

Kilobaud Microcomputing
Elm Street
Peterborough, NH 03458

Mathematics and Computer Education
(formerly *MATYC Journal*)
P.O. Box 158
Old Bethpage, Long Island, NY 11804

Mathematics Magazine
Mathematical Association of America

Mathematics Teacher
National Council of Teachers of
Mathematics

Mathematics Teaching
Association of Teachers of
Mathematics
King's Chambers
Queens Street
Derby DE1 3DA, England

MATYC Journal (see *Mathematics and
Computer Education*)

Periodical Guide for Computerists
E. Berg Publications
622 East 3d Street
Kimbal, NE 69145

Popular Computing
P.O. Box 228
Hanover, NH 03449

School Science and Mathematics
School Science and Mathematics
Association
126 Life Science Building
Bowling Green State University
Bowling Green, OH 43403

SIGCUE Bulletin
Association for Computing Machinery
(Special Interest Group on Computer
Uses in Education)

Teacher (see *Instructor and Teacher*)

Two-Year College Mathematics Journal
Mathematical Association of America